Feudal America

Feudal America

Elements of the Middle Ages in Contemporary Society

Vladimir Shlapentokh

and

Joshua Woods

The Pennsylvania State University Press
University Park, Pennsylvania

Library of Congress Cataloging-in-Publication Data

Shlapentokh, Vladimir.
Feudal America : elements of the middle ages in contemporary society / Vladimir Shlapentokh and Joshua Woods.
p. cm.
Includes bibliographical references and index.
Summary: "Uses a feudal model to analyze contemporary American society, comparing its essential characteristics to those of medieval European societies"—Provided by publisher.
ISBN 978-0-271-03781-3 (cloth : alk. paper)
1. United States—Social conditions—21st century.
2. United States—Politics and government—21st century.
3. United States—Economic conditions—21st century.
I. Woods, Joshua.
II. Title.

HN59.2.S55 2011
306.0973'09051—dc22
2010039062

Printed in the United States of America
Published by The Pennsylvania State University Press,
University Park, PA 16802–1003

It is the policy of The Pennsylvania State University Press to use acid-free paper. Publications on uncoated stock satisfy the minimum requirements of American National Standard for Information Sciences—Permanence of Paper for Printed Library Material, ANSI Z39.48–1992.

This book is printed on Natures Natural, which contains 50% post-consumer waste.

Contents

Preface vii

Acknowledgments xi

1
The Feudal Model in Social Analysis:
From Medieval Europe to Contemporary America 1

2
Feudal, Liberal, and Authoritarian Models as
Tools for Analyzing the Middle Ages and
Contemporary American Society 18

3
Big Money and Corporations as Promoters
of Feudal Tendencies 33

4
The Feudal Model and the
Organizational Level of Analysis 56

5
Private Coercion:
A Feudal Aspect of Contemporary American Society 78

6
Personal Relations in American Politics and Business:
A Feudal Phenomenon 99

Conclusion 122

References 133

Index 163

Preface

Judging by their commentary on American public opinion, their sharp debates on key social issues, and the wide variety of labels they place on society, the critics and observers of the United States seem to be talking about several different countries. Indeed, their portrayals of the country range from fascist state to ideal democracy.

The United States is certainly not the only country to have stimulated debate over its defining characteristics. The Soviet Union, for instance, was the subject of a wide range of commentary and analysis. Until its collapse in 1991, many observers—both inside and outside the country—treated the USSR as a true socialist society, while others regarded it as a brutal totalitarian regime (Shlapentokh, Shiraev, and Carroll 2008). In the post-Soviet period, debates over Russia and other postcommunist countries continued. If some were eager to accept the official definition of Russia as a "normal" liberal capitalist country, others were no less insistent that labels such as "authoritarian" and "oligarchic" should be applied (Shlapentokh with Woods 2007).

Similarly, is France the motor of European integration, a deeply nationalist country in search of "grandeur," a true democracy, a champion of egalitarianism, or a society with growing authoritarian and discriminatory tendencies? Italy, in its turn, has been described as a "normal" democratic society and an oligarchy, as well as a criminal society ruled by mafias. Iran is seen by some as a healthy Islamic democracy and by others as a highly repressive theocracy. Popular labels for China range from a "normal" totalitarian regime to a fledgling liberal capitalist society.

Returning to the United States, we see sharp disagreements among journalists, scholars, and politicians on whether or to what extent the term "liberal capitalism," including genuine political and economic competition, accurately describes U.S. society. It is difficult to deny the considerable influence of corporations and political clans on the election process, the importance of personal relations in business and politics, the frequent disregard of merit in the hiring and selection procedures of public and private organizations, the privatization of public space, the walling of wealthy American neighborhoods, the widespread use of private security, and the independent control of violent force. While there is agreement that deviations from ideal liberalism exist, there is general disagreement about the seriousness of these problems, how long they will persist, and how they became problems in the first place.

One camp, the true believers in liberal capitalism, suggests that all such problems are temporary, accidental deviations from the liberal model. While every society faces considerable challenges, U.S. society is led, for the most part, by honest and able people who can meet these challenges. In other words, the problems derive not from the barrel, but from a few bad apples.

This optimistic vision of liberal capitalism has been attacked from all sides. Those on the far right believe that the country has moved toward an authoritarian model, in which corrupt bureaucrats and government officials violate the principles of liberalism in all spheres of life, while those on the far left insist that American society has never fit the liberal mold and is currently dominated by big corporations that use the government as a tool for achieving their private interests.

We disagree with all three camps. Many aspects of American society fall into the category of liberalism, and the economy is, for the most part, competitive. The problems that plague the country, however, are not temporary or accidental, but are deeply ingrained in the fabric of society. To an extent, we agree with the position of those on the left but disagree with their views on the origin of these problems and their exaggerated claim that liberal elements do not exist. While U.S. corporations weaken the bureaucracy, encourage corruption, and damage the democratic process, the American people still have a great deal of influence on their leaders. The election of President Barack Obama stands as evidence in favor of the democratic vision of society.

We also question the notion that corporations represent a united front in their dealings with government and the public. Some radicals on the left underestimate the rivalries between individual corporations, the autonomy of the state, the role of the media as critics of corporations, the power of the grassroots organizations scrutinizing corporate activities, and the independence of government officials.

While the country's social, political, and economic ills are endemic and enduring, they do not derive from a fatal flaw in the essence of liberal democracy. The cause, rather, should be traced to the coexistence of other types of social organization. As seen in many countries, past and present, the United States is a hybrid or segmented society, one that comprises several universal social forms. To glimpse the whole—its functions, dysfunctions, and general characteristics—we need multiple models, including liberal, authoritarian, criminal, religious, and others. Each of these ideal types deserves the attention of scholars. In an effort to fill gaps in the literature, this book focuses on the feudal model, and draws primarily on the liberal and authoritarian models for the sake of comparison.

The idea that "feudal" elements can be found in contemporary U.S. society may seem historically discordant. After all, the United States, unlike European countries, did not experience a feudal stage in its history. At the same time, feudal developments need not be associated only with the European Middle Ages. Societies encounter feudal tendencies whenever the egotistical interests of the few challenge democratic principles, and do so within the rules of competition in the political and economic spheres.

Our approach is intended to underscore the weakness of describing American society, or any society, with a single model or system. A tendency among scholars and, particularly, politicians to label societies as either liberal or authoritarian rose to prominence in the postwar period. This dichotomous framework—imbued as it was with cold war ideological leanings—sometimes made it difficult to see other forms of social organization in the United States and elsewhere.

Furthermore, two tendencies—the grand theoretical tradition and the enduring interest in explaining everything in society with a single set of principles—are deeply rooted in the social sciences. Marx in the nineteenth century and Parsons in the twentieth century were notable among sociologists who believed that one theory alone could explain all aspects of a given subject. Scholars of the natural sciences are probably even more eager than social scientists to develop grand theories.

The propensity to simplify information and give straightforward answers to complicated questions was epitomized by the medieval thinker William Occam in the fourteenth century. The rule of Occam's razor insisted that "entities should not be multiplied unnecessarily." As the history of science has shown, the systematic process of reducing complex problems to relatively simple ideas, though a reasonable path for science, can result in serious mistakes. A noteworthy rejoinder to Occam's razor is Einstein's famous quip that "theories should be as simple as possible, but no simpler."

The trouble with simplicity came to light rather glaringly during the financial crisis of 2008–9, when the public's trust in market mechanisms was put into question. Even professional economists found themselves in a general state of bewilderment as they watched the faltering financial institutions unravel. During a congressional deposition in 2008, former Federal Reserve chairman Alan Greenspan said, "Those of us who have looked to the self-interest of lending institutions to protect shareholders' equity, myself included, are in a state of shocked disbelief" (Andrews 2008).

Representative Waxman of California pressed Greenspan to clarify his statement: "In other words, you found that your view of the world, your ideology, was not right, it was not working."

"Absolutely, precisely," Greenspan replied. "You know, that's precisely the reason I was shocked, because I have been going for forty years or more with very considerable evidence that it was working exceptionally well."

The misreading of financial institutions during the economic crisis of 2008–9 is only one of many examples that demonstrate the dangers of relying on the simplistic assumptions of a single model, in this case liberal capitalism. One of the underlying goals of this book is to show how a multimodel analysis—what we call the segmented approach—may help us avoid, at least in part, potential pitfalls. A second aim is to outline, delimit, and apply the feudal model to the United States. While feudalism reveals only one part of this multifarious society, it has been largely neglected by contemporary observers and deserves a careful investigation.

Acknowledgments

We would like to convey our deep gratitude to Larry Busch, Peter Manning, Roger Kanet, and Chris Oliver for their helpful comments and ideas related to this book. We are particularly grateful to Sandy Thatcher, who supported this project from the very beginning. Our sincere thanks also go to Vera Bondartsova, Julie Gold, and Judy Spangole for their important editorial work.

1

The Feudal Model in Social Analysis: From Medieval Europe to Contemporary America

The concept of feudalism has received an increasing amount of attention in recent years but remains largely undeveloped and undertheorized. For us, the terms *feudal, feudalism,* and the *feudal model* refer to an ideal type of social organization—that is, a theoretical construct that generally corresponds to the essential features of concrete reality but never replicates them precisely. Such a model, as Weber (1949, 93) wrote, is a "limiting concept with which the real situation or action is compared and surveyed for the explication of certain of its significant components." Following Weber, we suggest that feudalism can be found in a range of societies across different time periods. Medieval France serves as the empirical basis of the feudal model, but even this society merely approximates the ideal-typical feudalism.

The model suggests that the feudal state manages to persist over long periods of time, in spite of the problems associated with political fragmentation, instability, and the state's dependence on other social actors and organizations. In this way, ideal feudalism is neither "ideal" in the conventional sense nor a metaphor for social chaos and disorder. It is a dialectical construct, at the center of which lies a suboptimal yet sustainable brand of central authority.

In order to develop the feudal model as a tool of analysis, we begin by reviewing how it has been used by other investigators, past and present, and then synthesize some of these treatments in a cohesive conceptual framework. This treatment of feudalism builds on several of our previous works (Shlapentokh with Woods 2007; Shlapentokh 1996a, 1996b, 1997a, 1997b, 2003, 2004; Shlapentokh, Levita, and Loiberg 1997; Woods and Shlapentokh 2009).

"Feudalism" in Contemporary Social Analysis

The term *feudalism* is used in the discourse on contemporary society in a number of different ways. The "feudal perspective" cuts across a great deal of academic terrain, bridging the work of journalists, sociologists, political scientists, international relations experts, and historians. One group of authors includes journalists and pundits who, overlooking the scholarly research on feudalism, apply the term loosely to a range of corrupt, unsavory, or backward aspects of society. Judging from an electronic search of major world newspapers, these authors are more likely to associate feudalism with developing nations than with Western ones (Glionna 2008; Matthews and Nemsova 2006).

A second group offers a more cohesive conceptual framework and applies it to illustrate the problems of Western democracy and capitalism. A typical representative of this group is Farmer (2006), who paints a dark portrait of Walmart, the leading baron of big-box grocery stores. The founder of Walmart, Sam Walton, emerges as a "neo-feudal knight" who disregards social and legal standards and perpetuates a business climate "characterized by economic warfare, gold, and certainly significant autonomy" (Farmer 2006, 157).

The third group, composed mostly of American exceptionalists, is interested in how a society's feudal heritage, or lack thereof, influences its development and contemporary circumstances. Schlesinger (1999, 152), for instance, suggested that America was "uncontaminated by feudal reminiscences," while Hartz (1955, 99) wrote that the country "was unfamiliar with the heritage of feudalism" and that this circumstance defined "the American liberal experience."[1]

The final group draws on feudalism to describe the processes in both postcommunist societies and other non-Western countries that have recently undergone major political or economic transformations. By the late 1990s, the feudal perspective became quite fashionable in the analysis of so-called transition societies, postcommunist Russia in particular. Throughout the 1990s and early 2000s, the Russian state and several other former communist regimes were unable to regulate the new and very powerful social actors and organizations that emerged following the collapse of the Soviet Union. The new business

1. For similar arguments, see Weinberg and Shabat 1965; Kelly 2001; Rabkin 1999. Some members of this group did not completely deny the impact of feudalism on America, but associated it only with earlier periods of American history, such as the seventeenth and eighteenth centuries, when immigrants poured into the country, bringing with them a set of life experiences that were colored by the feudal past. One author, for instance, suggested that certain aspects of the Middle Ages influenced the framers of the U.S. Constitution (Bailyn 1967, 282).

moguls, regional governors, and criminal organizations further weakened the state, encouraged corruption, and hindered the transition to democracy and a market economy.

These "feudal" circumstances were regarded as similar to the social reality in Europe after the downfall of the Roman Empire (Shlapentokh with Woods 2007). Latynina (2000, 2001, 2002, 2005), a well-known Russian political commentator, regularly refers to Russia's "industrial feudalism" and labels big corporations as "feudal empires." A number of other well-known Russian scholars also use the feudal metaphor in their descriptions of post-Soviet Russia (Konchalovskii 2006; Grinberg 2006; Orekhovskii 2005; Danilov 2000; Guriev 2001). Though less popular outside the country, several foreign experts draw on feudalism as well. Ericson (2000), for instance, applies the feudal model in his analysis of the Russian economy. In *Shadow Politics,* Stavrakis (1997, 8) discusses the deinstitutionalization of the state, particularly in the peripheral regions, and argues that "Russia is now more nearly a feudal system rather than a federal one." Treisman (2002, 58) takes a similar line, noting that the provincial governors of the Yeltsin era possessed the power to contest and bargain with the Kremlin and to exploit their regions like "feudal fiefdoms." Although Russia receives the most attention in this respect, the feudal model (or direct comparison to medieval Europe) has also been used in analyses of Chechnya (Lieven 1998), Romania (Matei 2004), the former East Germany (Meier 1990), and Bosnia-Herzegovina (Deacon and Stubbs 1998).

Other scholars apply feudalism in broader discussions of East European (Verdery 1996) or postcommunist countries in general (Karstedt 2000, 2003). Fairbanks (1999, 2000), for instance, suggests that the weakness of many postcommunist states represents an unusual case in history. "Most transitions away from authoritarian rule in the last two hundred years, however revolutionary or disorderly, did not weaken the state. If they did not issue in democracy, a strong authoritarian regime usually emerged, sometimes after a brief period of anarchy" (Fairbanks 2000, 35). In contrast, almost all former communist regimes experienced a weakening of the state and the fragmentation of political power throughout the two decades following the start of *perestroika.* Fairbanks (2000, 35) further suggests that the closest historical comparison to these circumstances—"an overwhelming powerful and intrusive state succeeded by very weak states"—was the collapse of the Roman Empire, this being the justification for using "feudalism" in the analysis of postcommunist countries. Our approach is closely aligned with the views of Fairbanks and other post-Sovietologists.

As discussed below, however, our treatment of feudalism has a few important deviations from this group, as well as from the others.

Our Approach: "Ideal Feudalism"

While our interpretation of feudalism overlaps, to varying degrees, with the four groups discussed above, our key assumptions are best understood by how they contrast with these approaches. Not surprisingly, the feudal model deviates furthest from the loose, journalistic treatments of the term. Given the lack of consensus on the meaning of feudalism, its usage requires a careful definition.

Ideal feudalism also departs in meaningful ways from the other three groups. First, unlike most members of these groups, we do not make direct comparisons between the United States and the European Middle Ages, even if these parallels are, in some cases, extremely interesting. As mentioned, we compare certain aspects of contemporary America to the feudal model, which allows researchers to draw comparisons between societies and across time periods. Feudalism, according to Weber (1978, 1070), can be found not only in medieval Europe, but also in the preclassical period of Greece, in the last period of the Roman republic, in medieval China, and even in Ptolemaic Egypt. As suggested in *The Encyclopedia of the Middle Ages* (Cantor 1999, 164), feudalism can be used as "an abstract model or ideal type relevant not only to medieval Europe." This perspective is particularly at odds with the approach of American exceptionalists, whose emphasis on the sequence of historical events and the specific course of institutional development contrasts with the notion of universal models and leads them to draw only concrete comparisons between America and medieval Europe.

Our approach is inspired in part by Simmel's "formal sociology," a perspective that rejects the idea that new historical events change the essential nature of human interaction. Simmel argues that societies consist of universal patterns of interaction, which occur and reoccur throughout history and across different social and cultural settings. Two entirely different types of human behavior or interaction can be understood with the same formal concept or model. For instance, in many ways, conflicts between nations are similar to conflicts between husbands and wives. As another example more akin to the feudal model, the need for personal protection and the willingness of people to pay for it leads to a universal form of social interaction between providers and receivers of protection (Simmel 1968, 1978; see also Coser 1977).

A parallel perspective is shared, at least in part, by Simpson (1998), a historian of medieval law, who constructed a feudal model and used it to describe not only life in the Middle Ages, but certain aspects of American society as well. Among other things, he compared the ideal typical relations between medieval lords and vassals—their mutual rights and responsibilities, and sources of power—to the organized crime syndicate led by Al Capone in the 1920s and 1930s. Karstedt (2000) supported the universalistic perspective when suggesting that the patrimonial and feudal structural patterns of medieval Europe never disappeared. Smelser (1994) compared medieval developments to the circumstances in failing contemporary states. Webber and Wyldavsky (1994, 228), also consistent universalists, suggested that noncentralized governments, as seen in medieval times, have existed throughout history (in Mesopotamia during the Kassite period, in Egypt during the Middle Kingdom, in Japan between the ninth and eighteenth centuries).[2]

Another important distinction between our view and the others involves the "segmented approach" to social analysis, which emphasizes the need for multiple models to explain any society or complex organization, past or present (Shlapentokh 1997a, 1997b, 1998; Shlapentokh with Woods 2007). Concrete elements of society that do not fit a given model should not be seen merely as "deviations," but rather as empirical evidence that more than one model is needed for the analysis.

Some authors, particularly those who link feudalism to postcommunist societies, ignore other models and thereby overextend the explanatory power of the feudal model. While rejecting "one-system" approaches—or any type of totalizing perspective for that matter—our feudal model is designed merely to supplement other ideal types of social organization, such as the conventional models of liberal capitalism and authoritarianism. While feudalism may be one of the best parallels for describing contemporary Russia, particularly in the 1990s, it is not the only one and should not be considered as such.

The segmented approach breaks with the principles of "system analysis," as formulated in the 1950s and 1960s by Parsons and others (Parsons 1952, 1971; Trevino 2001; Ackoff, Emery, and Ruben 2005; Cortés, Przeworski, and Sprague 1974). The one-system or holistic approach, even in classic Parsonian terms, has remained somewhat popular in the United States (Jacob and Toscano 1964, 209–10, 243–44) and Europe (Luhmann 1995). Our approach is intended to

2. For other authors who discuss how the feudal model overlaps with both medieval and modern times, see Hall (1962), Duus (1993), Grinberg (2006), and Beck and Beck-Gernsheim (1995).

underscore the weakness of describing American society, or any society for that matter, with the use of a single model or system. A tendency to label societies as either liberal or authoritarian rose to prominence among scholars and particularly politicians in the postwar period (Curtis, Blondel, and Brown 1993; Mankiw and Harris 1998; Case and Fair 1996; Bornstein 1994). This dichotomous framework sometimes blurred the lines of otherwise subtle, nuanced comparative analyses of the United States and other countries.

The segmented approach is supported by those authors who have challenged the Parsonian vision of the United States as an integrated society and emphasized its deeply fragmented cultural and social patterns (Cascardi 1992; Kuper and Smith 1969). For instance, Robert Solo, a pioneer of this idea, refused to see the American economy as an integrative system that is effectively regulated by market laws. He characterized the economy as a combination of various types of economic organizations that pursue different goals and obey different laws (Solo 1967; Stiglitz and Walsh 2006).

In their analysis of various authoritarian regimes, several contemporary political scientists have abandoned the one-system approach to operate, instead, with the concept of a "hybrid" society, which is quite close to our methodology. However, proponents of the hybrid models look at society only in political terms. Thus, for them, a hybrid society is merely a mixture of different authoritarian and democratic institutions, while for us, the segmented approach supposes not only combinations of different political institutions, but also of economic and social institutions. To some degree, those political scientists who advocate "the graded approach" to authoritarianism and who try to measure the degree of democracy in society are close to the "hybrid" methodologists, sharing with them the same narrow perspective in their analysis of society (Levitsky and Way 2002; Diamond 2002).

Certain variants of the Marxist perspective can also be enrolled as supporters of the segmented approach. While some Marxists focus on the unifying role of a "mode of production" as the determinant of all aspects of society (in fact, like Parsons, they offer an "integrative" or holistic vision of society), others, such as Eric Olin Wright and Pierre Bourdieu, emphasize social stratification and the fissures between various classes and their lifestyles (Wright 1998; Bourdieu 1984; Harrington 1969; Greenberg 2004). Using Marxist terminology, Perry Anderson (1974a) developed a view that is similar to the segmented approach, suggesting that each society represents a combination of different modes of production. Using a segmented approach in the study of Latin American societies, Laclau (1971) talked about a "triple society," pointing out the existence of feudal, slave, and capitalist elements in these countries. The concept of a "triple society" was applied to Latin America by other scholars as well (Mills, Taylor, and Graham 2002; Stern 1988; Romano and Stein, 1984).

The segmented approach becomes all the more necessary when investigating the feudal elements of societies outside the postcommunist sphere, the United States in particular. The democratic model plays a crucial role in explaining many aspects of American political life, from grassroots community organizations to the national election system. The authoritarian model is also quite useful for understanding how many institutions function—bureaucracies, corporations, some churches, the penal system, the army, and even, to some extent, universities. Many key economic relationships may be explained by the market capitalist model (Mankiw 2001, 67). Rather than debunking these models, as many critics have done, we wish to expand current thinking about American society by adding the feudal model to the contemporary toolkit of social analysis.

The Feudal Model: State Weakness as a Key Characteristic

The feudal model may be sketched in a few succinct strokes for the sake of summarization. Although it is possible to create a more exhaustive list of features, we are focusing on six elements: (1) the weakness of the state and its inability to protect its territory, guarantee the security of its citizens, and enforce laws; (2) the collusion and conflicts between the central administration and major autonomous social actors possessing political and economic power; (3) conflicts and collusions between and within large organizations, involving corruption and other forms of illegal or semilegal actions; (4) the use of personal relations in political and economic life; (5) the prevalence of elitist ideology; and (6) the use of private agents and organizations for providing security and protection.

Again, while this model may have many parallels with the European societies of the Middle Ages, it is not meant to perfectly replicate either them or any other society. It is meant, rather, as a framework for studying certain aspects of almost all societies, from ninth-century France to contemporary America, which cannot be explained using the conventional models of social analysis, such as liberal capitalism and authoritarianism.

The most important and perhaps unique element of the feudal model is its assumption about the relative weakness of the state compared to other prominent social actors and organizations. While different models encompass different types of authority, most suppose that the central authority itself—whether based on democratic principles or the dictates of a single ruler—can enforce the principles of its organizational structure. Ideal feudalism, in contrast, does not assume an efficacious central authority, but rather a middle ground between purely functional and dysfunctional authority. The model is designed to reflect the real-life tensions between the center's efforts to establish order and operational efficiency, and the social forces and human appetites that fragment power structures and distort the formal coordination of society. Under such conditions, individual social actors and organizations—whether medieval lords or multinational corporations—systematically influence, manipulate, and contradict the state and each other, while pursuing their own interests—even when doing so conflicts with the interests of the state and society at large.

There are differing views on how to conceptualize and measure the strength of the state. According to Rotberg (2003), one option is to gauge the state's strength by its ability to enforce laws and preserve its monopoly on the use of violence and coercion, or, in Rotberg's terms, to effectively deliver crucial political goods—the most critical being "the supply of security, especially human security" (Agrawal 1990). The strength of the state depends on a range of factors, including the level of corruption and crime; the existence of independent (or near independent) centers of power that conflict with each other and with the central authority; the privatization of security; the prevalence of personal relations in business and politics, including kinship relations and nepotism; and the state's access to scarce resources (Rotberg 2003; Hopkins 1972, 275–76; Ullman-Margalit 1977, 20–25; Migdal 1988, 3–39, 258–86; Shlapentokh 2006).

We can discern three levels of state weakness, which are associated with varying levels of feudal elements in contemporary society. The first level is typically found in Western countries, such as the United States, in which large social actors, such as corporations, play an important role in politics, and the state is only moderately successful in fighting corruption, fraud, and other crimes. The second level is seen in some Latin American, African, and Asian countries, as well as in Russia, Ukraine, and other postcommunist countries. The central administration in these countries is unable to enforce laws, corruption is prevalent, and the local lords and oligarchs enjoy a high degree of autonomy. "Failed states" represent the third level of state weakness (Rotberg 2003). In this case, the central authority is close to losing control over its territory and is unable to stop severe internal conflicts between different actors (ethnic groups, regions, war lords, clans, tribes, companies). For countries such as Somalia, Sudan, and Afghanistan, the establishment of feudal relations would bring more stability to the political and economic arenas and greater observance of rules and laws (Osman 2007).

"Feudalism" in Medieval Historical Analysis

Thus far we have reviewed some of the prior applications of feudalism in the study of modern societies and described the general principles of our approach. The next task is to outline the specific content of the model itself and discuss the real-life social conditions it brings to light. To achieve this end, we turn to a discussion of feudalism in the context of medieval historical analysis.

Much of this literature falls into one of two groups: the socioeconomic school and the political school. The two schools are based on observations of the same or similar medieval European societies, but offer different models for understanding these societies. The socioeconomic school places social and economic relations at the center of its model, while the political school emphasizes power relations, military might, and the political structure in the given society. Although we argue that the political model is more relevant to contemporary American society, the two perspectives need not be seen as mutually exclusive. It is more important to differentiate them, as one is often mistaken for the other (Jha 2000; Mukhia 2000). To begin, however, we should first respond to a rather sizable group of authors who completely reject the use of models, in whatever form, in the analysis of medieval European societies.

Some authors have attempted to discredit the concept of feudalism altogether (e.g., Richardson and Sayles 1963; Brown 1974; Reynolds 1994; Backman 2003). They suggest that the concept should be dropped because the differences between any two so-called feudal societies (French, British, German) are so great that the term itself is meaningless. No feudal model, regardless of how it is constructed, can fully explain a medieval society, and they believe that any effort to use one does more to obfuscate reality than to reveal it (Reynolds 1994).

This critique has been raised against a wide range of ideal-typical social and historical analyses (Moore 1966). In the 1980s and 1990s, for instance, several authors suggested that capitalism had materialized in different forms in the United States, Europe, and Japan (Braudel 1992, 403). The range and diversity of these different types of capitalism were thought to diminish the general usefulness of any one ideal model of capitalism. Yet, as we suggest, a single model may be especially useful in revealing commonalities and differences in the concrete elements of capitalism across these nations.

Some of the criticism of the feudal model is aimed at the practice of using ideal types as tools of social analysis. The critique is directed not only against Weber's epistemological methodology, but also against the construction of grand theories, which have been regarded as "privileged" and "subjective." Some postmodern thinkers prefer "an ambiguous presentation," which "permits, even encourages, an 'infinity of interpretations'" (Rosenau 1992, 178). They tend to see the methods of the natural sciences as completely inapplicable to the social sciences.

The criticism of ideal types is not new. In the mid-1970s, Giddens (1976, 23) suggested that the whole Weberian methodology was "obsolete." Confirming his dispute with Weber as early as the 1980s, Collins (2005, 23; 1986) more recently suggested that the use of ideal types leads to the neglect of "process" in favor of "structure," an accusation directed at any scholar who describes or labels a society as a whole.

In spite of these attacks, many scholars, even some influenced by postmodern thinking, use ideal-typical analyses, explicitly or implicitly, in their study of contemporary societies. In line with Weber's definitions, Bauman praised the use of "models," "which aim to render intelligible the otherwise chaotic and scattered evidence of experience." He underscored, as we do, that "ideal types are not descriptions of social reality but the tools of analysis and—hopefully—its comprehension" (Bauman 2007, 23; see also other scholars who use ideal types, such as Blackshaw 2005; Kreps 1986; Luke 1989).

In fact, the real problem with using a model lies not in the characteristics of the model itself, but in the fact that most researchers use only one. If, as mentioned, some elements of the economies of the United States, Europe, and Japan cannot be considered "capitalist" in nature, then other ideal models are needed. As Braudel (1992, 280) argued, "the formation of any national market has therefore to be studied in the diversity of its elements: each new combination is likely to be a special case." A similar contention can be brought against those who used only one model—totalitarianism—to study Russia, China, or Cuba during the Soviet era (Gleason 1995; Fitzpatrick 1982; Lewin 1988; Hough 1980).

If we follow the argument made by feudalism's detractors to its logical end, we must throw out all the major concepts in the social sciences, from democracy to totalitarianism. Indeed, there are no pure societies, and each real society contains elements of many ideal models. Again, the solution here is to embrace the complicated task of simultaneously applying multiple models to a single society or complex organization.

The Socioeconomic School

Moving now to a group of scholars who accept the use of models in social and historical analysis, the socioeconomic school identifies the main features of feudalism as the dominance of a landed aristocracy, the agrarian character of society, and the low level of technology and trade. When Marx talked about "feudalism," he was usually referring to its economic structure. Other key concepts for Marx included small-scale "peasant agriculture," which was unable to produce surplus value, "bondage," and the "feudal services" that peasants provided to the lords (Marx 1906, 18). Marx and Engels (1906, 13), following the famous historians of the Restoration such as François Guizot and Augustin Thierry, focused on class stratification in medieval times and the differences in social status between "feudal lords, vassals, guild-masters, journeymen, apprentices, serfs." While Marx only rarely discussed medieval political institutions, he did point out that "the might of a feudal lord . . . depended not on the length of his rent roll, but on the number of his subjects"; he also discussed the social significance of "the great feudal wars" (Marx 1906, 93, 789–90).

The socioeconomic model of feudalism, with its emphasis on the economic dominance of the aristocracy and on social inequality, has been developed primarily by scholars with Marxist orientations and those with a special interest in medieval class struggle (Hobsbawm 1990; Hilton 1966; Wallerstein 1974; Morton 2005; Laffey 2004). The advocates of this approach usually extended the "Middle Ages" far beyond the classic period, which fell roughly between the ninth and thirteenth centuries (Bloch 1989; Ganshof 1964, xv; Ullmann 1961, 1988). Among other things, they considered absolute monarchy, which emerged in the seventeenth century, to be a medieval institution and emphasized its support for the hereditary aristocracy, as well as for social and political inequality. This school generally disregarded the role of absolute monarchy as a unifying force in society, not to mention the higher levels of conflict and political fragmentation in the early Middle Ages.

Even though it emerged many centuries after the classic feudal period, the socioeconomic school, with its underestimation of the political nature of feudalism, characterized the French Revolution as "antifeudal," because it was directed against landowners and inequality. This antifeudal view of the French Revolution was developed by the famous French historian Lefebvre (2005) and several others (Markoff 1996; Mackrell 1973; Cobban 1999; Tonsor 1979). The same take on the French Revolution dominated the debates over the transition from feudalism that prevailed in England during the 1960s and 1970s, particularly among Marxist historians such as Sweezy (1978), Dobb (1947), Holton (1985), and others (Cornforth 1978; Kaye 1984). These authors tended to avoid the political dimensions of feudalism and concentrate on class struggle, technological innovation, and the market as the mechanisms of transition.

This disregard of the political dimension of feudalism is also typical for scholars who apply a feudal perspective to the analysis of developing countries. They have used the feudal model, for instance, to elucidate the social processes and structures in Latin American countries, though they ignored the roles of the state and noneconomic coercion. In the transition debate, they emphasized production relations from a Marxist perspective and focused only on the relations between peasants and landlords (Brewer 1980; Wiarda and Kline 1979; Wiarda 1992). Another group of Marxist scholars who also ignored the political dimension suggested that economic exploitation by the world capitalist metropolis, as formulated in Wallerstein's dependence theory, was the driving force behind feudal relations in the Latin American context (Frank 1967; Cain and Harrison 2001).

The Political School

Our model of feudalism is more in line with the political school, which focuses on political fragmentation and the relative weakness of the central authority. The key advocates of this approach include Coulanges (1923), Vinogradoff (1908), Ganshof (1964), and Bloch (1961, 1989).[3] The political school diverges from the socioeconomic school in the way it characterizes power relations in medieval societies. It treats socioeconomic phenomena, such as landed

3. Other contemporary historians of the twentieth century who side with the political model of feudalism and focus on the relative weakness of the state include Dubuis (1995, 161), Chibnall (1986, 125), Le Goff (1988, 40), and Théis (1992). Even some Marxist scholars see the agrarian relations in the Middle Ages as a product of the fragmentation of political power. Perry Anderson, for instance, underscored that the specific organization of the seigniorial and serf classes were shaped by the "system of parcellised sovereignty," which made it possible for landlords to use "extra-economic coercion . . . over the direct producers" (Anderson 1974b, 413–17).

property, as products of the political structure, while the socioeconomic school argues just the opposite—that economic relations explain the characteristics of political institutions.

As a second difference, the political school directs its historical gaze at an earlier period of medieval society, focusing on the deep political fragmentation that existed after the collapse of the Roman Empire. In an effort to establish some order in society and protect themselves from foreign enemies, the most powerful rulers created networks of knights and endowed them with land and laborers. Prior to the rise of absolute monarchy, however, social order and stability remained tenuous. With few resources at their disposal, kings of the early Middle Ages were forced to yield part of their power to local emissaries, and ultimately to make them landowners with the right to bequest their property to their descendants. This was the price they paid to establish a modicum of order in the kingdom's territory. The central authority resorted to decentralizing power as a way to secure order in society and tap local resources.

The feudal model is mostly based on the classic period of feudalism, between roughly the ninth and thirteenth centuries (Bloch 1989; Ganshof 1964, xv; Ullmann 1961, 1988). Following the death of Charlemagne, the decline of his empire, and the incursions of Vikings, Magyars, and Moslems, the central authority in European societies was extremely weak. An assortment of powerful landholders established regional hegemonies, or "kingdoms," within the former boundaries of the empire. In many cases, however, the power of kings was only marginally greater than that of lower lords, the church, and various tribes and warrior clans.

Although a hierarchical relationship existed between lords and vassals, "power was not a pyramid; it was scattered" (Barendse 2003, 525). Societies of the Middle Ages were marked by "a dispersal of political authority amongst a hierarchy of persons who exercise in their own interest powers normally attributed to the state, which are often, in fact, derived from its break-up" (Ganshof 1952, xv). The vassal, or lower lord, was at once "subject and master" (Bloch 1989, 220), which naturally weakened and fragmented central authority. As a rule, lower lords attempted to limit their obligations to the higher lords, while at the same time trying to increase the obligations of their dependents.

Adding to the social instability, the state (or kingdom) lacked the resources to establish a coherent and effective judicial system. Although laws did exist and were, to some extent, respected by the people, many areas of life were unregulated or beyond the reach of the central authority. The judicial powers of the state, according to Bloch (1989), were fragmented, ineffective, and often overlapped or contradicted the powers of independent regional courts. The lord of a given territory often claimed the right to judicial authority. In other words, the lord's legal or "public" right to judge others in court was rooted in his personal power and ability to protect his lands with military force and to dominate those who depended on it (Donovan et al. 1993, 30–31). As Bloch (1989, 372) suggested, "it is characteristic that the jurisdiction of the lord who exercised high justice ordinarily acquired the name of 'castellany'—as if the only source of judicial rights that common opinion now recognized was the possession of a fortified dwelling, at once the origin and the symbol of actual power." Power holders, for this reason, often went unpunished for even the most egregious offenses.

What is more, the central authority did not possess a monopoly on violence. All the major actors in society—from kings and lords to tiny chieftains—claimed the right to use military force to protect their jurisdictions. Given the state's inability to establish social order throughout the territory, medieval societies experienced high levels of crime and violent conflict. This social instability, in turn, caused people to place a premium on security. Protecting one's life and property was a central preoccupation of all members of society and played a key role in the development of political relationships and social structure (Volckart 2002). To ensure their security, lords supplied land to their vassals in exchange for military service, while vassals supplied protection to peasants in exchange for labor (Bloch 1989).[4]

What modern Western societies now regard as "corruption" (the exchange of money for political power) was a standard form of interaction between political and economic elites in medieval Europe. Given the king's tenuous grasp on power, "illegal" bribes and gift giving in politics, as well as the outright purchase of public offices, were commonplace (Pirenne 1937; Davis 2000; Pollock and Maitland 1968). Corruption played a persistent role in the major institutions of medieval society, including the judicial system (Prest 1991; Dean 2001), customs agencies and other tax administrations (Baker 1961), the offices of sheriffs and bailiffs (Janin 2004), and the Church (Frank 1995).

The classic medieval period was a time of permanent conflicts, even if the feudal model does not adhere to the more extreme, Hobbesian vision of society as "a war of all against all." As Tocqueville (1904, 211) suggested, the members of the ruling class, the feudal aristocracy, were always at war, and the idea

4. A few authors (e.g., Rosenwein 2005, 147) treat vassalage as "voluntary and public," disregarding the fact that it was a form of protection against disorder in the absence of a strong, centralized state.

of a national interest hardly existed. The concept of *patrie,* the fatherland, was not used in France until the sixteenth century.

Under these generally unstable political conditions, roving bands of mercenaries offered "protection" to nobles and monasteries in the countryside (Cantor 1993). Illegitimate means of personal gain and power grabbing—such as patronage, conflicts of interest, bribery, extortion, graft, embezzlement, grand-scale thievery, and violent raids—were widespread in society until the rise of absolute monarchies in the seventeenth century. Circumscribing written and verbal agreements, the big social actors and organizations clashed and colluded, betrayed and befriended each other in a high-stakes contest to grab as much power, money, and land as possible.

Notions of a common good, social justice, or even a national interest were often neglected by elites in the Middle Ages. Instead, power holders created and maintained an elitist ideology that valued the status quo, extolled feudal aristocracy—particularly its paternal hierarchy, code of honor, and independence from the state—and commended the medieval "division of labor" between the knight, the parson, and the ploughman (see Hammond and Hammond 1969, 215). This ideology also held contempt for the members of the "third estate"—merchants, bankers, and shopkeepers (Clark 2000, 70, 72).

Given the state's inability to enforce laws and regulate society, most political and economic activities were channeled through personal relationships, "connections," kinship ties, and nepotism; transactions, in other words, that were based largely on mutual trust and loyalty. The importance of personal relations was beyond question in the Middle Ages. Power was often exercised not through formal institutions, but through private agreements and personal prerogatives (Freeman 2001).

Although these power relations were quite unstable and inefficient, they endured for long periods and sustained a semblance of normality in society. There existed a sort of "feudal order," which reflected the need for greater safety, predictability, and efficiency in everyday life across all strata of the population. Following this reasoning, Tocqueville discussed the strong ties that "united the vassal to the lord under the feudal system" and the code of honor, which helped the aristocracy establish social order (1904, 178, 209; see Gibbs 1953). Contract-based military services (Douglas 1969; Duby 1998) and some elements of the legal system (Ganshof 1964) were also known to be somewhat reliable. From this perspective, medieval societies can be seen as an unstable network of powerful agents who were often at odds with each other, yet coexisted and, in some cases, cooperated quite effectively.

Weber, the Feudal Model, and Modernity

Weber occupies a special place in the debate over feudalism. Taken as a whole, his work seems to oscillate between two models (political and socioeconomic). On one hand, Weber suggested that feudalism involved the rule of the "landed aristocracy" (1978, 1070), and associated it with the "manorial system" (1978, 67–68) or "patrimonial structure" (1978, 239). While Weber drew a distinction between "fief" ("contractual" or "occidental") and "fiscal" ("patrimonial") feudalism, he argued that the difference between them should not be exaggerated, because both assumed that ruling elites held a monopoly over land (1978, 259–62). Following the socioeconomic school, Weber asserted that the French Revolution "put an end to the feudal system with one blow on the night of August 4, 1789" (1978, 98).

On the other hand, in some cases Weber demonstrated his interest in the political structure of medieval society. He generally described "fiefs" in political terms "as any grant of rights, especially of land use or of political territorial rights, in exchange for military or administrative service" (1978, 1071). He also underscored that "French feudal law" was intended, first and foremost, to "increase the political power of the territory" (1978, 70).

Weber's ambiguity toward feudalism may be linked to his treatment of rationalism and modernity, and his belief in a linear form of social and historical progression. Weber (1978, 162, 192, 225) extolled a new époque of rationality in all spheres of life, beginning with the market economy, and on through to the new professional bureaucratic state (Brubaker 1984; Martin 2005). He and others who associated modernity with progress, such as Parsons, Habermas, and Foucault, believed that, with the rise of rationalism, the Middle Ages had retreated into the past. Parsons, for instance, suggested that regional and cultural particularism (features of medieval societies) had yielded to the pressure of universalism (Giddens 1991, 256). In fact, such a contention had been raised as early as the Enlightenment, when several thinkers—including the founders of the famous eighteenth-century French *Encyclopedia*—mocked feudalism as an obsolete system, given its obscurantism, mythology, religion, traditions, and irrational bureaucracy.

While modernity and modernization certainly brought radical social changes, Weber and his followers exaggerated the scale of modernization—a typical example of a "one-system" approach to the study of social phenomena—and encouraged later scholars to relegate feudalism, in its entirety, to the past (Turner 1992, 5). Giddens's notion of a "postfeudal Europe," for instance, is incompatible with the segmented approach and its central premise that different types of social organization—some old, some new—coexist in contemporary society. Under the spell of modernism, few general sociological works or textbooks discuss the "feudal" form of social organization (Horowitz and Strong 1971; Turner 1985; Gordon and Harvey 1978; Eitzen and Zinn 1993; Fichter 1971; Babbie 1983; Light and Keller 1982). Any simplified concept of "modernity" obscures the fact that multiple forms of organization and social relations can be found in almost any society, from ancient Rome and medieval Europe to the contemporary United States.

Of course, our critique of the exaggeration of modernity's break with the past should not be understood as support for the admirers of medieval culture or romanticism's rejection of modernity. "Medievalism" still exists among many people, particularly nationalist and separatist groups, and in many countries, such as England and France (Agrawal 1990, 254; Ortenberg 2006, 240).

Conclusion

Ideal feudalism supposes that the central authority in society is relatively weak and unable to fully regulate other power centers; a sort of pluralism of "the few," to use Aristotle's terminology. The model anticipates frequent conflicts and a low level of state-provided security for individuals and groups, though it does not suppose a complete absence of social order or stateless anarchy.

Our use of ideal types follows the intellectual tradition of Weber and Simmel. This approach has become common in the contemporary social sciences, particularly in the area of comparative analysis. Medieval France serves as the empirical basis of the feudal model, because its concrete political and social characteristics were quite similar to the abstract constructs of feudalism. However, the feudal model is, by definition, a simplification of reality. As such, it cannot explain all of the developments in medieval societies, or any other social context, across time and space. Nevertheless, we refute the claims of some historians who fail to distinguish between models of reality and reality itself, and who generally reject the use of the term *feudalism* as a tool of social and historical analysis. The feudal model, by itself, is a powerful instrument, but it is designed merely to supplement other ideal types of social organization. It stands as only one tool in the segmented approach to the study of society, which suggests the use of not one but several models.

2

Feudal, Liberal, and Authoritarian Models as Tools for Analyzing the Middle Ages and Contemporary American Society

The segmented approach outlined in chapter 1 assumes that most types of social organization that exist today can also be found in the past. The number of these is actually quite small. The most important forms of political organization are the authoritarian, feudal, and liberal capitalist models, which roughly overlap with the famous Aristotelian typology: the rule of one (authoritarian), the few (oligarchic or feudal), and the many (liberal).

The liberal capitalist model supposes a division of power, political freedoms, free elections, perfect market competition, and a state that has the power to enforce the rule of law. The authoritarian model comprises hierarchical management, highly concentrated decision making, strong police forces (conventional and political), and state-controlled social and economic institutions. The feudal model, as discussed, consists of a weak state and multiple centers of power. Other types of social organization include the criminal layer, where violence is the major governing instrument, and the theocratic model, with the church serving as the basis of social organization.

The segmented character of most societies, past and present, demands the use of multiple models simultaneously. Social outcomes are determined by the relative role of each pure type and by the nature of their interactions. Similar patterns of behavior can be found across history, which explains in part why the great texts of the remote past, such as Thucydides' *History of the Peloponnesian War* and Machiavelli's *The Prince,* continue to interest contemporary readers. In medieval societies, with their aristocratic pluralism, many key developments, such as the election of kings and popes, can be best understood through the prism of the liberal model, while other aspects require the authoritarian model.

Although this book as a whole is devoted to applying the segmented approach (with an emphasis on the feudal model) to contemporary American society, we begin this chapter by demonstrating how the same approach can be used for analyzing medieval societies. Our second objective is to show how this approach is not only useful for describing diverse societies, but also for explaining how societies change. The use of ideal types or models does not imply that societies are static or rigid. On the contrary, models should be seen as analytical tools for describing societies, as well as for illustrating the dynamic interaction between its different parts, and identifying where and under what conditions societies transform. The segmented approach and the use of multiple models, far from encouraging determinism, help identify social transformation without buying into simplified notions of historical progression or one-system functional analysis.

The Liberal Model and the Internal Dynamics of Medieval Societies

The idea that medieval society is antithetical to liberalism and democracy stands as a problematic simplification of history. The political pluralism of the "few"—the existence of multiple centers of power in the same society—should be seen as a liberal element, and one that led to further liberal processes in society. The major social actors of the time (lords, universities, churches, guilds, cities, and others) often challenged the king and each other as they struggled for autonomy. One outcome of these conflicts was the establishment of numerous official documents and practices that protected their rights. Among these documents, the Magna Carta (1215), with its sixty-three clauses, was used by British barons to force King John to respect the law, the rights of his subjects, and the "liberties and free customs" of London. This document would become a symbol of civil rights and play an important role in the building of democracy in England and other countries (Ehrlich 1982). Also important was an article in the Treaty of Leek (1312), between the king and lords, which established a Council of Lords to advise the monarch (Neillands 2001).

The fight for political freedom was a typical element of medieval life. Cities such as Bruges in the Netherlands, Lübeck in Germany, or even Novgorod in Russia advanced the concept of freedom through their conflicts with kings and each other. The famous medieval aphorism "the city air makes people free" epitomized this struggle. Graf von Kleve recognized the special rights of the city of Kleve (now the Netherlands) for the first time in 1232.[1] In spite of an intervening period of absolutism, the cities transferred their democratic ideas to the nascent democracies of later periods.

The medieval Catholic and Protestant Churches also contributed to the development of democracy. Some popes resisted the arbitrariness of the king and supported the idea of limiting royal power. The famous struggle between the German King Henry IV and Pope Gregory VII, in "the investiture conflict" of the late eleventh century, over who should appoint bishops (the pope or king) was one striking example of a political conflict in the Middle Ages that restrained the power of the king. The duel between the pope and the king was viewed with great delight by the German aristocracy, which wanted to limit royal power (Duffy 1997; Rosenwein 2005). On the other hand, the struggle between the popes and the French kings resulted in victory for the royals. The fight against Church intervention in the lives of individuals, a postulate of Protestantism, also helped forge the premises for liberalism and democracy in medieval times. The Church's strong dependence on the central authority helps to explain why democracy did not develop in Russia and other countries (Eagles, Johnston, and Holoman 2004).

Even though a caste system existed in medieval society, ordinary people still had certain rights. The Middle Ages also bequeathed lessons on elections, which bridged Athenian democracy and the modern state. Even though elections were controlled by "the few," they can be seen as liberal elements that played an important role in medieval societies. In several cases, lords even elected kings. In France, Pepin the Short was elected as the founder of the new Carolingian dynasty by an assembly of magnates, and was consecrated by the bishops in 754. The same thing happened in 834 when feudal magnates, rejecting the will of Louis the Pious (Charlemagne's son), did not give Aquitaine, a subordinate kingdom of the empire, to Charles's preferred heir, but to another son, Pepin.

The election of Polish kings was another example of medieval pluralism. The Polish king Wladyslaw Jagiello was elected for the first time in 1386. Between 1572 and 1791, the election of Polish kings by the nobles (sometimes forty thousand to fifty thousand of them) was the norm. The elected king was forced to accept *pacta conventa* (an agreed-upon contract), which hashed out the king's obligations to the nobles. The power of elected kings also restrained the

1. See the conference devoted to this aphorism in the Institute of Sociology in Linz, Austria, in 2002, www.nt.tuwien.ac.at/nthft/temp/oefg/text/veranstaltungen/stadtluft.pdf; see http://www.heimat-kleve.de/geschichte/chronik/05_08.htm.

parliament (*sejm*), which convened regularly in medieval Poland. It was divided into two chambers—the senate (mostly bishops) and the chamber of envoys (the representatives of landed nobility). The power of the great lords was so strong that in the late Middle Ages each member of the sejm had the right to veto any proposal advanced by members of the parliament (*liberum veto*).

There were other divisions of power in medieval society. The judicial system enjoyed some autonomy. The Magna Carta placed the law above royal power. Even such an aggressive and cruel English king as Edward the First, who was described by his contemporaries as "inconstant and treacherous," respected the will of his great council and parliament. His compliance with the law earned him the title of the English Justinian (Fraser 2000, 82).

According to some scholars, such as Ganshof (1964) and Duby (1998), the medieval legal system was quite sophisticated and functioned well under most circumstances. The social actors of the time, they suggest, followed a strict code of conduct in their everyday lives. In our view, they exaggerate, to some extent, the level of order and the degree to which laws were observed. They give the impression that medieval France, around the year 1000, was an orderly society. In a large volume by Duby, little is said about the banditry and violence in France during this period. The twelve-page table of contents contains sections about numerous religious and intellectual phenomena of the time, but never mentions the level of order in society. Another group of historians embrace the opposing perspective, suggesting that a general disrespect for law characterized much of the Middle Ages (Janin 2004; Hanawalt and Wallace 1999; Gauvard 1999; Davis 2000). These conflicting perspectives can be resolved, at least in part, by adopting a segmented approach, which anticipates the real-life manifestations of multiple models (liberal, feudal, and authoritarian) in any society or large social unit.

Private Interests in Medieval Society

Feudal political pluralism encouraged the role of private interests in the Middle Ages, which led to the strengthening of liberal tendencies. Some authors have suggested—wrongly by our estimation—that a distinction between public and private interests was not made until the eighteenth century (Sennett 1992, 17–18; Johnson 1995, 216; Outhwaite 1994, 531; Sales 1991). In fact, the public-private distinction, a liberal element, can be seen, if to varying degrees, in any society—medieval France, the Soviet Union, and twenty-first-century America.

The task is to ascertain the extent to which this distinction functioned in a given time period and regime. The collapse of Roman society, along with the sophisticated laws that coordinated private and public interests, had a lasting impact on social relations in early medieval Europe. The barbaric societies that emerged from the ruins of the Roman Empire mostly ignored individual private interests. Ordinary people were given no option but to obey the king or ruler. Until the ninth century, in fact, French kings did not make a distinction between their own property and the property of "others." For a long time there was no such thing as "public finance," and the king was not held accountable for the public's needs. The king was allowed to collect taxes only when "the nation" was at war, and he often used his own wealth to finance the government (Cantor 1993, 487; Wolfe 1966; Henneman 1971).

The tendency of the ruler to see the country as his own property was typical for almost all despotic, totalitarian regimes. For instance, the Russian tsars, almost up until the nineteenth century, considered themselves the owners of everything in the country (Braudel 1992). This particularity of Russian society, as suggested by some scholars such as Richard Pipes, postponed the development of private property and liberalism for centuries (Pipes 1999).

In the case of ninth-century France, however, the decline of royal power and the emergence of autonomous social actors (lords, bishops, guilds, and universities, among others) led to the development of private property, and clarified the distinction between public and private interests. Subsequent to the ninth century, the king's property was strictly separated from the public wealth in all new post-Roman states. As suggested by the contemporary British historian Antonia Fraser, following Edward I's ascension to the throne in 1274, his first task was "to determine more clearly the boundaries between royal and private power" (Fraser 2000, 82).

Officials of the royal administration considered their jobs to be a sort of private fief, which could be used for extracting income in addition to their official salaries (Aries and Dubuis 1985). The division between private and public life in the Middle Ages became so strong that, as Webb (2007) showed, privacy was an important phenomenon in this era, even if "constant company was the general rule."

Of course, the private interests of individuals in medieval society were restricted by feudal contracts, laws, customs, and the interests of "others." However, these restraints were not sufficient for protecting national interests. Indeed, with the dominance of private interests, permanent wars raged. The confiscation of private property was a fixture in social life. As suggested by Cantor (1993,

486), "The barons paid little attention to the necessary details of government, and their constant infighting for personal advantages made the failure of baronial government inevitable." Ultimately, feudal private interests had a devastating impact on society, the economy, and, of course, the country's ability to defend itself against foreign invasions.

During the Hundred Years' War, France suffered one defeat after another, as the lords "were intent in following their own policies and whims" and did not obey the king in his fight against the English invaders (Neillands 2001, 49). No less suffering fell upon medieval Germany, where thirty years of war against foreign armies (Swedish and French, among others) stood as a remarkable example of the indifference of German princes to the well-being of their country. The story was similar in medieval Poland, where the lords refused to give up their private interests for the sake of the nation, which suffered three partitions in the eighteenth century, and finally ceased to exist in 1795.

The importance of private interests in medieval times can also be seen in the marketplace. Market transactions supposed the existence of two individual partners who acted with their own interests in mind. Those authors who ignore the distinction between "private" and "public" also tend to ignore the importance of the market in medieval society. Such was the position of many Marxists (McNally 1993) and several other contemporary authors, such as Karl Polanyi (1944). In fact, feudal relations coexisted with imperfect markets and with money playing an essential role. The royal administration and regional lords needed money to buy land and arms, pay soldiers, and purchase entertainment and luxury items. Kings and lords received money from taxes and customs, the sale of privileges and offices, and the illegal extortion of money from cities and individual merchants (Spufford 1988).

The subsistence economy, which many scholars treated as a central characteristic of the Middle Ages, was mostly related to the activities of peasants and was only partially relevant to the upper class, considering its consumption of luxury foreign goods. In general, as suggested by the well-known economic historian Michael Postan (1944), "economies wholly natural never existed and money always played an important role in Middle Ages life."

Medieval Contracts as the Basis for Liberal Institutions

The importance of private interests made contracts necessary, which further encouraged the development of liberal elements in medieval society (Gordley

1991). While the influence of Roman law on medieval contracts should not be disregarded, it was a particular medieval practice to focus on trust as the basis of agreements. Several contemporary authors have suggested that the roots of contracts as an institution lie in medieval society (Mayhew 1984). Some authors have even suggested, referring to the role of contracts in the Middle Ages, that nineteenth-century liberalism and twentieth-century libertarianism owed their basic premises to feudalism (Painter 1961; Benton 1962). Cantor (1993, 318) insisted that the "effect of the heritage of 12th century law is felt to the present times." As underscored by other authors, the spread of contractual practices in the Middle Ages led to freedom, free choices, and bourgeois property, even if this practice benefited only a small minority of the population (Scheiber 1998; Nörr 2000). Summarizing the history of British law, Maine offered the pithy expression "from status to contract," which referred to the move from the constraints of social status, which limited the conduct of individuals, to contracts, which offered them freedom (Kahn 2004).

By the twelfth century, the institution of contracts permitted an enhancement of the rights of vassals at the expense of their lords (Simpson 1998). Later, contracts were extended to ordinary people, and respect for the participants of contracts spread throughout society. The important task of hiring mercenary troops would have been impossible without contractual deals (Neillands 2001). Bloch (1961) interpreted feudalism as a set of relations between a vassal and his lord, as if those relations assumed equality between the agents. Contractual relations were also typically found between landlords and free tenants. Following Bloch, Simpson underscored that contractual relations were "the basis of the system of social organization which has come to be called feudalism" (Simpson 1998, 20). The same line was supported by Douglas, with his focus on contractual military service as the major feature of feudalism (at least in its Norman version) (Douglas 1969), and to some degree by Ganshof, given his emphasis on the legalistic elements of feudalism (Ganshof 1964). Contemporary historians of law also supported the view that feudal relations were inherently contractual (Carson 2006).

Well-known thinkers such as Hobbes and Locke were inspired by medieval practices (Buckle 1991; Gordley 1991). While Hobbes is correctly seen as the apologist of Leviathan, which he treated as the antidote to feudal fragmentation, he "liberalized" the totalitarian monster by suggesting that ordinary people contracted with the absolutist state in order to protect peace. This circumstance persuaded some scholars to see Hobbes as "a contractual political scientist," and to refer to him as the founder of liberal thought (Hampton 1986).

It was not Hobbes, however, but two other thinkers who made the feudal institution of contracts a main postulate in their vision of a "good society." One was Locke, who insisted that the state yield to civil society and function only on the basis of contracts with free people. In his treatise on government, Locke suggested the idea of extending the feudal contract to everybody (Cazel 1961). The second author to connect his name indelibly to the idea of contracts was Jean-Jacques Rousseau, in his important book *The Social Contract* ([1762] 2006). More than any other publication, it turned the medieval contract into the symbol of democracy, because contracts between a sovereign and ordinary people, or between individuals, supposed equality. Several twentieth-century authors, such as Parsons (1967), Hayek (1973, 35–46), and Oliver Williamson (1985), with their Lockean, utilitarian approach to human relations, identified contracts as a key element of free society (Ellickson 1991).

The Authoritarian Model and Medieval Societies

While the liberal elements were quite important in medieval society, authoritarian elements were much more pronounced. This was obvious even before absolutism took hold in France, Russia, Austria, Sweden, and Prussia (Moore 1966). Even a weak royal power still had an extensive bureaucracy, which operated like a typical authoritarian organization, with the king or his proxy making final decisions.

It goes without saying that the Carolingian monarchy of the ninth century was a typical authoritarian entity, with a well-developed bureaucratic machine. Its capitularies (edicts of the head of state) dealt with various issues of the country, and were addressed to, among others, the Church, the stewards of the royal manors, and the villages, which were obliged to send knights to the army. The royal administration sent emissaries, the *missi*, to supervise the provinces and guarantee the efficiency of local administrations. After Charlemagne's death and until the triumph of absolutism, most French kings were much weaker than the Carolingian emperor. However, many of them, such as Louis IX and Louis XI, headed a bureaucracy that was an important factor in a feudal country such as medieval France, which collected taxes, supervised the police and court systems, and took care of the army (Cantor 1999, 289–91).

The state created by William the Conqueror in England was another example of a combination of authoritarian and feudal elements in medieval society. First, the king obliged the lords to provide his army with knights. The lords were also obliged to make an appearance three times a year in order to be familiar with the king's plans, and to advise him on domestic and foreign policy. The king had a staff of nobles and clerks that ran everyday business. The local agents of the king (sheriffs) represented the central government in the provinces and did not tolerate disobedience of the royal will, even from the lords. The king (and not only William the Conqueror, but also the kings that followed) taxed the population, even if the major source of income was the royal estates (Cantor 1999, 277–84).

Each feudal lord, within the context of his estate or manor, was an absolute ruler whose power was not restrained much by the king or the Church. With his staff, the owner of a manor oversaw the economic, political, and spiritual life of the people who lived in his territory. The police and courts were under his control. The village community enjoyed some autonomy, but ultimately control was superimposed by the manorial administration. The lord formally owned the forests and pastures, even if they were used by peasants, according to custom. The peasants, whatever their status, were obliged to deliver their rents—in kind or in money—to the lord, as well as perform some labor within the lord's demesne (Vinogradoff 1924).

The Catholic Church in medieval society was, of course, a strongly authoritarian organization. The Church was governed by a multirung hierarchy, from the pope to the common monk, and everybody had to obey the priests of a higher rung. The Church issued its own rules, which regulated property relations inside the Church. It was the Reformation that challenged the hierarchy inside the Church and demanded that ecclesiastic people be subordinate to the government (Cantor 1999, 38; Guenée 1991; Beard 1968).

Feudal Tendencies in American Society

We have enumerated the liberal and authoritarian elements in medieval society and discussed how the social significance of these elements changed over time. Now we apply the same segmented approach to an analysis of American society, with an emphasis placed on feudal tendencies.

Private Interests in American Society

Capitalism, as described by Locke and Smith, supposes that the private interests and activities of individuals in a free market economy produce prosperity and ultimately contribute to the general welfare of the nation. The importance of private interests has been highlighted throughout American history by a variety of leaders and luminaries, including the framers of the U.S. Constitution. *The Federalist,* for instance, uses the term *private* no less than thirty times (Hamilton, Madison, and Jay 1788).

The liberal capitalist model, however, supposes that restraints should be placed on private interests. Two instruments are crucial for this purpose: perfect competition and the government, both of which should guarantee the equality of each actor in pursuing his or her interests. These instruments supposedly prevent the emergence of monopolies—political and economic, material and nonmaterial. Yet, as soon as the private interests of one prevails over others, that is, as soon as one person or group benefits from a monopoly of any sort, temporary or permanent, feudal elements enter society and undermine liberal principles. When the private interests and greed of elites are let loose, liberal societies suffer and the role of feudal elements in life increases (Phillips 2003).

American Representative Democracy

Feudal tendencies in democratic societies, however, emerge not simply due to an unequal distribution of resources and the accumulation of wealth in the hands of the "few." Almost all so-called democracies in the world function not as "direct" but as "representative" democracies. The closest representative of ideal-typical democracy (the liberal model) is Athenian or Jeffersonian democracy. Representative democracies are, in comparison, more prone to feudal tendencies. Even reasonably well-functioning representative democracies with strong market mechanisms generate very large political and economic actors who, under some circumstances, pursue their own interests and policies without regard to the public or the market, resulting in weakened political equality and imperfect competition. The executive power and state apparatus, despite the congressional and judicial restraints, has a great deal of autonomy, as well as the ability to influence elections and sell its services to corporations and other major social actors.

The predisposition of democratic institutions to generate feudal elements was analyzed by Robert Michels in his studies of democratic parties in the early twentieth century. He discovered the "iron law of oligarchy," which suggests that even democratic organizations tend to develop into oligarchies. Michels contends that "the leaders" are "technically indispensable" to society, while the masses are "immobile and passive" and have a tendency to "organize themselves and consolidate their interests." Discussing the degeneration of democratic principles by the "few," or by "oligarchs," Michels, with some exaggeration, suggested that "the power of elected leaders over electing masses is almost unlimited." He continues, "The formation of oligarchs within the various forms of democracy is the outcome of organic necessity, and consequently affects every organization." And he claims that "when democracies have gained a certain stage of development, they undergo a gradual transformation, adopting an aristocratic spirit, and in many cases also the aristocratic forms, against which at the outset they struggle so fiercely" (Michels 1915, 400–401, 408).

A typical feature in many democratic countries is the very limited involvement of ordinary people in the political process, elections in particular. This passivity increases the political role of big organizations. With their money and political connections, they influence the outcomes of elections and gain other advantages that would not be possible if the system was close to the liberal model (Berelson, Lazarsfeld, and McPhee 1954; Donovan et al. 1993).

The Case of Privatization

The nature of privatization, and the extent to which the liberal, feudal, and authoritarian models can explain it, depends on who or what controls the process (the market, government, a small group of powerful social actors) and whether or not bureaucrats use it for their own interests. Whatever the political, social, and economic consequences of privatization, the process itself shrinks state power. From the 1980s to the early 2000s, privatization was seen by many as the best solution to many economic and social problems. During this period, state power in several countries declined, reversing the growth trend of the 1930s through the 1950s (Feigenbaum, Henig, and Hamnett 1999; Bushnell et al. 1991). A detailed consideration of the changing role of the state in American history, though an important topic, goes beyond the scope of this text.

The reduction of state power through privatization leads to two different results. If a privatized company becomes part of a well-functioning competitive market, the society moves toward the liberal capitalist model. During the euphoria of the Reagan-Thatcher revolution in the 1980s and 1990s, many observers believed that privatization expanded the role of the market, enhanced the efficiency of the economy, diminished bureaucratic intervention in economic processes, and promoted "shareholder democracy."

One of the strong advocates of privatization during this period was Lawrence Summers, treasury secretary during the Clinton administration. Later, as the president of Harvard, he proclaimed at a World Bank conference in 1992 the merits of privatization and practically refused to cite any of its negative consequences (Galal and Shirley 1994). In 1996, another Harvard economist, Andrei Shleifer, along with his coauthors, said that "corruption generally raises efficiency, in that it allows private investors to buy their way out of some of the inefficiencies demanded by politicians, but it does not always lead to first best," and that corruption is an efficient way to "renegotiate to a more efficient resource allocation" (Boycko, Shleifer, and Vishny 1996, 313).

A belief in privatization as a panacea to all social problems was typical in the first years after the collapse of the Soviet Union, particularly among Western analysts. It took several years for some economists, such as Joseph Stiglitz (2002) and Jeffrey Sachs (2003, 2008), to understand that privatization, under some circumstances, results in unwanted outcomes: low efficiency and an increase in corruption.[2]

Capitalist privatization should be distinguished from feudal privatization, which leads to the transformation of a state company into an organization that operates outside both market competition and state control. The feudal character of privatization is particularly strong when privatization leads to the concentration of economic power and to the monopoly of resources, which makes owners into feudal actors who mostly ignore the market and even challenge the state and law (Feigenbaum, Henig, and Hamnett 1999, 23). The official agencies that supposedly supervise privatized companies sometimes are co-opted in the process of feudal privatization (ibid., 21). This form of privatization bolsters monopolistic tendencies in the economy and leads to the deterioration of services.

Recently, some authors, discussing the political aspects of privatization, have observed that it can produce negative results for society. Vickers and Yarrow named seven reasons that state organizations are privatized, and while most of them are economic, the authors also noted the government and its interest in "gaining political advantage" (Hodge 2000). Adding to the list of political motives behind privatization, Feigenbaum and his coauthors (1999, 154) pointed to legislators who help sell public utilities and various lucrative contracts to "friends" in exchange for contributions to election campaigns. As suggested

2. For more about the feudal character of privatization in Russia, see Shlapentokh (1996a, 1996b, 2004); Clarke and Pitelis (1993).

by several researchers, political considerations, corruption, and personal relations play important roles in the decision-making process of privatization in developing capitalist countries (Weizsäcker, Young, and Finger 2005; Parker and Saal 2003).

Public choice theory contributes to the analysis of different types of privatization and the role of politics in this process. As one public choice theorist wrote, bureaucrats seek to maximize "salary, perquisites of the office, public reputation, power, patronage, output of the bureau, ease of making changes, and ease in managing the bureau" (Niskanen 1971, 108). However, most researchers of privatization largely ignore the public choice approach. As Feigenbaum and his coauthors (1999, 2) wrote, "privatization is typically portrayed in narrow, almost apolitical terms, as little more than a vehicle for helping government balance their budgets, or, at best, improving the overall performance of the economy."

The Case of Privatizing Public Services

The privatization of public services became a hot topic in the 1980s and 1990s when the President's Commission on Privatization was created (Linowes 1988). A considerable number of authors praised the privatization of public services for increasing efficiency and reducing the cost of services (Savas 1990). In the last decades, federal and local governments have transferred many of their functions to private organizations; such areas of responsibility include public safety, prisons, education, judicial services, health issues and programs, environmental protection, and garbage collection (Auger 1999; Dilger, Moffett, and Struyk 1997; Metzger 2003; Finn, Manno, and Vanourek 2000; Dunham 1986; Harding 2001; Provine and Seron 1991).

We do not wish to judge these developments from a normative perspective, but rather to delineate their feudal and liberal elements. The delegation of state functions to private companies fits the liberal model if several firms bid for state contracts and the winning company is controlled by free market relations. In other cases, privatization leads to a situation in which a company is not effectively controlled by the market or the state (Sullivan 1987; Donahue 1989).

As the trend of privatization took root, ordinary people became concerned about the accountability of the privatized firms. In a nationwide survey by the U.S. Advisory Commission of Intergovernmental Relations (ACIR) in 1986, a majority of people preferred local governments to private companies in the delivery of many services, including ambulance services, garbage collection, and others. A survey conducted by PEW in 1998 brought similar results about the importance of the role of federal and local governments in delivering many services. A study of the attitudes of Michigan residents in 1996 yielded similar results: among fourteen services, the respondents gave preference to private contractors in only five cases (cleaning streets, performing clerical services in governmental buildings, providing emergency medical services, performing janitorial services in the same buildings, and collecting garbage).

The privatization of services, according to Michigan residents, increases "political corruption or favoritism" from 2.52 to 3.12; each item was measured based on a five-point scale ranging from 5 (strongly agree) to 1 (strongly disagree) (Thompson and Elling 2000). This survey confirmed the conclusion that Ronald Moe made in 1987 when he contended, "Possibly the most potent of the actors limiting the spread of privatization in the American context is the specter of corruption" (Moe 1987, 458).

The analysis of specific cases of privatization in America is beyond the goal of this chapter. The real character of privatization can be established only in the process of empirical analysis that shows what sort of privatization is taking place (capitalist or feudal). It depends on various factors, including the impact of corruption and the existence of competition (Hart, Shleifer, and Vishny 1997).

The Authoritarian Model in the Analysis of Contemporary American Society

The authoritarian model is also important for the study of contemporary society. Labor is largely based on relations between superiors and subordinates. The hierarchical principle dominates the relations between managers and employees in America factories, offices, and shopping malls; between doctors and nurses; between teachers and students. Several leading organizations, including the army and the Catholic Church, are also based on hierarchical principles. The same is true of most corporations and midsize businesses. The American government bureaucracy at the national and local level is strongly influenced by elected officials and the right of legislators to control its activity. Most of the everyday activities of the executive branch of government follow the principles of hierarchical organizations. The same is true of trade unions, which combine democratic and authoritarian rules in their activities. American universities are complicated organizations in which liberal rules play an important role (for instance, the election of several categories of officials and voting procedure in the tenure process), but the hierarchical principle still shapes the relations between the provost's office and the deans, and between deans and departments.

The hierarchical principle supposes the pivotal role of sanctions and punishment for rule violation, as well as the fear of superiors. Many authors in the last decades showed their disgust for the spread of fear in American society, including Garland (1990), Shklar (1998), Ryan and Oestreich (1998), and Robin (2004). However, they do not consider the role of fear in the authoritarian organizations of American society and do not recognize that, so long as this type of social organization exists in society, fear will remain an organic instrument for running these organizations (Shlapentokh 2006). More consistent are those writers who propose the elimination of authoritarian principles in the functioning of any unit of society, from the factory to the classroom, and the replacement of them with democratic rules (Busch 2000).

Conclusion

This chapter showed how the analysis of any society, past or present, requires a segmented approach and the use of at least three models (liberal, authoritarian, and feudal). Contrary to conventional wisdom, some liberal tendencies existed in medieval societies. The political competition of the "few" made the emergence of liberal elements inevitable. Private interests and contracts also played important roles in medieval society and laid the groundwork for the liberal institutions of a later age. No less important were authoritarian tendencies, as seen in the development of absolute monarchy in the late Middle Ages. The conflict between these tendencies reflected the essence of historical processes until the bourgeois revolution.

The segmented approach also fits contemporary American society. Unrestrained private interests generate monopolistic tendencies, and big corporations emerge as feudal social actors. Representative democracies often fail, in some respects, to bar corporations from using their resources to influence elections and diminish political equality. Authoritarian elements can also be found in contemporary America, particularly in organizations that are structured by hierarchical or command principles. All three models are needed for the analysis of privatization. Depending on various circumstances, privatization can enhance the market or increase feudal or authoritarian elements in society.

3

Big Money and Corporations as Promoters of Feudal Tendencies

Feudal elements tend to emerge when the state is unable or unwilling to maintain order in society. This inability may stem from a lack of resources or from problems associated with corruption. One such tendency occurs when social actors, from individuals to large organizations, use their private resources to extract privileges from the state in a way that is incompatible with the public goals advanced by the central administration or electorate. More generally, a monopoly on any scarce resource—a typical feudal phenomenon—generates corruption and creates a basis for collecting extra "rent" through modes of behavior that violate hierarchical, democratic, and market principles. Essentially, each piece of private property and each public office is a monopoly, even if only a temporary one, for those who control it.

As Coase and Williamson suggested, monopolies can be found in all spheres of social life (Williamson 1996, 288). Churches, for instance, have a monopoly on religious rituals. A church can use various forms of religious approval or disapproval to influence its members. The Catholic Church still uses the fear of excommunication to temper any challenge to the pope's monopoly on truth and the various rules of the Church. The power basis of many theological regimes in history resided in their monopolies on the right to approve or disapprove behavior. This instrument was often more effective than physical coercion.

The employees of large firms are well aware of the monopoly on decision making held by top executives or CEOs. Even the secretaries and close advisers of executives enjoy a sort of monopoly on access to the leader. Such power can be exchanged for a variety of rents, from simple acts of kindness to valuable gifts and lucrative jobs. The boards of directors of large organizations also hold a monopolistic position, given their control over rewards and decision making, and the difficulties of challenging their official verdicts.

As a matter of fact, all privileges, by definition, have an exclusive and monopolistic character, which implies an unequal distribution of some good or opportunity. The privileges that some actors receive can range from the perks of nepotism and the use of offices as sources of additional income, to tax concessions and export licenses.

These relations challenge the principles of both the authoritarian and liberal models. The authoritarian model supposes that each member of society is rewarded only for contributing to the might of the state or to the power of its leaders. The liberal model supposes that the well-being of each individual depends on the success of perfect economic and political competition. No one is entitled to privileges stemming from the abuse of property or positions in bureaucracy. Economic inequality encourages feudal tendencies, a point that was noted by the advocates of Jeffersonian democracy who suggested that democracy is threatened by large concentrations of wealth. Robert Dahl, in *On Political Equality*, wrote that in countries such as the United States and Britain, the importance of "minority money" in political life makes the idea of fair democratic competition nonsense, because elected politicians answer more to big money donors than to voters (Dahl 2006; Ringen 2006).

Of course, people with few resources have less access to privileges than those individuals who control major assets—such as political or religious power, money, and prestige—which can be used to extract benefits in interpersonal relations. Most people with limited incomes have no chance of receiving significant privileges in economic or political life, whereas those with deep financial resources, property, or high positions in government function both as givers and receivers of privileges that contradict the official structure, whether authoritarian or liberal.

Corruption as the Basis for Feudal Tendencies

Corruption in contemporary society is a "normal" channel that makes the exchange of political privileges for money possible. According to Treisman (2000, 399), corruption can be defined as "the misuse of a public office for private gain." The level of corruption explains the extent to which contemporary society overlaps with the feudal model. "Corruption" should be seen as a universal phenomenon that plays an important role in almost all societies.

As mentioned, corruption is rarely treated as a normal part of society in the contemporary literature. As noted by Lambsdorff (2007, 1), the founder of Transparency International, "corruption . . . turns out to be a relatively new challenge for social science." In an otherwise impressive collection of articles on corruption edited by Glaeser and Goldin, one cannot find an attempt to examine corruption from a general theoretical perspective. In the introduction, the editors emphasize the illegality of corruption, its redistributive character, and the usual list of possible causes of corruption, even where laws adopted under the pressure of ruling elites make corruption look legal in many instances (Glaeser and Goldin 2006). In speaking of "white-collar crimes," Braithwaite (1985) wrote that almost no one has tried to connect these crimes with a general sociological theory. The same diagnosis can be extended to most studies of corruption.

The feudal model offers a broad theoretical framework, which juxtaposes corruption vis-à-vis the liberal and authoritarian models. Our approach is similar to that of historians and other scholars who study the "market relations" of ancient Rome or the totalitarian elements of Western society. Corruption is a normal element in practically all societies, past and present, from totalitarian societies, where it plays a limited role, to societies with weak states in which corruption is a central form of social interaction and exchange.[1]

Henry Chamberlain (1932) wrote that "organized crime is as ancient as civilization." The same is true about corruption. In a related book by Lee-Chai and Bargh (2001, 57), the authors titled one of their chapters "From Moses to Marcos." In the 2,500-year-old Indian manuscript *Arthshastra,* a demand was made of the king to fight corruption (Jain 1998). Corruption was also widespread in ancient Rome (Wallace-Hadrill 1989; Wilson 1989).

In the Middle Ages, corruption became a key part of social relations, even if this term has only recently been applied to this époque (Dean 2001; Waquet 1991). Bribes represented an important part of the income of judges and sheriffs in thirteenth-century England. Janin found that people in Nottingham were forced to pay their judges a hundred shillings to gain immunity from criminal prosecution (Janin 2004).

Surveying various studies on the judicial system in several medieval European countries, Dean suggested that the nobles were rarely punished for their

1. There are different views on the size of corruption in the Soviet totalitarian society. Some contemporary Russian authors, in order to diminish the responsibility of the current ruling elite for the rampant corruption in post-Soviet society, suggest that corruption was even higher in Soviet times (see Chubais 2002; Gudkov 2000).

criminal deeds (Dean 2001). Gift giving, a clear form of corruption, was another important feudal element. In the kingdom of Charlemagne, for instance, gifts from nobles, which were separate from taxes, were an important source of royal revenue (Rubin 1987; Rutz and Orlove 1989).

Corruption as a Feudal Aspect of American Society

Corruption has a long history in American society. As asserted by Henry Adams, corruption posed a serious problem to the country in the second half of the nineteenth century, when even President Grant was suspected of taking bribes. At that time, executives, the judiciary, banks, professionals, and people in general all operated "in one dirty cesspool of vulgar corruption" (Josephson 1962). At the beginning of the twentieth century, corruption was widespread in the major cities. It became a central object of investigations by muckrakers such as Lincoln Steffens (Zinn 2003). Corruption was also widespread during the "roaring Twenties" (Perrett 1985). In the early 2000s, according to Transparency International, corruption was a more serious problem in the United States than in several other countries. In 2007, however, seventeen countries ranked higher than the United States on Transparency's corruption scale.

Based on an index of public perceptions of corruption, the United States' ranking of 7.2 was only slightly higher than that of Belgium (7.1), Chile (7.0), and Spain (6.7) (Transparency International 2007). Numerous publications in the last few decades vividly describe corruption at all levels of the federal and local governments (Grossman 2003). Contemporary history describes several major scandals involving corrupt activities, including the savings and loan scandal, the ABSCAM scandal (1978–80) (Grossman 2003),[2] the collapse of Enron,[3] and the Abramoff affairs (Weisman 2006).[4]

2. The case involved several congressmen and U.S. senators. In 1978, FBI agents, posing as representatives of a phony corporation called "Abdul Enterprises," asked some congressmen and senators to help them purchase casinos in the United States. Seven of them were enmeshed in bribery charges and indicted in 1980. One congressman, Michael Myers, was expelled from the House of Representatives as a result of the scandal.

3. The central figure of this scandal was Kenneth Lay, the CEO and chairman of Enron from 1986 until his resignation in 2002. He was indicted in 2004. Lay was a major Wnancial donor to the election campaign of President George W. Bush and had been named a leading candidate for the secretary of treasury.

4. The case involved Michael Scanlon, a Republican political operative and the spokesman for House majority leader Tom DeLay, who planned with Jack Abramoff to bribe a congressman in order to cheat American Indian tribes. He pled guilty. In fact, several legislators and officials were involved in Abramoff's schemes.

Among the politicians who were indicted or resigned from their posts due to involvement in corruption, including bribery cases and illegal campaign-financing schemes, were members of Congress, including majority leader Bill Frist, who was labeled as one of the most corrupt politicians in America (he was forced to retire after being fined for improprieties related to the financing of his 2000 election), Jim Traficant (indicted in 2002), Robert Torricelli (indicted in 2002), Randy "Duke" Cunningham (pled guilty in 2006), William Jefferson (indicted in 2006), and Ted Stevens (indicted in 2008).

The list of local politicians indicted for taking bribes after 2000 is quite long. It includes Alaskan legislator Tom Anderson (indicted in 2006), California assembly speaker Fabian Nuñez (2007), Connecticut governor John Rowland (resigned in 2004), Louisiana governor Edwin Edwards (convicted in 2000), and New Jersey state senator and former Newark mayor Sharpe James (accused in 2008) (Craven 2008). Some American states, such as Illinois, are known to have particularly serious problems with corruption, in the past and the present. Even before the case of Illinois governor Rod Blagojevich in December 2008, several officials from this state had been linked to corruption. Even considering only cases of the recent past, we can mention Congressman Dan Rostenkowski (April 1996), Governor George Ryan (April 2006), Robert Sorich, the patronage chief for Governor Richard Daley (July 2006), and Antoin Rezko, a fundraiser for Illinois governor Blagojevich and senator Barack Obama (June 2008) (McIntire and Zeleny 2008).

The American public is aware of the high level of corruption. When asked in a 2006 *USA Today/Gallup* poll, "How important for you will each of these issues be to your vote for Congress this year," 49 percent of Americans said that "government corruption" is "extremely important." Only concern about the Iraq War was higher; people were more worried about corruption than about terrorism and the economy (Parker 2006). In another Gallup poll in 2006, 83 percent thought that "corruption in Congress" is a "very serious" or "somewhat serious" problem; 47 percent believed that most members of Congress are corrupt (Gallup).

The high level of corruption in Washington is, according to the views of many observers, one of the main reasons for the extremely low overall approval rating of Congress (21 percent in 2006). It is important to note that the three branches of government have always tried to curb corruption. Congress has attempted to regulate the amount of money that its members can accept. In 2008, the value of gifts received by members of Congress from one person could not exceed $100 per year (Public Citizen 2007). Corporations, as suggested in the next sections, are the leading actors in fostering feudal relations in society. Their access to gigantic amounts of money provides them with a similar level of political power as the medieval manor.

The Landlord and the Corporation

The landlord was a major player in medieval society. Its role matches that of the corporation in a capitalist society. Both tend(ed) to create their own worlds while trying to be as self-sufficient as possible (Vinogradoff 1924). Both possess(ed) tremendous political power, making them partners and, in some cases, opponents of the central administration. Both actors enjoy(ed) a great deal of autonomy, particularly with regard to internal processes and controlling the people within their territories. The interaction between internal and external dimensions and the dynamics of this interaction shaped (or shapes) the function of both the manor and the corporation (Bowman 1996, 127–37). Those who ran feudal estates and those who run corporations determine(d) the level of their personal income, as well as the number and size of their numerous perks.

The main resources of medieval barons were land and the territories they controlled. Their landholdings determined the size of their private armies, the number of knights with heavy arms and horses, and the size of their clientele, or, to use Wickham's (2005, 192) terminology, their "network of sworn military dependants." Of course, though important, the size of the estate was not the only factor determining the status of medieval aristocrats. Other factors included their place or position in the hierarchy, kinship with the king, alliances with other feudal barons, and participation in various gatherings, such as tournaments and royal festivities. Conspicuous consumption bloomed in the early Middle Ages and included expensive castles, decorations, fine clothing, jewels, and personal servants (Wickham 2005, 201). The structure and management of the manor was almost as complex as that of a midsized corporation. The division of labor in medieval castles was quite sophisticated; servants performed a variety of very different functions to satisfy the needs of the lord and his retinue.

Church relations and participation in church endeavors (the Crusades, for instance) were important to feudal barons, since the actions of bishops and the pope could enhance or diminish their prestige, as well as legitimize or delegitimize their property. Each big land property (manor or fiefdom) had its own church. Some landlords founded and patronized their own monasteries, in the same way as the head of a corporation might patronize universities or other groups. In some ways, the media plays a similar role for corporations as the Church did for landlords. The attitudes of journalists toward corporate America are as important to today's firms as the attitudes of bishops were toward local barons.

The military performance of barons in wars and tournaments greatly affected their prestige. The number of people who lived in the territory of their fiefs—including peasants of various types, vassals, and villagers—was also an important determinant of a landlord's political power. The property of the feudal baron—"long-distance landowning," to use Wickham's term (2005, 188)—was often dispersed over a big territory, not unlike the local branches of a large contemporary corporation. The feudal lord considered infrastructure construction and maintenance in villages and cities in his region to be his responsibility; for instance, he was concerned about the state of dikes and the security of roads.

Whereas money played a secondary role in medieval times (Innes 2000), financial resources serve as the basis of a contemporary corporation's political power and autonomy. A corporation's political power is also based on the number of employees and branches the organization manages (equivalent to the number of knights and peasants under the control of feudal bosses). Indicators of the corporation's power include its financial performance, the degree of market control, and the level of salaries and bonuses paid. These well-known signs of the political power held by managers and owners of corporations correspond to success in war in medieval times.

The number of branches a corporation controls is an important indicator of its power, in the same way as the number and size of the patronage network of a medieval baron determined the extent of his influence (Wickham 2005, 191). A contemporary corporation's clientele is quite similar to the networks run by medieval barons (Kawata 2006). The number of employees in a corporation is akin to the number of peasants who depended on a medieval lord. A company's control over its workers, including their wealth, pensions, and health insurance benefits, is comparable to medieval relationships between a landlord and his peasants. The services offered by a landlord to his peasants, which included judicial protection and help during disasters, could be compared to the activities of a corporation, which provides its employees with a variety of services (medical, educational, and legal, as well as entertainment benefits). Of course, we should not forget that peasants were barred from leaving their residences, while today's corporate employees can and do leave on a regular basis (Lindblom 1988; Jouvenel 1951; Kanter 1993).

Corporate power is also seen in the level of influence a firm has on the local community or its surrounding city. Big corporations, like medieval manors, are sometimes involved in maintaining city infrastructure, parks, transportation, and a range of other city-level services. The greater a corporation's involvement in a city's well-being, the higher its public prestige. A corporation, as the main employer in a city, maintains close relations with the local authorities. The same was true of big landlords in medieval France or England. Vinogradoff (1924, 458) suggested that manorial administrations maintained relations with village communities and their "peculiar self-government."

Personal connections between corporate owners or leaders and government officials (similar to the connections between lords and kings), as well as between corporations via their interlocking directorates, play an important role in society (Bowman 1996, 19–20). For medieval barons, marriage was the interlocking device. The concept of networks is as necessary for describing social relations in medieval France as it is in contemporary America. The participation of corporate managers in various meetings, including at the White House or on Capitol Hill, is just as important to them as the attendance at tournaments, various ceremonies, and the royal court was for knights. Some authors, following Mills, have pointed to the personal backgrounds of owners and top managers of big corporations, and suggested that their "aristocratic" heritage and ties to members of the economic and political elite determine their career paths (Dogan 2003, 1–3).

Of great importance to the political power of corporations is the number of elected officials who defend their interests in Congress, and the number of "friendly" media outlets. For corporations, the media are as important today as the Church's opinion was for barons. Media sources can establish a company's image as a pro-social organization that willingly takes some responsibility for the nation and its people (for instance, campaigns against smoking or obesity). In a similar fashion, the medieval Church would spread the view of powerful lords as good Christians, illuminating their contributions to the Church. The lords would then, in turn, support the Church with donations of money and land. Contemporary corporations perform essentially the same exchange with the media by paying for commercial advertisements.

As discussed in the next sections, corporations acquire privileges from the government both directly and indirectly. In some cases, they use their material resources—money to begin with—to obtain privileges from the executive, legislative, and judicial branches. In others, they use the election process to promote people who will later reward the corporation with various privileges.

Rent-Seeking Activity

The rent-seeking theory explains how corruption helps corporations gain various advantages from the government. The idealization of money and the disregard of its political and often destructive role explain, in part, why the rent-seeking theory did not emerge until the late 1960s (Tullock 1967, 1989). A rent-seeking activity is considered by many authors to be a particular case of corruption, in which corporations bribe government officials to receive privileges (Treisman 2000; Ades and Di Tella 1999). The concept that was later termed *rent seeking* entered the economic literature in the 1960s. However, the term was proposed by Anne Krueger in 1974. In fact, the first author to write a major book about the interaction between the government and corporations was Rudolf Hilferding (1981), an Austro-Hungarian Marxist who talked about the increasing role of banks in capitalist economies. Hilferding entered the history of economic thought with his ideas about the coalescence of financial capital and government, which were later widely used by Vladimir Lenin in his famous work *Imperialism: The Highest Stage of Capitalism* (1917).

Jain (1998) has noted that the neoclassical mainstream scholars have mostly ignored the concepts of rent seeking and corruption (Keim and Zeithaml 1986; Colander 1984). Mark Mizruchi (Mizruchi and Koenig 1986, 1988; Mizruchi 2004), who wrote abundantly about the social issues of corporations, ignored relations between corporations and the government. Even Scott Bowman, in an important book that critically analyzed corporations, did not mention rent-seeking activities or corporate involvement in corruption (Bowman 1996). It is remarkable that Reich, an economist and politician who is critical of the American economic system, almost completely ignores corruption and rent-seeking activities, judging from his numerous publications and recent book *Super Capitalism* (Reich 2007). Sociologists who study corporations and white-collar crime also tend to ignore rent seeking.

Rent Seeking in the Middle Ages

Rent seeking can be found in any place or time in which money plays an important social and political role. According to the economic historian Postan (1944, 123), "economies wholly natural never existed and money always played an important role in Middle Age life." The royal administration and medieval lords yearned for money, which they used for a variety of purposes, including expanding the royal domain, strengthening its military forces, and supporting a high lifestyle. The need for money pushed social actors to sell various privileges to each other, and to common people as well (Cantor 1993, 464). The government, the barons, and the Church each possessed a monopoly on various resources, which they exchanged for money. Tollison and his colleagues showed how this concept could be used for analyzing the Roman Catholic Church as "the dominant firm in the salvation industry" (Ekelund, Hebert, and Tollison 1989, 309).

Along with demanding taxes, the state frequently forced the bourgeoisie and cities to "borrow" money. The central administration could also draw money from other big actors, such as guilds, through negotiations or promises of autonomy and other privileges. Another source of money came from the sale of positions in the royal administration, a common practice (Pirenne 1937).

Privileges from Rent Seeking

Rent-seeking activities are usually defined as those political activities of organizations, groups, or individuals that extricate special monopoly privileges from the government by compensating officials in various ways. The concept of rent seeking supposes a high level of autonomy for the state, an idea that is incompatible with Marxist and radical views of the state. An orthodox Marxist perspective would insist that the United States government is "a committee for managing the common affairs of the whole bourgeoisie." Even neo-Marxists—such as Poulantzas—who suggest that the state machine has some autonomy still ultimately contend that it is no more than a mechanism for coordinating corporate interests (Poulantzas 2000).

Rent seeking is not always illegal. The privileges that corporations receive include government contracts, which are especially valuable in the defense industry; the exemption from or lowering of taxes; "redistributive legislation" (laws favorable to corporations); concessions in regulations; immunity against judicial prosecution; the speeding up of registration processes; autonomy in management, including the waiving of national laws; licenses for foreign trade; easy credit; and the elimination of competitors during the sale of state property, which makes it easy to bankrupt one's rivals or block their entry in the market. A bank, for instance, may gain a great advantage over its competitors when government officials select it as the agent who distributes budget money (Lindahl and Carter 1959).

A special type of rent-seeking activity is the buying and selling of official political positions, from ambassadorships to memberships in Congress or parliament (Buchanan, Tollison, and Tullock 1981; Mitchell and Munger 1991). The case of Illinois governor Blagojevich is a clear illustration of feudal elements in American political life. Blagojevich was arrested in December 2008 on federal corruption charges. Prosecutors said that he had conspired to profit from his authority to appoint a successor to Barack Obama, who resigned his U.S. Senate seat after being elected president (Davey 2008). Like a feudal boss, the governor attempted to use his official powers to extract compensation from local organizations and individuals, in exchange for subsidies or government contracts (*New York Times* blog, 2009). Blagojevich was the fifth of the last eight Illinois governors to be charged with a crime. Since 1971, one thousand Illinois public servants have been convicted of corruption (Zernike 2008).

Pork-barrel practices, in which legislators manage to attach expenditures to special bills that are useful for their constituency as a sort of payment for their election or reelection, are a form of rent seeking. Pork barreling, which has been an important social and political issue over the years, emerged prominently during the 2008 presidential election campaigns.[5] The borders between rent-seeking activities and legislators performing their duties as representatives of a single territory are indeed gray. Still, acquiring special privileges for individual territories, whatever the opportunity cost, is at least similar to rent seeking (Tullock 1989; Mueller 1990; Harris 1995). As suggested by one author, perhaps with some exaggeration, recent increases in rent seeking have destroyed the reputation of Congress (Parker 1996). An important sphere of rent-seeking activity is the government's provision of public goods. Powerful political actors, such as corporations and universities, are able to acquire public goods, such as free land, in exchange for supporting legislators or other officials (Gradstein 1993).

Rent Givers

Those who pursue rent-seeking activities (corporations and other major social actors) spend money and other resources in order to receive privileges from officials. The money used to bribe officials is considered a transaction cost, which reflects the expenditures of the firm on its public activities. Of course, transaction costs influence the price of goods and services (Williamson 1996, 25–28).

5. "Pork barrel" spending, or earmarking, is a practice by which legislators secure federal funding for their home districts. See, for instance, the article, "Pork Barrel Spending Emerging as Presidential Campaign Issue: Candidates, Critics Differ on Definition of and Remedies for the Practice," by Michael W. Drudge (Drudge 2008).

Responding to the Blagojevich scandal, a journalist from the *New York Times* suggested that "politicians routinely receive political contributions in return for their decisions, whether they involve making appointments or taking a stand on legislation. Lawmakers vote in favor of bills and steer appropriations backed by their donors without fear that prosecutors will bug their offices and homes" (Johnston 2008).

Blagojevich is a product of Chicago's notorious political machine, which has roots going back to the late nineteenth century, when immigrants, predominantly from Ireland, Poland, and Italy, were often discriminated against and sought protection from local political bosses. In exchange for food, housing, and jobs, immigrants promised their loyalty and votes to their benefactors. The feudal character of the Chicago political machine became well known in the era of Mayor Richard Daley (1955–76). His contemporaries talked about him as "the wily machine boss who ruled Chicago like a feudal preserve," as a tyrant who maintained "a feudal political system of patronage and fear," and as a "feudal boss" (Cohen and Taylor 2000, 3, 496–97). Even before Daley, however, Otto Kerner, who served as governor in the 1960s, was found to have accepted bribes in racetrack stock. And the ascension to power by Richard Daley's son, Richard Jr. (who has ruled the city since 1989, having been reelected five times, the last in 2007), fits the feudal model as well.

Following the 1970 death of Paul Powell, an Illinois secretary of state from 1965 until his death, the police discovered $800,000 in cash hidden in his closet—a considerable amount of savings for a man whose salary was about $30,000 a year (Zernike 2008). What other analytical tool can explain this and other similar aspects of big-city politics, where semilegal rent-seeking activities mix with pure corruption as organic parts of urban society (Bennett 1997)?

Chicago is not a feudal island, of course. Many other cities and regional governments have their feudal elements as well. According to the Corporate Crime Reporter, the ten most corrupt states (in order) are Louisiana, Mississippi, Kentucky, Alabama, Ohio, Illinois, Pennsylvania, Florida, New Jersey, and New York (Corporate Crime Reporter 2009).

The costs and efficiencies of rent-seeking activities vary greatly. The costs may include expenditures on lobbying and bribing officials with cash, gifts, the transfer of corporate stock, the provision of apartments, and high-class entertainments. Providing lucrative jobs in the private sector to officials following their retirement from government is another important form of corruption. Some officials have tried to confront this development. President Obama, for instance, prohibited officials from resigning from government and immediately taking certain positions in business (Reich 2007).[6] Donations to political campaigns are also an effective form of rent-seeking activity.

Enron's connections to the White House are an excellent example of rent seeking. There is a great deal of evidence showing that Enron, in the person of Kenneth Lay, participated in the formulation of President Bush's energy policy. This was vitally important to Enron, the nation's largest buyer and seller of natural gas. Lay met privately with Vice President Dick Cheney in 2001, when Cheney led the National Energy Policy Development Group, which drafted Bush's energy policies (Simon 2002, 50, 52). The company's influence on the White House was illustrated by the fact that Bush's economic counselor, Lawrence Lindsey, had been a paid adviser to Enron. Karl Rove, Bush's political strategist, was a big investor in Enron, and the Republican national chairman, Marc Racicot, was a paid lobbyist for Enron (Simon 2002, 49). The company had a long relationship with powerful members of Congress from Texas. Senator Phil Gramm's wife was an Enron director. The company also had connections to House majority whip Tom DeLay and others. President George H. W. Bush was hired by Enron as a consultant (Simon 2002, 52). Enron always supported George W. Bush and his political allies.

The employees and directors of Enron gave Bush $623,000 over the course of his political career, which began in 1994. The Bush presidential campaign in 2000 received $74,200 in contributions from two dozen top executives and board members. From 1999 to 2001, Enron also gave $1,895,964 in soft money contributions to the Republican and Democratic national parties (Simon 2002, 47–48). In essence, rent-seeking activities are not aimed at creating resources, but at redistributing them. For this reason, rent seeking is a political instrument used by management, and it depends on the political environment. In fact, rent seeking is a mechanism that provides one actor with a monopoly on some limited resource and deprives this resource from others, even if these others could use it more effectively.

The Consequences of Rent Seeking

Rent-seeking activities are mostly illegal and lead to an unproductive allocation of resources (Colander 1984). Some authors use stronger statements, insisting

6. As discussed by Reich, after leaving office, more than half of the senior people in the Clinton administration became lobbyists. Tom Daschle, Democratic minority leader of the Senate, after his fiasco in the election of 2004, found a very well-paying position in a lobbying firm that served mostly Republican clients (Reich 2007, 138–39).

that "rent seeking in the form of bribes and corruption can lead to a nation's economic decline" (Mueller 2003, 358). Of course, rent seeking also has a tremendously negative effect on democracy and social order. As Jomo wrote, "rent-seeking activities thus impose avoidable costs involving resource transfers or, alternatively, resource use on socially unnecessary and unproductive activities, which are deemed socially wasteful" (Jomo 2003, 338; see Diamond 2003). Meanwhile, rent seeking is almost totally ignored in most economic textbooks. One exception can be seen in the work of Galambos and colleagues (Galambos 1988; Galambos and Pratt 1988).

Regulation and Rent Seeking

The government's regulation of corporations generates a complex set of relations between public agencies and private businesses; much of this interaction can be interpreted best using the feudal model.[7] As many researchers have noted, corporations participate in politics in order to protect and expand their economic welfare and ensure their survival (Epstein 1969; Williamson 1975, 1981; Sitkoff 2003–4; McChesney 1997). As suggested by Cheung (1987), a corporation's participation in politics can be thought of as a transaction cost (see Williamson 1985). The importance of rent seeking is proportionate to the influence of federal and local regulations on corporations. Rent-seeking activities attempt to mitigate relations between government and corporations, which can be very antagonistic.[8] As David Vogel suggests, "nearly every corporate department developed a counterpart in the regulatory bureaucracy: decisions as to what to produce, where to produce it, whom to hire and promote, how to allocate research and development funds and—even for a brief period—how much to charge customers and pay employees became subject to a highly complex process of negotiations and bargaining between corporate officials and regulators, congressmen and judges" (Vogel 1983, 26–27; Weidenbaum 1986, 285–89).

The Technology of Rent Seeking

In the United States, where lobbying is a legal business, rent seeking has become a substantial economic sector that employs thousands of people. From

7. For instance, by the mid-1970s, nearly every aspect of the automobile was regulated, including its exhaust levels, fuel efficiency, and safety; a major share of the car industry's research and development became devoted to compliance with government directives, while the cumulative impact of eighteen government-mandated specifications adopted between 1968 and 1974 was estimated to have increased the retail price of the average car by $300 (Vogel 1981, 27).

8. For a summary of social regulatory issues in Europe and the United States, see Vogel (1981, 24).

time to time, lobbying in the United States has been a target of criminal investigation, some of which has led to prison terms, as in the case of Jack Abramoff in 2006 (Epstein 1969).

Rent-seeking activities demand that corporations create their own bureaucracy and network of organizations in order to influence the government. Between 1975 and 2005, the number of registered lobbyists in Washington increased almost tenfold from 3,400 to 32,890. In 1950, fewer than one hundred companies had an office in the capital. By the 1990s, this number had increased by five times. These companies employed more than 60,000 lawyers. In 2006, the initial salary for a lobbyist with good connections in Washington was about $500,000 (Reich 2007, 134–35, 139; McGrath 1979).

Legislators, whose decisions can influence business, are often the target of rent-seeking activities (Keim and Zeithaml 1986). A good example is the case of Frank Lorenzo, chairman of Eastern and Continental Airlines. He was a generous donor to the Republican Party. As soon as the senior Bush became president, he helped Lorenzo in his dispute with the unions, taking Lorenzo's side in the conflict, despite the recommendation of the National Mediation Board to create a federal emergency strike settlement board and provide a sixty-day cooling-off period (Eitzen and Baca Zinn 2004, 408).

Direct Corporate Influence on Politics: The Academic Debate

A number of mainstream sociologists have conspicuously ignored the role of corporations when it comes to describing political life in America. (We put aside here the important and highly debated issue illustrated in Berle and Means's *The Modern Corporation and Private Property* [1968], which described the political and social character of contemporary corporations as being the relative role of their managers, boards of directors, and stockholders.) Mark Mizruchi, a prominent author on the role of corporations in American life, noted in 2004 that sociologists recently lost interest in the study of the role of corporations in American political life (Mizruchi 2004).

Several sociology and political science textbooks, notwithstanding their various critiques of American society, do not discuss corporations as political actors at all (see, for instance, Stark 2001; Andersen and Taylor 2002). Take, for example, two sociology textbooks edited by Neil Smelser. In one (1994), the term *corporation* was never used. In the other, his noted *Handbook of Sociology*, corporations were mentioned only in the context of international relations (see Evans and Stephens 1988, 755–56).

Political scientists also tend to ignore corporations as leading political actors in American society, as seen in Rodee's *Introduction to Political Science* (1983) or Burns, Peltason, and Cronin's *Government by the People* (2000). You will not find the term *corporation* in *Politics in Three Words: An Introduction to Political Science* (Best, Rai, and Walsh 1986) or in *Sociology: Micro, Macro, and Mega Structures* by Jones, Gallagher, and McFalls (1995).

Some political scientists even ignore the political activities of corporations when describing elections in American society. The authors of *People, Power, and Politics* devote twenty pages to the election process in the United States, but never mention the role of corporations as donors (Donovan et al. 1993). The political activities of corporations even go unnoticed in *The Role of the Modern Corporation in a Free Society,* a book devoted to this institution (Danley 1994). No less surprising is the absence of this subject in Mueller's eight-hundred-page *Public Choice III* (2003), which pays much attention to rent-seeking activities and lobbying—and the influence of these phenomena on political processes such as elections—but talks only about "interest groups," without specifying them and without making distinctions between big corporations, dairy farmers, and small political parties.

As mentioned earlier, economists often sidestep this subject as well. For instance, the prominent economist Gregory Mankiw, in his popular textbook *Principles of Macroeconomics* (2007), almost completely ignores the subject of corporations. The government is discussed in the book only in relation to government debt, governmental purchases, and the level of taxes. Nothing is said about rent-seeking activities and the complex relations between government and business (Mankiw 2007).

Other textbooks on macroeconomics follow a similar template, ignoring the political role of corporations and rent seeking (Case and Fair 2002; McConnell and Brue 2006; Blanchard 2003). The economist Oliver Williamson only pays minor attention to the state, and ignores other institutions in his discussion of market mechanisms. In fact, given his focus on transaction costs, Williamson—not unlike Coase and Simon—supports contemporary institutionalism. One of his major books, *The Economic Institutions of Capitalism* (1985), contains a chapter titled "The Modern Corporation," yet there is no mention of rent-seeking activities or corruption or even a general statement about corporate-government relations. In a more recent book, *The Mechanism of Governance,*

Williamson (1996) continued to ignore the political and social context of big business.

Only a few economists have focused on the political dimension of large corporations. Among them, Joseph Stiglitz (2003, 76) suggested that corporations "are often associated with bribing governments and contributing to corruption." More credit should go to the economist Robert Solo (1967), who described the American economy as a "hybrid system" and as a network of autonomous organizations, such as corporations, governments, trade unions, and households. He also discussed the influence of corporations on public policy.

While the contemporary discussion is lacking, there has been some debate over the role of corporations in American politics, particularly in the rather distant past. Interest in this issue emerged as corporations became the leading economic force in society in the early twentieth century. Two opposing views rose to prominence. In one camp, the advocates of "corporate liberalism" treated corporations as "corporate individuals" and saw them as "normal" actors in the competitive world of politics. This group suggested that freedom of speech protected the rights of corporations to spend as much money as they wished to circulate their views. Close to this camp were those who advocated a "pluralistic model" of American political order and conceptualized the corporation as just one of many different interest groups operating in a "competitive democratic market" (Bowman 1996, 27).

In the opposing camp were some politicians and scholars who, while recognizing the importance of corporations as promoters of technological progress, regarded them as "special actors" that, given their high concentration of economic power, presented a significant danger not only to economic competition, but also to democratic institutions and liberal freedoms. Among others, Herbert Croly talked about the destructive consequences of economic concentration to American democracy in his book *The Promise of American Life* (1909). A few years later, with a focus on corruption, Walter Weyl (1912) seconded Croly's concern about the impact of corporations on political order in society. These and a few other classic writers even labeled corporations as "feudal," "oligarchic," or "plutocratic," and called for restraints on corporate intrusion in the political process (Arnold 1940).

Several other prominent writers of the time were active in denouncing the political activities of corporations. Lincoln Steffens was an ardent critic of the political party machines of the early twentieth century (Steffens 1931). Lippmann, Lewis, and others highlighted the problems created by corporate activities in politics. Edwin Sutherland, a well-known sociologist and a pioneer in the study of white-collar crime, wrote that illegal business contributions to political candidates, even if infrequent, "tear at the social fabric more insidiously than do crimes of the common street variety" (Sutherland 1949, 83–88, 109–10).

There are many contemporary authors who stress the pernicious impact of corporate political activities on society. Peter DeLeon stated, "The corruptive political behavior of corporations seems omnipresent in contemporary American political systems" (DeLeon 1993). Bowman (1996, 281) talked about "the displacement of democracy by oligarchic rule throughout society." Among contemporary authors, Cavanagh strongly rejects attempts to justify the political activity of corporations in any period of American history. He bluntly states that "corporations have no natural rights" to participate in political processes, "nor do corporations have the right to use shareholder monies for political purposes that may be contrary to individual shareholder's preferences" (in Cavanagh and Mander 2002, 141).

Several other authors, with various political affiliations, have shared a similar view, including Dahl (2006) and Polsby (1963). Politicians have taken this position as well. Feingold suggested that corporate executives, with their tremendous power, permanently threaten "ideal, or pluralistic democracy" (see Sitkoff 2003–4, 30–36). Lindblom was quite explicit about the negative role of corporations in political processes when he contended that corporations have neither an ethical nor a logical legitimate role in the democratic process (Lindblom 1988). Reich is another politician who strongly condemns the political activities of corporations (Reich 2007).

Sitkoff argues against the thesis that corporate election donations damage investment activities or the interests of stockholders. He suggests, rather, that political donations have a positive effect on business, and opposed laws that limit campaign donations. Of course, Sitkoff's argument, which at least recognizes the existence of rent seeking, has little to do with the impact donations have on democratic principles and the honesty of elections. He may be right that the donations have a favorable effect on business. It may also be true, as he suggests, that some individuals, such as Ross Perot or Jon Corzine, make even bigger contributions to election campaigns than many corporations, but this misses the point (Sitkoff 2003–4).

A number of authors have exonerated or even praised corporations for their political activities. Some deny the accusation that corporations have threatened democracy. They tend to stress the separation between the business of lobbying, which is legal, and what is essentially illegal interference in elections.

Others suggest that the participation of big business in the election process is necessary to balance the power of trade unions.

Peter Drucker insisted that the political activities of corporations were "normal," because a corporation is an autonomous institution possessing "a triple personality"—economic, governmental, and social. He insisted that political activity is a normal element of corporate life (Drucker 1993). This view is shared, to some extent, by supporters of the various concepts of managerialism. Many prominent authors, such as Schumpeter (1954) and Galbraith (1952), have followed Berle and Means's (1968) analysis of the motivation of top managers. They discussed the leading role managers have played in the economy (the technostructure in Galbraith's terms), and recognized that managers yearn to play an active political role in society (Burris 2001; Pindyck and Rubinfeld 1998). Some advocates of managerialism have even contended that many CEOs are "more bipartisan," "closer to the political center," "less estranged from big government," and more "convinced of the necessity to expand the role of government to prevent deep depressions and possible radicalism" (Monson and Cannon 1965, 46–48). At the same time, critics of managerialism, such as Peter DeLeon (1993) and Scott Bowman (1996), have insisted that most managers, with their oligarchic, antidemocratic ideology, push the American political system away from the Jeffersonian ideals of democracy.

Participation in the Election Process

In society, corporations play a political role, acting as activists in election campaigns (Johnson-Cartee and Copeland 1991; Middleton and Chamberlin 1988). While hundreds of publications in recent years have been devoted to the topic of campaign financing by private businesses, this issue has only rarely been discussed in terms of a general theory of society (see Ferguson 1995; Berg 1994). Public choice theorists represent an exception to this rule.

Meanwhile, in the last two decades, the role of corporations in campaigns increased enormously, as the election process at all levels became more expensive. In a 1997 speech, President Bill Clinton reported that spending in congressional campaigns had increased sixfold in the last two decades (Gibbs et al. 1997). As suggested by many authors, corporations and wealthy people often play a crucial role in election outcomes (Green 2004). The defenders of the unlimited use of money in election campaigns use the free-speech argument—any restraint placed on spending money contradicts the First Amendment—

which was supported to some extent by *Buckley v. Valeo,* the Supreme Court decision of January 1976 (Bowie 2007; Lange and Rose 2007).

The role of corporations and wealthy individuals in election campaigns is particularly important when the candidates refuse to take public money and rely only on private money (Broder 2008). After the adoption of the McCain-Feingold Act of 2002, a corporation could not directly contribute soft money to a campaign in order to promote a particular candidate, but it could spend money for promoting "the issue" or for some other purposes, such as voter registration. For this reason, a corporation can finance the election campaign through political action committees (PACs), which directly participate in the campaign on the side of one or another candidate. However, a corporation cannot spend more than $5,000 on one candidate (Behan 2001).

Corporations can also mobilize their employees, shareholders, and all of their families for this purpose; each individual can make a contribution of up to $2,300 to each candidate and $28,500 to a national party committee (Fisch 1991; Khanna 2003). The role of PACs increased tremendously in the 1970s. In 1974, there were only 608 PACs in the United States. In 1989, there were 4,234. Among them, 1,802 were corporate and 349 were labor (Johnson-Cartee and Copeland 1991). Corporations can also cover the operational costs of independent PACs, which collect money from the general public (Etzioni 1988; Drew 1983; Sabato 1984).

During the federal election cycle of 2000, as data from the Center for Responsive Politics show, "large individual donors" gave one-third of all contributions. The contributions of "big donors" surpassed the contributions of "small" donors (those who gave less than $200) by almost two times. At the same time, in comparison with 1996, the contribution of big donors also increased by almost two times, while that of small donors diminished by one-third (Phillips 2003). By the end of June 2008, donations above $2,299 made up 22 percent of all donations to Obama's campaign and 39 percent of McCain's. It should be noted that wealthy individuals can also finance their own campaigns, which makes them stronger candidates than their rivals who do not have the same assets.[9]

Corporations and the wealthy know how to get around laws that limit their

9. As Marc Green wrote, "In 2000, twenty-seven House and Senate candidates spent at least $500,000 of their own money on their own campaigns. Self-financing is especially pronounced for challengers and for candidates in open-seat races. Challengers in the 1996 House elections spent an average of over $40,000 of their own money, one sixth of their total campaign costs; candidates in open-seat races spent over $90,000. The average Senate challenger that year spent $645,000—one quarter of his/her total campaign costs—out of his/her own pocket" (Green 2004, 158).

contributions. For instance, the 2002 campaign finance laws restricted the use of "soft money" from corporations and other big donors, which was channeled through political party campaign committees, but the mechanics of "bundling" and the use of lobbyists for this purpose allowed candidates to circumvent the new legislation. George W. Bush used these strategies for the first time during the 2000 presidential election. Bundling allows candidates to bypass the $2,300 cap on individual contributions. A campaign's strongest supporters go beyond simply offering donations, by attempting to collect or "bundle" money from other donors (Green 2004; Reich 2007; Kirkpatrick 2007). In some cases, political donations can be disguised as charitable donations or as tickets for fund-raising dinners organized on behalf of the party (Handler, Godtfredsen, and Mulkern 1980; Malbin 1979; Mulkern, Handler, and Godtfredsen 1981; Swanson 1981; Chappell 1982; Herndon 1982; Kau and Rubin 1982).

Yet another way to make large donations is to create special organizations called 527s, which are free to accept unlimited "soft" money (Luo 2008a). These organizations received their name from Section 527 of the federal tax code. While many groups fall into this category, election observers tend to be most concerned about independent 527s that are not connected to a PAC or a party, which means they exist outside the government's strictest regulations, as dictated by the 1971 Federal Election Campaign Act (Cantor 2006). Wealthy people and corporations can also use paid advertisements that claim to support "the issue" but, in fact, promote a chosen candidate (Reich 2007).

The existing laws contain loopholes that allow corporations to receive privileges in exchange for money without formally violating the law. For example, the Democratic National Committee, during the presidential campaign of 2008, was not permitted to solicit soft money from corporations and managers. There was one important exception, however: corporations and unions could send as much money as they wanted to the party's convention. As reported in the *New York Times*, "donors who give $1 million or more at the 'Presidential Sponsor' level are given convention credentials to all hospitality suites and are assured of invitations to private events." The author continues, "One key fund-raiser for the Democratic convention is Steve Farber, a founding partner of one of Washington's leading lobbying firms and a major Democratic donor who has played golf with former President Bill Clinton and raised money for his presidential library." The newspaper cites a DNC brochure that promised to bring together "a unique group of business leaders, high-level lawmakers, members of the national and international media, and prominent academics" (Wayne 2008).

In conclusion, the report suggested that "more recently, with the nominees selected months in advance, they have turned into giant festivals promoting their nominee and providing opportunities for members of Congress and high-level corporate executives and lobbyists to meet in social settings—and for corporations to write large checks to support the party" (Wayne 2008). While federal elections are regulated by strong laws, the rules about donations in states are much more lenient. As Scott Turow writes, "in Illinois . . . there are literally no limits on political donations—neither on how big they can be nor who can give them. Anybody—union officials, regulated industries, corporations, lobbyists—can throw as much money as they like at Illinois politicians" (Turow 2008).

The impact of corporate donations on the outcome of elections is usually high. Such donations are especially beneficial for incumbents, given their established relations with corporations (Green 2004). As Ashford (1986) demonstrated, there was a link between the magnitude of corporate campaign contributions and the success of candidates in the 1980 congressional election. Burns, Peltason, and Cronin, in *Government by the People,* wrote that "those who give most are those who have the most." This situation is contrary to the ideals of democracy. Corporations, as these authors suggest, achieve all sorts of goals through elected officials, from idealistic ones to very egotistical ones—such as obtaining ambassadorships or invitations to a White House dinner for high-level administrators—which ignore even the interests of corporations (Behan 2001; Burns, Peltason, and Cronin 2000). Several authors have supported the idea that corporations have a major impact on the results of elections (Frendreis and Waterman 1985), while some have refuted this view (Grenzke 1988).

Obama's presidential campaign claimed that the American public had financed its efforts and that "small donors" ($200 or less) were the main contributors. As reported in the *New York Times,* however, these suggestions were exaggerated. In fact, small donors made up only 26 percent of contributions, while those giving $1,000 or more made up 47 percent. The difference between Obama's big donor contributions and McCain's big donors (59 percent) was not as great as initially reported. Kerry's campaign, at 56 percent, and Bush's second campaign, at 60 percent, were also mostly supported by big donors (Luo 2008b).

Conclusion

The feudal model is a useful tool for understanding the social circumstances in which people and organizations use their financial resources to acquire additional (often illegal) revenues that they do not deserve, according to the principles of the liberal and authoritarian models. In the Middle Ages, landed property permitted the aristocracy to receive feudal rents. In contemporary liberal society, big money is the basis of feudal relations. The concentration of money diminishes competition in the economy and in politics, and fosters corruption in society.

The manor was the key feudal actor in medieval times, while the corporation plays this role in contemporary society. The two actors have much in common, as they exert their power on individuals and society using similar techniques. Both actors extract monopolistic privileges from the central government in exchange for various resources. The political activities of corporations are not in line with the principles of political equality or the liberal model. While big corporations impair the election process, they do not, contrary to the Marxist perspective, always behave as a united front in politics. Feudal conflicts between firms, and between firms and the state, play an important role in corporate politics.

The feudal behaviors of corporations and public officials, which result in special privileges for corporations, are a danger to liberal society that harms the public interest and the efficiency of the market. Corporations also participate in political processes, elections in particular, and damage the democratic principle of political equality. Feudal behavior is normal and natural in the sense that it represents a recurrent and patterned social phenomenon. For a society to move toward the liberal model, it must first examine and come to understand these feudal tendencies.

4

The Feudal Model and the Organizational Level of Analysis

In chapter 3, we applied the feudal model to an examination of interorganizational relations. We discussed, in particular, how corporations and governments collude and conflict with each other, resulting in various "feudal" elements, such as the purchase of political influence and the use of money in election campaigns. In this chapter, we pursue a similar approach, but apply the feudal model to the study of social relations between individuals, departments, and other units inside organizations.

To begin with a classic definition, an organization can be understood as a group of individuals who work together toward a common interest or goal. A formal set of rules and a fixed understanding of authority, occupational roles, and responsibilities shape the actions of individuals (or organizational subunits) (Handel 2003). Ideally, in other words, all members of an organization use officially established means to achieve officially established goals.

This definition is consistent with the bureaucratic model of organizations formulated by Weber (1978). Organizational structures, according to the model, are hierarchical; communication is limited to superior-subordinate relations; occupational jurisdictions are clearly marked; and daily operations are coordinated and guided by explicit, impersonal rules, written documents, scientific research, and expertise. Writing in the early twentieth century, Weber argued that bureaucratic organization was more efficient and technically superior to all other organizational forms, and that its future success and proliferation was inevitable.

The usefulness of Weber's model to contemporary social scientists, however, lies not in what it predicts or what it says about organizations per se.

Rather, it contributes most as a tool of comparative analysis. Weber himself used "bureaucracy" to elucidate the characteristics of the "patrimonial" model of government organizations, and vice versa. The bureaucratic model has served as a point of departure, comparison, and criticism for a number of major theoretical perspectives, such as the human relations school, humanistic management, open systems perspectives, and organizational culture (DiMaggio and Powell 1983; Pfeffer and Salancik 1978; Mizruchi 1996). In this chapter, we examine intraorganizational conflicts, which contrast with the expectations of the bureaucratic model and other functional, rationalistic approaches to the study of modern organizations.

Starting in the 1950s—not long after Weber's work first appeared in English—organizational researchers began investigating conflicts within organizations. It soon became clear that much of the behavior generated by conflict processes and outcomes could not be understood with the classic bureaucratic model (Handel 2003). Since then, the study of intraorganizational conflict has produced numerous empirical and theoretical contributions (e.g., Benson 1973; Kolb and Putnam 1992; Lewicki, Weiss, and Lewin 1992; Morgan 1981; Pondy 1967; Walton and Dutton 1969). This chapter offers a conceptual framework that synthesizes some of these perspectives into a cohesive whole, the feudal model.

Uses of the Feudal Model in the Study of Organizations

We have two aims in mind as we apply feudalism to the study of intraorganizational conflict. First, we use the feudal model as a general theoretical framework to clarify a number of recurrent conditions under which intraorganizational conflicts emerge. Several researchers have offered answers to the question of what causes conflict inside organizations. Moving back and forth between empirical evidence and two ideal types (feudalism and bureaucracy), we aim, as in earlier chapters, to expose these answers to a wider range of historical cases, to conceptualize them as universal social patterns, and to delimit their application to modern organizations. By showing that people in both the medieval and modern contexts have responded in similar ways to similar circumstances, we attempt to identify and illuminate what Bendix (1963, 535) calls "sociological universals."

This approach should be distinguished from an attempt to use historical parallels to build predictive models and validate causal relationships.[1] Less ambitious and deductive, our aim is not to reveal the organizational factors that, taken together, *determine* feudalism. Rather, it is to reveal the social patterns that belie conventional, rationalistic models of contemporary organizations (bureaucracy in particular), and demonstrate that these patterns are recurrent in diverse historical contexts. Our comparative approach, in other words, is more akin to the logic of descriptive analysis than that of causal, statistical analysis.

Second, though we do not pursue this point extensively, we suggest that feudalism, and the medieval kingdom in particular, may be a useful metaphor in the context of organizational analysis. As many linguists and other social scientists have suggested, metaphors play an important role in the way people structure their thoughts and perceptions in everyday life (Lakoff and Johnson 1980; Maasen and Weingart 2000). We suggest that the same logic holds in the process of social scientific inquiry. Metaphors are indeed prevalent in the organizational literature and in social science generally. Metaphors such as the *machine,* the *organism,* and the *pyramid* have been used to highlight a particular set of ideas about the nature of organizations, and to make them more available and understandable to observers. This availability, in turn, shapes the way students learn about organizations and the way scholars investigate them. We hope our references to medieval social actors and organizations—and the feudal model in particular—will make a small contribution merely by directing attention to an alternative set of ideas and encouraging organizational inquiry on useful, and sometimes new, questions.

Characteristics of the Feudal Model

All complex organizations are composed of several differentiated parts (departments, branches, work groups, task forces, and so forth). The subunits may differ in size and function, but members of the organization generally recognize the borders between them. Based on the bureaucratic model, each subunit is defined by official tasks and objectives, as well as by official means to

1. For example, in *Social Origins of Dictatorship and Democracy,* Moore (1966) shows that several historical cases have a certain social phenomenon in common, as well as the same set of hypothesized causal factors explaining the phenomenon. In a similar vein, Parsons (1951) offered detailed, deductive historical parallels (and contrasts) to support his assumptions about the function of societies as "social systems."

achieve these objectives—including specified procedures and protocols, formalized levels of authority, and other mechanisms. Of course, the character of goals and means differs across organizations, along with the given bureaucratic structures (from loosely coupled systems to rigid hierarchies), but the idea that the subunits should operate within the bounds of official goals and means represents a basic assumption for any model of bureaucracy. The individuals within each subunit are also responsible for different tasks and objectives, but for now we will treat the "subunit" as the main subject of analysis.

In short, the bureaucratic model suggests that the subunits of organizations pursue official goals using official means. In actuality, as many researchers have found, they often operate in ways that contradict one or both of these criteria. As illustrated in table 1, a subunit may use unofficial means to pursue official goals, use official means to pursue unofficial goals, or use unofficial means to pursue unofficial goals.

We refer to these patterns as "feudal conflicts," or as parts of the feudal model, because they were especially common in western European societies during the early Middle Ages, when the central authority (the king) was often too weak or disorganized to fully regulate the feudal lords and other powerful social actors residing in the territory. Although the lords were technically bound by written, verbal, and implied agreements, they often ignored or rejected the dictates of the king, particularly in times when their level of military power or political influence was relatively high (Shlapentokh with Woods 2007). Applying the feudal model to modern organizations, the king represents the central authority or top management, while the feudal lords symbolize the disparate subunits of the organization.

In each of the three variants of the feudal model, some form of conflict occurs as a subunit disregards or contradicts the organization's official goals, means, or both. While there are numerous definitions of "conflict" (Fink 1968), we follow Deutsch's (1973) conceptualization, which emphasizes the behavioral aspect. Using behavior as the defining characteristic of feudal conflict is important for at least two reasons.

Table 1 Three variants of feudalism, categorized by goals and means.

	Pursues official goals	Pursues unofficial goals
Uses official means	Bureaucratic models of various types	Dysfunctional semifeudal model
Uses unofficial means	Functional semifeudal model	Feudal model

First, the subunits of an organization may be deeply divided on a given issue and harbor negative attitudes toward other subunits or the central authority, but their activities may remain clearly within the boundaries of the organization's official means and goals. As discussed by Kolb and Putnam (1992, 132), divisiveness and confrontation between subunits may "occur informally and out of sight," or at least remain latent until a breaking point, at which time the conflict results in feudal elements.

Second, some conflict-driven organizational environments may, under some conditions, have positive effects (Smith 1966). Many organizations are intentionally structured as highly competitive settings in which individuals and subunits vie for the organization's limited resources, without transgressing official means or goals (Butler 1973). In addition to the motivational benefits, disagreements may also help to illuminate all sides of an organization's problems and reveal a range of creative solutions (Landsberger 1961). A conflict of this sort can produce innovation without breaching normative boundaries, and can be resolved through conventional bureaucratic mechanisms.

Feudal conflicts, in contrast, involve behavior that goes beyond the official means and/or goals of an organization. This is not to say that all feudal conflicts are damaging, illegal, or even "deviant," according to the unofficial norms of the organization. As illustrated by the "functional semifeudal" variant (see table 1), a subunit may use unofficial modes of conduct to pursue official objectives. In this chapter, however, we place greater emphasis on feudal conflicts that reflect the "dysfunctional semifeudal model" or the pure "feudal model," which have received less attention in the literature and represent the clearest contrasts with the rational, organismic models.

A note should also be made about the parties involved in feudal conflicts. From a classical sociological perspective, conflicts are primarily driven by structural inequalities. The orthodox Marxist perspective, for instance, anticipates class struggles or conflicts between groups of disproportionate socioeconomic status. On the one hand, the feudal model follows this line of thinking, which rightly emphasizes conflicts between two important organizational subunits: workers and management. On the other hand, the Marxist perspective disregards conflicts between subunits of the same social class. The feudal model, in contrast, anticipates these conflicts, as well as the struggles between subunits that comprise multiple classes of workers and personnel. In short, the feudal model focuses on both the Marxist and non-Marxist dividing lines of intraorganizational clashes.

Drawing on a broad range of studies, the remainder of this chapter attempts to identify some of the conditions under which feudal conflicts arise in both modern and medieval organizations, and to discuss the consequences of these developments. This model builds on a number of earlier works on intraorganizational conflict (Walton and Dutton 1969; Benson 1973; Kolb and Putnam 1992; Morgan 1981), as well as the classic and contemporary research on the principal-agent problem (Brehm and Gates 1999). We also owe a special debt to Dalton, who was a trailblazer in feudal analysis, if by another name. His work, though dated, is vital for understanding modern organizations from the feudal perspective.

Decentralization Versus Feudalization

As discussed in previous chapters, the territorial integrity of the medieval state was limited. In western Europe, following the death of Charlemagne in the ninth century, a number of powerful, autonomous agents emerged, often clashing in their efforts to seize land and wealth from each other and from the crumbling Frankish kingdom (Duby 1977; James 1982; Jones 1999; Elias 1982). As discussed by Elias, "after the fall of the Roman Empire in Western Europe, centrifugal forces prevailed for a long time. Even if Charlemagne managed to unite a huge empire during his lifetime, his successors lacked the means to keep it together. For many centuries, centripetal forces were too weak to sustain a stable central power over a large territory for any considerable period" (Elias 1998, 24).

Even powerful kings depended greatly on the cooperation of their vassals to govern. Until the rise of absolute monarchies in the seventeenth century, the lower lords enjoyed a wide span of control and often used their autonomy to maximize their own interests at the expense of the king. In short, the governing powers of medieval states were both highly decentralized and prone to feudal conflicts. Whether applied to relationships between organizations—as examined in the previous chapters—or relationships within them, the inability or unwillingness of the central authority to control smaller units is a key characteristic of the feudal model. Although not a synonym of feudalization, decentralization in medieval times was associated with feudal tendencies.

Not unlike the medieval kingdoms, some highly decentralized modern organizations also lack the ability to fully regulate their disparate units at times. The decentralization of corporate enterprises increased in the late twentieth century as many large firms responded to shifts in world markets by changing their strategies and loosening their hierarchical structures. As Kolb and Putnam

(1992, 313) suggest, firms moved from bureaucracy to *adhocracy,* that is, they became "less hierarchical, and more dominated by task forces, project teams, and product groups—entities which can respond more quickly to changes in strategy, markets, and technology." Similar to adhocracy is the notion of "loosely coupled systems" (Morgan 1981, 34). Loose coupling refers, among other things, to the tenuous connections between an organization's subunits, which preserve their identities and remain separate from each other or the central authority (Weick 1976).

Under some circumstances, expanding the autonomy of subunits creates "problems with coordination and control" (Miller and Gubin 2000, 79; Blau 1970, 1972), or, in other words, increases the potential for feudal conflicts. Given the weak and undefined structure of some decentralized organizations, or adhocracies, the subunits sometimes clash on issues of authority and responsibility (Mintzberg 1979). A link between adhocracy and conflict has been found in a number of different organizational contexts (Green 2003; Desveaux, Lindquist, and Toner 1994). The research on loose coupling also highlights the relative weakness of the central authority and the precarious relations between the subunits.

A prime example of loose coupling can be seen in business alliances or joint ventures, which are based on formal agreements between firms to undertake economic activities together. The number of these alliances grew dramatically in the last two decades of the twentieth century. Some American firms, such as Hewlett-Packard, Corning, and Coca-Cola, became known as effective managers of alliances. Business alliances are also known to achieve consistent success in foreign countries, particularly Japan (Gerlach 1992). In general, however, alliances are highly unstable. In the American market, the failure rate stands at roughly 50 percent (Kale, Dyer, and Singh 2002; Kogut 1989). Even when large departments are created to coordinate alliances, the relative weakness of the central authority, along with a number of associated factors, which we discuss later (opportunism, lack of trust, uncertainty, dependency, and rivalry), commonly lead to their downfall (Park and Ungson 2001; Khanna, Gulati, and Nohria 1994; Kogut 1988; Park and Russo 1996; Killing 1983).

The instability that arises in decentralized organizations is a universal phenomenon, seen in both modern and medieval contexts, which highlights the tension between a large, complex organization's efforts to establish order and operational efficiency, and the social forces and human appetites that fragment the power structure and distort formal mechanisms of coordination. As discussed in the next sections, however, decentralization is a general process, and it does not reveal the specific factors that lead to feudal conflicts. It is to these factors that we now turn.

Structural Interdependence and Feudal Conflict

Decentralization involves the dispersion of decision-making power across the subunits of an organization. This process does not, by definition, create feudal tendencies. In many cases, adhocracy is the most appropriate framework for coordinating organizational communication and other activities. It may, in fact, lead to greater creativity and innovation within the subunits, greater information flow between them, and greater overall productivity and efficiency, which clearly fall within the bounds of official goals and means (Chang and Harrington 2000; Weick 1976). Adhocracy or loose coupling, as Weick (1976) points out, may reduce conflicts between subunits by virtue of the diminished interaction between them and the looser demands placed on coordinating their activities.

Moreover, in the case of most American businesses, power remains concentrated at the top, even when the responsibility for decisions and profits is "decentralized" (Jackall 1988). Decentralization, from this perspective, may actually help a large organization increase its authoritarian dominion over its disparate parts.

For these reasons, feudalization is more germane than decentralization to the relative strength of the central authority, and to the organizational structures (formal and informal) that coordinate the subunits. Reflecting on the medieval context, we might suggest that decentralization was a less direct predictor of insubordination on the part of local lords than was the king's military might, and the formal and informal mechanisms he used to make his might felt throughout the territory.

From the time of the early Carolingians in the eighth century, responsibilities for governing the land were dispersed among numerous lower lords. The Frankish kingdom was indeed a decentralized political organization, yet feudal conflicts were less common under Frankish rule than in earlier and later periods of French history. Social order was especially well established under the powerful Charlemagne. At this time, the local actors were bestowed their powers as "honors," not "benefits." As Bloch explains (1989, 192), honors "were not granted for life," and "their occupants could always be removed from office even without any fault on their part." In spite of the evident decentralization of governing power, Charlemagne was able to keep the local lords in line.

Later, as the crown weakened, the holders of honors gradually transformed themselves into "territorial potentates," and their honors, in practice, became benefits "firmly rooted in the soil" (Bloch 1989). The lower lords of the provinces increased their military fortitude, acquired new estates, built castles at strategic junctures along trade routes, developed independent connections with other power holders—the Church in particular—and expanded their network of vassals. Considering the essential needs for security and control over land, there was still a great deal of dependency between the king and lower lords, as well as an official hierarchy in place. This interdependence became problematic, however, when the two parties enjoyed disproportionate privileges. The lower lords always had a greater incentive to betray or renegotiate the formal and informal agreements that united them, resulting in increased tension and feudal conflict.

In order to survive in a competitive environment, modern organizations, like medieval kingdoms, must coordinate their disparate parts and secure some degree of cooperation among them. To this end, most organizations establish a formal hierarchy and official procedures to facilitate mutual compliance. As a result, each subunit, no matter how powerful, relies on other subunits to achieve its goals. This reliance is commonly known as "structural interdependence" or "task dependency." Although there are great differences between the modern and medieval procedures used to instill cooperation, the challenge of succeeding in this respect, particularly when the central authority is weak, represents a universal organizational dilemma.

Line-Staff Conflicts

Dalton (1950a, 1959) provided a classic study on the struggles caused by structural interdependence (among other things) in three industrial plants. Responding to the need for greater specialization in a period of rapid technological expansion, top officials at these organizations called increasingly upon "staff officers" (specialists in a particular field) to facilitate greater efficiency and increase production. Staff officers controlled large financial resources in order to develop new means to increase productivity. To complete their tasks, however, they depended greatly on "line officers," who held formal authority over production processes.

Fueled in part by the high level of task dependency and the differences in their formal occupational roles and authority, the line and staff interacted in a "system of conflict," which led to a variety of feudal elements or conflicts. One type of feudal conflict occurred when the formal rules that coordinated line and staff activities were unevenly enforced. Permission to bypass or break the rules became a bargaining chip that could be used by the subunits to pursue their opposing interests. For instance, a staff officer might have allowed members of the line to break certain rules in order to gain their support on a different project (often one in which they had a personal stake) (Dalton 1950a). The rules themselves, in this case, created a situation that was the opposite of their intended effect. According to both classic (Gouldner 1954) and contemporary researchers (Handel 2003), the manipulation of formal rules is a common practice in other organizations as well.

The second feudal element discussed by Dalton was interdepartmental bribery. This form of corruption has been studied primarily as an interorganizational phenomenon, as in the case when a public official sells government property, permits, or licenses to a private firm for personal gain. Nevertheless, as Dalton found, a similar interaction sometimes occurred between subunits within a single organization, particularly when one subunit held power over decision making and the other controlled financial resources (a typical situation in line-staff conflicts). In order to gain the line officers' "cooperation," either to advance an official project or for their own personal benefit, staff officers would sometimes secretly "kick over" some of their funding to the line.

A third feudal element involved the direct sabotage of new production techniques. Staff officers were always concerned about how their plans to innovate the production process would be received by the line. Line officers, meanwhile, worried that any change in procedure would lead to personnel changes and ultimately diminish their authority. Both subunits, for this reason, used sabotage to protect their domains. As Dalton (1950a, 349) wrote, the staff officers "knew from experience that middle and lower line officers could always give a 'black eye' to staff contributions by deliberate malpractice."

More recent research has identified sabotage as a growing problem in many contemporary organizations, especially with their greater vulnerability to computer-based sabotage (Domingues, Sousa, and Silva 2007). Taking one form or another, sabotage costs U.S. firms an estimated $200 billion annually (Harris and Ogbonna 2006; Murphy 1993). Research on this feudal element is difficult, given the need for respondents to disclose sensitive information. Nevertheless, a number of empirical studies have shown that sabotage is a recurring form of social interaction that plays an important role in the informal power structure of many organizations. Research on sabotage has been conducted in the cases of manufacturing plants (Hodson 1997; Giacalone and Rosenfeld 1987; Juravich 1985; Pollert 1981); hospitals (Kerfoot 2007); an entertainment firm (Analoui 1995); restaurants (Harris and Ogbonna 2006); government bureaucracies (Brehm and Gates 1999); and several other firms (Harbring et al. 2007; Ambrosea, Seabright, and Schminke 2002; Sprouse 1992).

The three feudal elements discussed above should not be seen as abnormal or random acts, but rather as universal patterns of social interaction, which are shaped in part by the formal and informal structure, and the level of authority held by the organization itself. Given the nature of task dependency, feudal conflicts may occur even when one subunit holds more formal authority than the other. The lesser of the two almost always has access to alternative sources of power or leverage, such as financial resources, the directives from top managers, the manipulation of formal rules, personal relations, friendships, family ties, bribery, threats, and sabotage.

Professional-Bureaucratic Conflicts

In addition to the line-staff conflicts described by Dalton, structural interdependence has been identified as a key factor in explaining intraorganizational conflicts in a number of other contexts, including struggles between the operating and maintenance branches of industrial organizations (Dalton 1955); the production staff and auxiliary workers in an engine factory (Burawoy 1979); the purchasing department and other departments in several firms (Strauss 1962; Weigand 1968; Sheth 1973; Anderson and Chambers 1985); the various departments of a telephone company (Walton, Dutton, and Cafferty 1969); and the subunits of correctional institutions (Zald 1962).

Educational organizations are especially fertile grounds for feudal conflict (McGuire 1984; Kirst 1970; Wirt and Kirst 1972; Zeigler, Jennings, and Peak 1974; Falk, Grimes, and Lord 1982). All the key ingredients of feudalization—a host of powerful actors with overlapping spheres of influence, high structural interdependence, and divergent personal and group interests—can be found in most schools or educational institutions. The formal authority of a superintendent or principle is constantly challenged by the "lords" of the school board, the teachers, the parents, and even the students.

Corwin (1970) aptly used military metaphors in his analysis of interdepartmental conflicts in several Midwestern schools. Focusing on the clashes between teachers and administrators, he argued that those teachers who were more "professionally oriented" were more likely to seek and achieve autonomy, and engage in conflict to protect it. In essence, the professionalism of teachers balanced the power between the "lords" of teaching and administration and stimulated confrontations over the educational kingdom's limited resources (Larson 1977). Other studies supported Corwin's findings in the case of schools (Falk, Grimes, and Lord 1982; Jessup 1978; Fox and Wince 1976; Hellriegel, French, and Peterson 1970).

Benson (1973) identified professional-bureaucratic struggles as one of the "fundamental contradictions" in many types of organizations. Drawing on previous works (Bucher and Stelling 1969; Bucher 1970; Freidson 1970a, 1970b), he proposed a "dialectical approach," as opposed to a functional scheme, to analyze confrontations between professionals and bureaucrats.

Benson's perspective is similar, in at least three respects, to the feudal model. First, it suggests that the central authority within organizations is often unstable. As in the case of conflicts between lower and higher lords in a medieval kingdom, modern organizational instability "grows out of inconsistencies and incompatibilities which are never fully resolved" (Benson 1973, 383). These "inconsistencies" include material conflicts of interest, organizational or geographical separation, and divergent values, beliefs, and ideologies. Second, social order in modern firms, as in medieval kingdoms, is often established through political maneuvers and informal negotiations, as opposed to purely bureaucratic, democratic, or market mechanisms. All complex organizations are influenced, to some extent, by the struggles between subunits and the informal strategies each employs to grab as much prestige, authority, autonomy, and financial reward as possible. And third, these contradictions, while usually masked or hidden by various devices, play a major role in "reshaping organizations," particularly in times of crisis (1973, 383–84). Conflicts between subunits may, in some cases, bring about organizational change or even disintegration.

Corporate Conflicts of Interest

Conflicts of interest emerge when the leaders of an organization have an opportunity to benefit personally from their official acts or decisions. These conflicts produce feudal elements when they result in actions that go against the organization's official objectives or its standards for achieving these aims.

In the last decades, there have been several examples of such abuses in the corporate world. In the 1960s and 1970s, the financial conglomerate Equity Funding committed massive accounting fraud, including the complete falsification of sixty-four thousand insurance policies (Demski 2003, 51). Numerous top managers and even lower-level employees were involved in the scam. The fraud, which led to the collapse of the firm, cost investors hundreds of millions of dollars and brought the indictment of twenty-two company employees, along with Equity Funding's auditors (Wells 1993; Reinstein, Moehrle, and Reynolds-Moehrle 2006; Dirks and Gross 1974). Large-scale fraud, insider transactions, misstatements on financial records, and accounting irregularities played a major role in the savings-and-loan crisis of the 1980s (Erickson, Mayhew, and Felix 2000), as well as many other high-profile corporate scandals, including the cases of the Cendent Corporation, ESM Government Securities, the HIH Insurance Group, the Barings Bank and WorldCom (Reinstein, Moehrle, and Reynolds-Moehrle 2006; Demski 2003).

By bringing these cases into the fold of the feudal model, we suggest that the subunits involved should not be treated as "isolated rogues" or a "few bad apples," but rather as patterned manifestations of corporate structure and governance (formal and informal). To further this point, let us briefly consider the case of Enron, one of the most complex and well-known scandals in recent years. There were a number of organizational factors that engendered the feudalization of this firm.

First, members of Enron's top management received a substantial portion of their salaries in stock options. At the time, there were no government or company regulations that controlled how or when they sold these valuable assets. In effect, Enron's stock compensation program motivated managers to make decisions that stimulated short-term stock performance at the expense of the company's long-term outlook and survival (Healy and Palepu 2003).

Second, the leadership at Enron promoted a particular culture or value system that encouraged rule breaking and aggressive tactics to maximize company profits. As a result, managers used both official and unofficial means (much of it illegal) to "create" earnings that artificially improved its bottom line and elevated its stock price in the short term (Sims and Brinkmann 2003). Top officials at Enron sold their shares before the company collapsed, leaving many investors—including pensioners and members of Enron's own workforce—with nothing when the stock dropped to zero.

The ideal models of democracy, bureaucracy, and capitalism include well-defined mechanisms (the rule of law, internal regulations, or perfect markets) that reduce conflicts of interest and limit their negative effects on organizations and society as a whole. The feudal model, in contrast, assumes that these mechanisms are relatively weak and systematically ineffective. This was certainly true in the case of Enron, given its ineffectual Internal Audit Committee, which was understaffed, inefficient, and consistently made mistakes (Healy and Palepu 2003).[2] In other words, the relative weakness of Enron's Internal Audit Committee increased the power and autonomy of top managers, just as the weak central authority in the Middle Ages allowed the local barons and great landowners to defy or manipulate the commands of the king. Enron can be seen as a weak and fragmented medieval kingdom, in which top managers, lawyers, and accountants (knights and local barons) pursued their personal interests, while jeopardizing the kingdom's long-term stability, along with the interests of many of its subjects.

Uncertainty

Many organizational researchers, contingency theorists in particular, have suggested that decision makers are often forced to act decisively in highly uncertain environments. These circumstances often result in conduct that does not fit either the classic bureaucratic model or rational-choice theories (Simon 1979; Downey and Slocum 1975).

In medieval times, given the turbulent social and political conditions, uncertainty characterized many different types of social interaction and relationships, from small matters such as the level of a knight's wages (Hollister 1960) or the specific boundaries between castellanies (Fischer 1992) to the most significant question of who owed homage to whom. One famous case of the latter was seen in Franco-Norman relations after the Vikings took control of Normandy in the ninth century. While the French king Charles the Simple regarded the Viking leaders, now Norman dukes, as "powerful yet essentially ordinary feudal vassals," the dukes themselves were reluctant to pay homage to the king (Hollister 1976, 203).

Prior to the Norman Conquest of England, there was only one act of homage made by a Norman duke to a French king, and even this one was ambiguous. In 1060, the Norman duke William the Bastard and the French king Philip I met at a neutral location on the Franco-Norman frontier and agreed to "a firm peace," but it remained unclear as to whether their agreement represented a solid feudal contract or simply a treaty, which left the structural hierarchy between the two groups uncertain. As Hollister (1976, 203) explained, these

2. As Healy and Palepu (2003, 14–15) suggested, the committee "did not challenge several important transactions that were primarily motivated by accounting goals, was not skeptical about potential conflicts in related party transactions, and did not require full disclosure of these transactions."

circumstances "reasonably raised the question of who was subordinate to whom." In the next centuries, the initial ambiguity in Franco-Norman power relations, not to mention their high structural interdependence, led to a great deal of conflict and war over the status of Normandy.

A number of empirical studies of modern organizations demonstrate how similar conflicts are caused in part by various types of uncertainty or ambiguity. In a study of industrial organizations, Barclay (1991, 154) found that "jurisdictional ambiguity" (that is, "the lack of clarity about which of two departments has responsibility for particular decisions or actions") is highly correlated with interdepartmental conflicts. Barclay's results confirm the findings of an earlier study by Walton, Dutton, and Cafferty (1969). These and other studies (Beck 1974; Jehn 1997) show that subunits are more likely to conflict when operational roles and the boundaries of authority are vague or uncertain. As in the case of the Franco-Norman power struggles, each side defines the relationship according to its own preferences, resulting in a greater potential for direct conflicts over scarce resources.

Ambiguous dividing lines between subunits also contribute to feudal battles over who should take the blame for organizational failures and the credit for success (Dalton 1950a, 1959; Dutton and Walton 1966; Walton and Dutton 1969). Similar problems arise when the criteria for evaluating the "effectiveness" of subunits are uncertain (Kahn 1964).

Perhaps the most destabilizing form of organizational uncertainty occurs when the subunits disagree about (or become indifferent toward) the formal objectives of the organization. Following the collapse of the Soviet Union, for instance, a number of experts argued that the North Atlantic Treaty Organization (NATO) would cease to exist without its clear mission of contending with the Soviet threat (Wallander 2000). Though NATO currently remains intact, international relations experts and commentators continue to cite "goal ambiguity" as a major obstacle to cohesive NATO activities, such as the provision of security in Afghanistan (Kulish and Shanker 2008).

Another example of the powerful effects of uncertainty has been seen in the newspaper industry, starting in the late 1990s. As news consumers turned increasingly to the Internet, there was a significant decline in circulation size and ad revenues at countless local, major metro, and national newspapers. To make matters worse, newspaper executives within and across news organizations disagreed about the strategic role of online publishing and the best plan for adapting to the Internet. Given the increased strategic and economic uncertainty, the famous turf wars between newspaper subunits, particularly the business side versus the journalism side of operations, only became more divisive (An and Bergen 2007).

One of the industry's most noted feudal conflicts was the newsroom revolt against the ownership at the *Los Angeles Times*. The ongoing struggle gained public attention in late 1999 over an ad revenue–sharing scheme that raised questions about the paper's journalistic integrity. Between 2005 and early 2008, a number of top editors, including Carroll, Baquet, O'Shea, and even the publisher, Johnson, were fired or resigned in protest of proposed staff cuts and other changes in the newsroom (Seelye 2006; Pérez-Peña 2008).

Informal Power Structures and Personal Relations

A distinction should be drawn between the uncertainty caused by imprecise rules and the uncertainty that derives from the subunits' intentional avoidance or transgression of the rules. In the latter case, ambiguity is systematically created and perpetuated by the members of the subunits themselves, either because they see the formal rules as too restrictive to allow them to fulfill their duties, or because they wish to capitalize on the various benefits of ambiguous power relations.

Uncertainty itself gives power holders leeway to pursue personal goals or unofficial group aims. This is not to say that uncertainty, by definition, leads to an abuse of power, but rather that uncertainty is a natural, enduring characteristic of both modern and medieval organizations, which elevates the potential for arbitrary actions. In Simon's terms, "when the production function can't be formulated in concrete terms," the actions of a leader may be "influenced in subtle, and not so subtle, ways by his self-interest and power drives" (1979, 500).

Uncertainty also may intensify the problems that arise from the structural factors discussed above, task dependency in particular. Dalton (1950b, 1959) stressed this point in his study of unofficial union-management relations in industrial factories. Representing the central authority in these plants, national union representatives and top management established formal contracts. The central authority assumed that the specific details of these agreements, like the edicts of a king, would be followed by the managers of the local plants.

The local leaders of both labor and management, however, "winked" at the contracts, just as the local lords in medieval times sometimes winked at their agreements with the king and with each other. The lords of labor and management saw the contractual details as either too general or too inflexible to be applied in their particular factory. They also anticipated the personal benefits of consolidating power in their local jurisdictions through informal negotiations and personal ties. As one committeeman commented, "the top people [policy makers] lay down too many hard and fast rules to follow. But we get around the contract by doing a lot of things that we can work out and keep off the record" (Dalton 1950b, 612).[3]

In many cases, the local lords were motivated less by the organization's mission than by their wish to "realize personal goals, deal with enemies, reward friends, protect themselves, increase their status, and the readiness to use expedients for these ends" (Dalton 1950b, 618). This sort of informal power structure was a common source of conflict between the subunits. Though we prefer the term *feudal,* Dalton used a near synonym, *oligarchical,* to describe these interactions. Other researchers have supported Dalton's findings in the case of industrial organizations and other contexts (Dubin 1957).

In a more recent line of research, Peter Manning (2008) discusses the role of personal relations in American and British police departments. Invoking the "feudal" model explicitly, Manning suggests that relations between superiors and subordinates follow the bureaucratic model on the surface—or in "front regions," to use Goffman's terms (1959)—but rely on personal relations in practice. "The basis for compliance to command is a mix of charismatic or 'personal' authority based on respect for the individual rather than or in addition to the office held and rational-legal authority based upon expertise and experience" (Manning 2008, 56). Manning identifies the existence of these dual forms of authority—bureaucratic and personal—as a source of internal conflict in police departments.

Functional and Dysfunctional Aspects of Informal Structure

While informal power structures and personal relations may generate feudal conflicts under many circumstances, they can also serve as a relative source of order, regularity and normalization. As illustrated by the functional semifeudal

3. Dalton provides a number of vivid illustrations on how operations at the local plants are dictated more by the informal, covert exchanges between the local lords (union committeemen, departmental superintendents, and the industrial engineering staff) than by the formal rules sent down by the central authority. He offers a model of industrial organizations wherein the classic dividing lines between union and management are intentionally muddled by the subunits themselves, both union consciousness and managerial commitment are weaker than the personal interests of the two parties, and the bureaucratic structures established by the central authority are systematically ignored (Dalton 1950b).

model (see table 1), the subunits may operate outside the organization's official rules and procedures, yet generally support its goals.

Burawoy (1979) developed this perspective in his noted study of an engine factory where informal relations dominated the production process. He suggested that the activities on the shop floor were guided by a "game" in which workers attempted to gain incentive pay by exceeding the baseline level of production.[4] The game of "making out," as the workers called it, was easier to win if the worker knew how to transgress the official rules, manipulate their managers and fellow workers, and capitalize on various informal relations and exchanges.[5] Even if the game involved deviations from the rules, its net result was higher productivity.

According to Burawoy (1979), the game of making out generated consent among workers, coordinated their interests with that of management, supported the status quo, and softened the subunits' opposition to the central authority. Although top-level managers would formally reject the means that some workers used to make out, higher productivity rates were no less acceptable, particularly in comparison to a deeply disgruntled, union-conscious workforce beset by protests, strikes, work stoppages, and conflict.

In some ways, medieval vassalage ("the mutual obligations of the armed retainer and his lord") was similar to the game of making out. On one hand, vassalage was quite functional for all parties involved, as it provided an effective means of defense and personal safety. For a time, the bonds of vassalage facilitated the organizing of a number of key social and political activities, including military defense, violent conquests, mutual consultations, membership activities in the lord's court, and participation in ceremonial parades (Bloch 1989, 221–22).

As confirmed by its eventual failure, however, vassalage also had its weaknesses. Not unlike the case of Burowoy's engine factory, an official hierarchical relationship existed between medieval lords and vassals, but, in practice, "power was not a pyramid; it was scattered" (Barendse 2003, 525; Ganshof 1952, xv). Almost all medieval social actors were at once "subjects and masters," competing in a contest of sorts, in which the lower lords, using any means available, attempted to limit their obligations to the higher lords while increasing the obligations of their dependents.

4. In a more current study, Espeland and Sauder (2007) applied Burawoy's notion of the "game" to a study of law schools and their reactions to the highly publicized law school ranking system (see also Sauder and Espeland 2009).

5. To make out, a worker might, for instance, bribe a crib attendant (a highly strategic person in the production process) with a "Christmas ham" (Burawoy 1979).

Over time, vassalage became more and more complex and contested. As Bloch (1989, 220) wrote, "gradually differences in rank and power, the development of inevitably divergent traditions, special agreements, and even abuses transformed into rights introduced innumerable variations into the obligations. This, in the long run, almost invariably tended to lighten them." In both medieval and modern times, informal "games" could weaken the central authority, encourage feudal conflicts, but also sustain a degree of social order and functionality.

Personal Loyalty

Loyalty to a person, as opposed to one's official position or formal responsibilities, represents a clear parallel between modern and medieval organizations. Without personal relations, the ceremonial bonds between medieval lords and vassals would have been even less stable, along with their collective ability to defend themselves against internal and external threats. These supposedly archaic forms of social interaction (favoritism, personal attachments, fealty relations, nepotism, and so forth) still play important roles in today's organizations.

Few researchers have made this point more definitively than Jackall (1988) in *Moral Mazes.* He argued that the power structure in modern corporations is highly personal and more akin, in many respects, to Weber's concept of patrimonialism than to his bureaucratic model. As opposed to being impersonally assigned to a formal position, subordinates are personally bound to their bosses, and must reinforce their subordination and demonstrate their acceptance of "the obligations of fealty" at every turn (19). In exchange for loyalty, subordinates receive protection when they make mistakes, promotions when their boss is elevated, financial rewards, and any number of ancillary benefits, such as "the nudging of a moveable panel to enlarge one's office, and perhaps a couch to fill the added space" (19).

Featly relations between individuals or groups are best described by the functional semifeudal or pure feudal models (see table 1), in which the parties involved use unofficial means, personal ties in particular, to achieve either official or unofficial goals. In the first case, a subordinate's loyalty to a boss encourages hard work, creativity, and the timely accomplishment of official tasks. Personal ties, mutual trust, favoritism, and nepotism may also generate stability, allow firms to respond well in uncertain environments, and help them repel threats from outside (Bellow 2003a, 2003b).

In the second case, fealty relations have deleterious effects on an organization and its ability to achieve its goals. If currying the favor of higher-ups is a subordinate's main ambition and prerequisite for advancement, the subordinate may be compelled to hide or obscure the failure or incompetence of the boss or withhold ideas and creative solutions that contradict the boss's judgments, especially in public settings (Jackall 1988). A manager may take a number of actions designed to ingratiate himself with a boss, but that may have negative, long-term effects on the performance of a given subunit or the organization as a whole. As Jackall wrote, "it is far more important to please the king today than to worry about the future economic state of one's fief, since, if one does not please the king, there may not be a fief to worry about or indeed vassals to do the worrying" (22).

A number of other researchers have considered the functional and dysfunctional characteristics of fealty relations between subunits or individuals within organizations. Like Jackall, Manning (2008) draws on Weber's patrimonial model in his explanation of the important role of loyalty in police departments. McPherson (1988) and others (Hoy and Rees 1974) looked at the effects of both personal and group fealty relations in schools, while Murray and Corenblum (1966) did the same with public utilities, and Adler and Adler (1988) considered college athletic programs. In this respect, the feudal model benefits the study of organizations by identifying informal constraints, loyalty relations, nepotism, and other personal ties as enduring social patterns that may, in some cases, facilitate the aims of the organization, but may produce suboptimal outcomes in others.

Loyalty can be understood not only as a set of behavioral intentions, but also as a part of an organization's culture. A culture of loyalty may emerge spontaneously, given the specific challenges, characteristics of labor, and other social conditions. As argued by institutional theorists, the wider culture may also impact the loyalty relations between subordinates and superiors within an organization (DiMaggio and Powell 1983). In a society such as Japan, where cultural norms and practices emphasize social status, the members of organizations are inclined to shape their interactions with others according to whether they are lower or higher in the social hierarchy (Sugimoto 2003). In many cases, as suggested by Etzioni (1964), the central authority of an organization intentionally develops and maintains a culture of loyalty in order to control its subunits (a subunit might also develop a subculture to reinforce its autonomy and disparate interests). Kunda (1992), for instance, explored this thesis in a noted study of a high-tech corporation.

In the Middle Ages, the culture of loyalty was generated by the violence and chronic warfare among the noble class. The cycles of military campaigns and the redistribution of conquered land fostered loyalty to superiors, which, in turn, stabilized the governing power of supreme warlords. As Teschke (1998, 343) pointed out, "the reputation and standing of Charles Martel, Henry Plantagenet, and Otto I, to name but a few, and the relative stability of their respective polities were directly predicated on such dynamic mechanisms of political accumulation." This same process, however, could also lead to fragmentation and feudal conflict. In a dialectical response to their accumulated fortunes and new estates, some lower lords turned inward, fostered their own internal loyalty relations, and emerged as rivals of their former leader. Functioning as a dynamic set of internalized values, the culture of loyalty in both medieval and modern times represents an enduring social phenomenon, which could bring order to an organization, as easily as it could sow the seeds of division and dissent.

Conclusion

Over the last several decades, as the size and global reach of many firms increased, organizational subunits often received greater authority and independence, while the relative strength of the central authority diminished. Although the current forces of globalization may be intensifying the fragmentation of authority in some organizations, the struggle for power within them is a universal phenomenon that can be found across organizations and in different time periods.

As elaborated in the foregoing pages, numerous researchers have proposed models to analyze this ongoing struggle, and to illuminate the sources and consequences of these conflicts. Drawing on previous research—and using Weber's classic bureaucratic model as a point of comparison—the feudal model identifies three circumstances in which the actions of subunits conflict with the official means or goals of the organization (see table 1). The different variants of the model are designed to reflect the complex system of tensions and strains within most large organizations, and to provide an approach to social analysis that avoids overestimating either the functional or dysfunctional nature of formal and informal power structures.

The feudal model brings attention to and synthesizes a number of empirical and theoretical treatments of intraorganizational conflict. The variables shown to be related (directly or indirectly) to such struggles include decentralization, structural interdependence, uncertainty, informal power, and personal relations. Greater attention to these factors is needed, given the general shortage of this analysis and its weighty implications for modern organizations. Although we have placed a greater emphasis on the disintegrative consequences of these factors, the feudal model also accounts for a range of integrative tendencies that is missing from most conventional models. The feudal model contributes to the literature on organizations by directing attention to an alternative set of ideas, identifying "sociological universals," and encouraging and directing further inquiry on intraorganizational conflict.

5

Private Coercion: A Feudal Aspect of Contemporary American Society

One of the key functions of any society is to provide its members with safety and security. While the methods of carrying out this task vary greatly between societies and across time, the given approach represents one of society's defining characteristics. Increasingly in the United States, private firms are performing the task of protecting individuals, groups, and assets. The safety and security of many Americans now depend in part on a range of private agents and organizations, from security guards, bodyguards, private investigators, and home security companies to commercial surveillance firms, massive in-house corporate security departments, private military companies, and other private-sector defense agencies and contractors (Wood and Shearing 2007; Loader and Walker 2007). These services not only secure life and property, but also aid in the expansion of wealth and power.

The "individualization of security," as Rose (1999, 236) puts it, may be a contemporary trend, but it has deep roots in human history. The independent control of violent force—what we refer to as "private coercion"—played an especially important role in the political and economic arenas of western Europe in the Middle Ages. Drawing on the medieval context, this chapter explains why the feudal model is necessary for understanding the nature and consequences of private coercion in the twenty-first century. More specifically, it makes four contributions to the literature on private security.

First, we provide a unique historical lens through which to reexamine the previous research. Several articles and books have analyzed the meaning of private security in contemporary society. Moving back and forth between empirical evidence and two ideal types (the feudal and liberal models), we aim to expose these explanations to a wider range of historical cases, conceptualize them as universal social patterns, and delimit their application to modern society.

Second, although much has been written about the private security industry, it has been primarily conceptualized as an instrument of defense or protection. In contrast, we suggest that private social actors utilize violence (or the threat of violence) not only to protect life and property, but also to expand power and wealth. Put differently, we argue that private coercion plays an important role in creating and maintaining pathways to power in the United States. For instance, to maximize profits, private collection agencies use aggressive psychological tactics and threats to force lenders to pay their debts. The detention of immigrants—"the fastest-growing form of incarceration in this country" (Talbot 2008)—has become a lucrative business for private prison companies, which have proven to be less transparent than the public jail system. Urban enclaves and gated communities represent miniature sovereignties, with independent security operations that restrict the rights of nonmembers to public space in order to protect and increase property values. Across the globe, private military companies (PMCs) perform a range of profitable security tasks in unstable regimes with little government oversight.

Third, while we agree that, in historical terms, the increased role of private coercion is linked to the rise of corporate capitalism (Spitzer and Scull 1977), we argue that it should not be seen primarily as a modern social phenomenon, nor as one found exclusively in the age of capitalist development. The feudal model is not only intended to highlight the analogous relationships in medieval times, but also to dispute the supposed novelty of contemporary social conditions.

Fourth, while previous theoretical approaches have examined particular types of private security, such as private policing (Forst and Manning 1999), PMCs (Scahill 2007), and gated enclaves (Alsayyad and Roy 2006), few have offered a general framework for understanding the broad spectrum of activities related to the private sector's use of violence. We suggest that further theorizing and conceptualization are needed to guide research on this topic and to develop a fuller, more comprehensive explanation of private coercion, its antecedent conditions, and its consequences for society. In this chapter, we offer a framework that highlights the defensive and offensive nature of private coercion in the specific context of the United States. We understand, at the same time, that such coercion is a global phenomenon (Avant 2005).

Medieval Security

With the fall of the Roman Empire, as well as after the collapse of the Frankish kingdom in the ninth century, political power fragmented in western Europe, conflicts ensued, and security became a great concern for all strata of the population. Transportation routes on both land and sea were treacherous. Travelers were vulnerable to a range of serious dangers, from lone criminals and rogue sheriffs to large bands of raiders. Economic activities diminished significantly in the early Middle Ages. Faced with external threats and invasions, much of the population in cities retreated to the countryside. The fear of crime and pillaging was felt strongly by all, though most severely by the peasants. As Bloch (1989, 41) suggested, "the incursions, whether of Arabs, Hungarians, or Scandinavians, were certainly not wholly responsible for the shadow that lay so heavy on men's minds, but they were without doubt largely responsible."

The early Middle Ages were a time of military insecurity, and the need for reversing this vulnerability became a driving force of social development and the basis of feudal institutions and exchange processes (Shlapentokh with Woods 2007). Commendation—the voluntary submission of small landowners to the feudal lord in exchange for protection—was a key institution in medieval society. The receivers of security regularly paid for it in the form of goods, labor, and military service. Attempting to live outside the feudal security system was dangerous. As suggested by Vinogradoff (1924), the bare existence of most peasants depended on their ability to find support from a lord.

Castles and fortified towns were vital aspects of medieval security technology. In addition to their obvious military function, castles provided a number of other services to power holders. They served as the residences of royals, military headquarters, and centers of political administration, law enforcement, prisons, and treasuries (Colvin 1982; Heiser 2000). They also stood as symbols of authority and social status for those who inhabited them. These architectural strongholds were, above all else, instruments of social control, often located along key trade routes, which allowed the lords to defend their lives and property, oversee and maintain their territory, fulfill their obligations to higher lords, and expand their spheres of influence through violent means (Stokstad 2005).

Although some aspects of medieval security can be seen as public, especially as governments became more established in the late Middle Ages, protection and military power were, for the most part, private goods, provided not only by the king but also by a number of independent actors. Mercenary groups—some well organized, others loosely coupled—were used to expand territories and pursue immediate financial gain through raids, extortion, and conquest. The systematic use of private coercion was not driven by the public's interest or a common social goal, but by a small number of powerful and largely independent lords.

The mercenary trade was indeed a popular medieval occupation, at times serving as a significant source of wealth and land for people of varying socioeconomic backgrounds. The younger sons of nobles, finding themselves disinherited from their fathers' wealth, often became soldiers of fortune. As independent agents, mercenaries served in both defensive and offensive capacities. In many cases, they fortified the armies of great lords and kings. Among other notable undertakings, mercenaries played an important role in the Crusades, as well as in the Norman Conquest under William the Conqueror, who seized the throne of England in the eleventh century. In the late Middle Ages, mercenary groups became better organized, forming what became known as the "great companies," which made war for their own benefit, unless hired and paid by a king, pope, or city republic (Fowler 2001).

Well-developed tax systems did not exist in the early Middle Ages. For this reason, entrepreneurs were able to purchase the right to collect taxes in their local areas from kings, sometimes through auctions. After paying a flat fee to the king, tax collectors used a variety of coercive means to maximize their investments in the form of tax revenues (Kiser and Kane 2001; Murphy 2003; Jones 1999).

The use or threat of violence, whether posed in defense of life and property or for pursuing wealth and conquest, was the basis of every leader's authority. As Bloch (1989, 151) put it, "of all the problems besetting the governing classes in those days, the most urgent by far was not that of administering the country or a private estate in times of peace, but that of procuring the means to wage war." By participating in the military marketplace, the lords competed for land, strengthened their autonomy, established localized economies, and eventually aligned their military forces, to form fledgling political systems and public institutions.

As suggest in the next sections, the various roles of medieval agents of private coercion can also be found, if to a lesser degree, in contemporary American society. Today, private coercion is vital to a range of political and economic spheres, such as transportation, housing, entertainment, urban development, commerce, international relations, military conquest, and more generally to the ongoing contest among private organizations, groups, and individuals to secure scarce resources. The medieval link between private coercion and the public's fear of crime and social disorder also remains relevant to contemporary society.

Medieval Authority and the Modern State

According to the feudal model, the provision of security and military force is a purely private affair. By treating it as such, however, we do not wish to encourage a dichotomous conceptualization of security as either "public" or "private." Rather, the feudal model represents one side of a continuum. With respect to the provision of security and the use of force, the feudal model is opposed to the liberal model, which presumes that the state holds a monopoly on violence and operates, with the public's consent, as the sole legitimate provider of security. Using these points of comparison, certain aspects of society may be described as being closer to, or more associated with, one ideal type than another.

European societies of the Middle Ages were closer to the feudal model than the liberal or authoritarian models. As mentioned, the relative weakness of medieval kings allowed some lords to maintain their autonomy and wield a great deal of influence on social developments. Ultimately, their authority was determined less by the law or the possession of land per se than by their ability to use, or threaten to use, physical coercion and violence in the monitoring, protection, and enlargement of their landholdings and wealth. The strength of these external forces made them indispensable to the king, while at once bestowing them with meaningful levels of independence and unaccountability.

While medieval societies may be best understood using the feudal model, no society perfectly replicates any model. Moreover, almost all societies exhibit some elements of multiple models. Even some aspects of security in the Middle Ages can be better understood with the liberal model than the feudal one. For instance, the Magna Carta of 1215, which was forced on King John of England by his disgruntled barons, outlawed the use of foreign mercenaries. The document stated that the king would "remove from the kingdom all foreign-born soldiers, cross-bow men, servants, and mercenaries who have come with horses and arms for the injury of the realm" (Lee 1900, 169; see Drew 2004). This was, in essence, a call for limiting the use of private security contractors—a typical aspect of the liberal model, which is further discussed below (Percy 2007).

The Liberal Model

The goal of this chapter is to use both the feudal and liberal lenses to analyze the modes of security in contemporary American society. As mentioned, the objective here is not to classify the entire security apparatus as either feudal or liberal. Rather, it is to sort out which aspects of this complex system fall closer to the feudal model than the liberal one. To pursue this task, however, we must further define the "liberal model."

Our treatment, as it relates to security, is based on Weber's (1965) definition of the modern state and his well-known assertion that it possesses a monopoly on the exercise of legitimate violence. This notion has been developed by a number of more recent scholars (Evans, Rueschemeyer, and Skocpol 1985; Tilly 1992), and rests firmly on the ideas of classical liberal thinkers such as Hobbes and Locke. From Hobbes's perspective, the state receives its monopoly on violence out of necessity, given the mutual need of citizens to maintain conditions of peace. Without a sole proprietor of coercive means, embodied by the state and the rule of law, life would be, as Hobbes famously noted, "nasty, brutish and short . . . a war of every man against every man." Locke also recognized the necessity of the state's monopoly on violence, but placed limits on its power and described its relationship with citizens as a social contract involving mutual obligations. Locke's writing stresses the need for normative judgments of state actions and the use of reason to distinguish between legitimate and illegitimate functions of institutions.

From Locke's perspective, the state does not exist simply for the physical safety of citizens, but because people need security and order to build a civil society. As Bislev (2004) writes in his treatment of Locke, "society is an association of citizens, and the maintenance of security is a necessary function for that association, something without which it cannot exist and thrive." In this way, the state's monopoly on violence supports the common good and represents a building block of democratic society. The legitimacy of the state's use of violence is ultimately based on its accountability to the public at large, as opposed to nonstate organizations that answer to private interests.

Although Weber was clearly influenced by his predecessor, his thinking sidesteps Locke's normative arguments about what the state should or should not do, and treats the monopoly on violence as part of his idealized conceptualization of the state. The control over violence is one aspect, according to Weber (1965), which distinguishes modern states from earlier forms of social organization—such as the unstable European kingdoms of the ninth century, in which the security function was fragmented and often used more for the sake of personal gain than for the common good.

Again, this is not to say that Weber's concept of the state *should* be put into practice or that all people necessarily accept the state's monopoly on violence. Rather, it is merely an observation on Weber's part, which serves as the basis of his ideal type. Such concepts are thought to be valuable to social scientists who wish to elucidate and compare societies, based on the extent to which they reflect one ideal type or another. Societies, in this case, can be differentiated in part by whether (or to what extent) the use of violence is controlled by private interests (the feudal model), or by the legitimate instruments of the state (liberal model). We embrace the Weberian approach because our aim is to understand the current security trends in American society, not pass judgments on them.

The independent control of coercive or violent force, what we refer to as "private coercion," was an important political tool and aspect of power in medieval Europe. Let us now turn to a discussion of the similar roles of private coercion in contemporary society.

Private Military Companies and International Security

The aspect of private coercion that captured the most attention from scholars, politicians, and journalists at the start of the twenty-first century was that many functions that have traditionally been carried out by the United States military were being outsourced to private contractors. Private military companies (PMCs) not only provide meals to troops and dispose of their garbage, but also work in areas of recruitment and interrogation. PMCs also fulfill guarding posts that put them in highly dangerous situations and that require a great amount of training and accountability. Private contractors of this sort work all around the world for government and nongovernment organizations, offering military consultation, training of troops in foreign lands, antikidnapping and counterterrorism operations, and the protection of vital assets, such as oil fields, oceangoing ships, and mining concerns.

Private military companies emerged prominently in the public eye during the Iraq war in the mid-2000s. Thousands of heavily armed soldiers worked in Iraq for private contractors, which received immunity from Iraqi courts and faced little serious oversight from officials in the United States (Miller 2005; Tyson 2005). Hired guns were involved in hundreds of violent encounters, but no one—neither media organizations, military experts, nor the American government—has clearly calculated and defined the number of unwarranted killings of the Iraqi population.

Nevertheless, public outrage against mercenary groups has been widespread, especially among local populations, throughout the course of American involvement in Iraq and Afghanistan. In September 2007, employees of Blackwater Worldwide killed seventeen Iraqi civilians and wounded twenty-three, which intensified public dismay and created a furor in Congress over the administration's failure to hold security contractors accountable for their misdeeds (Blackwater shootings 2007; Johnston and Broder 2007). Although the incident underwent a series of investigations by the FBI, the State Department, and the Pentagon, Blackwater weathered the storm and managed to stay in business (Risen 2008). In April 2008, the State Department renewed its contract in Iraq for another year.

The aggressive operations of private military companies have been discussed in great detail by scholars (Singer 2003; Scahill 2007). Viewing these firms through the feudal lens, however, sheds new light on an old subject. The feudal model places the emphasis not only on the power, fierceness, and unaccountability of today's soldiers of fortune, but also the relative weakness of the state and the deep interdependencies between the state and PMCs. For a variety of reasons, the United States government simply could not function in Iraq without PMCs. As reported in the *New York Times,* Patrick Kennedy, the undersecretary of state for management, bluntly confirmed that "we cannot operate without private security firms in Iraq. If the contractors were removed, we would have to leave Iraq" (Risen 2008).

Just as mercenaries stabilized the royal armies of the Middle Ages, in the early twenty-first century they represented an essential component of the military campaign in Iraq and other actions related to the "war on terrorism." While the liberal model tells us much about the official use of military force in foreign lands—after all, a majority of Americans and legislators initially supported the wars in Afghanistan and Iraq—it does not elucidate the social significance of the thirty thousand hired guns in Iraq who plug the holes of a tattered and understaffed official military force (*New York Times* 2008a).

The liberal model also fails to anticipate the potential competition between PMCs and state-sponsored military services, as they assemble their respective forces. A number of military experts, senior commanders, and Pentagon officials have raised serious concerns about the lavish salaries and benefits offered by PMCs, suggesting that the United States military's most talented and highly trained soldiers are being increasingly recruited into the ranks of the private military (Schmitt and Shanker 2004). The role of PMCs in international affairs is likely to expand as they continue to commandeer the nation's best and brightest military minds.

If it is true, even in part, that the American government depends on private coercion to uphold its interests abroad, it is not hard to imagine that the same dependence is felt by multinational corporations. Decades before 9/11, overseas firms faced what they saw as grave dangers from terrorism and other forms of violence, crime, and social unrest in foreign lands. Given the inability or unwillingness of local governments to protect them, they relied instead on mercenary forces. The great sums they paid for such services were treated merely as the calculated cost of tapping the given country's vital resources. In the early 1980s, James Nathan (1981, 156) identified this trend as the start of a "new international feudalism" and warned us that "a medieval situation may emerge in which the security function of the state is usurped by private contractors."

Given the intense social forces of globalization, privatization, increased concerns about terrorism, and the expanding capabilities of PMCs, Nathan's warning seems all the more prescient today. The rise of PMCs has fragmented the state's monopoly on legitimate violence and empowered the twenty-first century's new feudal actors. As Singer (2002, 212) puts it, "The unrestricted access to military services ushered in by the rise of the privatized military industry has clearly enhanced the role of non-state groups, which at one time had been at a significant disadvantage in a system dominated by states." Global corporations and other nonstate actors have access to "new options and new paths to power not imagined until very recently" (Singer 2002, 212). Interestingly enough, these "new" pathways are the conventional avenues through which medieval social actors gathered and maintained power in the Middle Ages.

The Size of the Private Security Industry in the United States

Given the high level of media coverage on this issue, the social significance of PMCs as agents of private coercion may seem obvious. The role of private coercion within the United States, however, rarely captures as much attention from politicians, the public, or the press. Even scholars have been slow to fully explore this crucial element of American society. The major textbooks of sociology, criminology, and political science almost always offer thorough discussions on the public police and law enforcement, but rarely cover the private security industry and the social consequences of its activities. Some observers have taken this argument one step further, suggesting that sociologists work from a "kindly bias," therefore denying the importance of physical coercion and the extent to which it props up social systems (Kleck 1988; Goode 1972).

Meanwhile, the size and scope of the private system of social control have increased significantly over the last decades. Although precise and reliable historical data about its growth are difficult to come by, Shearing and Stenning (1983, 1981) have contributed a great deal to our understanding of historical trends. In 1960, the number of private security personnel was roughly equivalent to the number of public police. Ten years later, public policing gained ground, even though there was continued growth in the private security sector as well.

Shearing and Stenning (1981, 1983) identify the early 1970s as a turning point in the evolution of private security, when the industry grew dramatically in size and outpaced the growth of public police forces. There was also an important shift in the organizational structure of this type of security. "Between 1960 and 1975 the ratio of in-house to contract security diminished from 6:1 to 1.5:1, indicating a major restructuring of the organization of private security" (Shearing and Stenning 1983, 495). In the next years, individual private security contractors would expand their operations, consolidate their interests, and reduce their dependence on any one client or organization, including government institutions.

The industry continued its rapid growth throughout the 1980s. As discussed by Pastor (2003, 42), between 1981 and 1991 there was a 140 percent increase in spending on private security (from $21.7 billion to $52 billion) and a 117 percent increase in expenditures on public policing (from $13.8 billion to $30 billion). By the year 2000, spending on private security had increased again, by 100 percent to $104 billion, while expenditures on public policing increased by only 47 percent to $44 billion. There is further evidence that the annual growth rate for private security has been roughly double the growth rate for public policing (Cunningham, Strauchs, and Van Meter 1990). To put it another way, at the dawn of the twenty-first century, 70 percent of the nation's investment in crime prevention and law enforcement was spent on private security. The latest available data from the Economic Census (2002) confirm the recent increase in the size of the private security industry.[1]

1. Using comparable data from 1997 and 2002, the number of establishments in the area of investigation and security services (guards, armored car services, investigation services, security system installers, and locksmiths) increased from 21,494 to 22,957, and the number of paid employees

The Nature of Private Coercion

Aggregated economic data, while necessary for understanding the social significance of private security in the United States, does not reveal the nature and diversity of the services offered by this industry. In the next sections, we consider the specific functions and qualitative meanings of these services in the context of both the liberal and feudal models.

Security Guards

The private security industry is perhaps most commonly associated with guards. In 2003, there were roughly 1 million guards working in the United States, and the vast majority of them (87 percent) were employed by the private sector (Parfomak 2004). The popular image of security guards tends to be rather benign and nondescript: unarmed men and women in semiofficial-looking uniforms, whose low-paying jobs demand little more than the presentation of security and the casual monitoring of behavior in a few isolated establishments, such as shopping malls and parking lots. In fact, security guards draw on a range of professional experiences, education, and training and operate in almost all aspects of commercial infrastructure—office and residential buildings, gated communities, banks, armored cars, hospitals, factories, plants, laboratories, data processing centers, universities, sports stadiums, casinos, and parks. The nation's air, sea, and rail terminals also receive some protection, surveillance, and other services from private organizations.

The duties of private security personnel are as varied as the interests of those who employee them. In the context of corporations, retailers in particular, security professionals work within a private system of justice. This system monitors, investigates, and prosecutes both those who work for the given firm and all those who come into contact with it (Davis, Lundman, and Martinez 1991; Shearing and Stenning 1981). Challenging the liberal model, the lords of private justice receive less public scrutiny and greater legal authority to search and detain suspected perpetrators, from shoplifters to their own employees, than do those in the public system of justice (Bishop 1988).

Moreover, private security companies, like PMCs, have taken over some of the traditional functions of the state. Among the total number of guards

---

increased from 682,891 to 761,291. See http://www.census.gov/econ/census02/. These numbers only include establishments with payrolls. The absolute numbers would be greater if small, single-person businesses were included.

employed in 2003, roughly 5 percent protected "critical" infrastructure and assets (Parfomak 2004). As defined by Congress and formalized in the USA Patriot Act, critical infrastructure refers to "systems and assets, whether physical or virtual, so vital to the United States that the incapacity or destruction of such systems and assets would have a debilitating impact on security, national economic security, national public health or safety, or any combination of those matters" (USA Patriot Act 2001).

In essence, then, private guards have not only supported official fighting forces abroad, but also protected much of the homeland against foreign and domestic enemies in the "war on terrorism" (Sauter and Carafano 2005). If private security companies function in strict accordance with state regulations and operate in the same ways as public institutions, they can and should be seen, in Weberian terms, as a legitimate arm of the state and a key element of the liberal model.

In practice, however, this is often not the case. While operating in a public capacity, private guards are primarily obligated to serve private interests, not public ones. To save costs, for instance, security contractors sometimes hire poorly educated guards, who are paid less than half the average salary of the public police and receive far less training (Parfomak 2004). Moreover, the state has been unable or unwilling to oversee and regulate the lords of private security and make its powers known to them. There are no federal training requirements for most guards; regulations involving the background checks of guards vary across states (sixteen states have no such regulations) and enforcement is often lax (Parfomak 2004). Part of the weakness of government regulators can be explained by the lack of public support for increasing state funding.

The Case of Airport Security Prior to 9/11

Even in the few "critical infrastructure" areas in which federal regulations do exist, the quality of private security often falls short of public needs. Airport security prior to the 9/11 tragedy clearly and painfully demonstrated that market mechanisms do not always meet the requirements of national security. Before 9/11, the system of security in airports was as fragmented as that in a medieval European kingdom. Security was controlled by three actors, whose aims and interests often diverged: commercial airports, which controlled access to the airport and surrounding area; commercial airlines, which protected the aircraft; and the Federal Aviation Administration (FAA), which held regulatory responsibility for airport safety in general.

In explaining why this system failed to prevent the hijackings on 9/11, the feudal model stresses two underlying factors: the relative weakness of the state, and the desire of other social actors to free themselves from the state's authority and pursue their own aims. These two factors have been highlighted by a number of government policy experts and economists. First, prior to 9/11, although government agencies were aware of "serious gaps in security procedures" at airports, "most of the proposals to tighten security measure were not adopted" (Seidenstat 2004, 277). Breaches in the private security network were common; the response of the FAA was weak and ineffective. Between 1990 and 2000, the FAA levied only $1.1 million in fines, despite the thousands of breaches. During this time period, there were 897 breaches at the Kennedy Airport alone (Seidenstat 2004).

Meanwhile, the lords of the commercial airline industry regarded the FAA and its regulations more as obstacles than as helpful instruments to secure the safety of air travel. Given the fact that tightening security would cut into profits, private security firms were constantly looking to cut corners, even when it meant violating government regulations at the expense of national security (Moss and Eaton 2001).

To be sure, prior to 9/11, commercial airlines had a strong incentive to avoid the losses associated with a terrorist attack on their facilities or operations. In general, however, that incentive was not compelling enough to encourage the appropriate level of security. Public and private interests were not aligned, and the state lacked the power to enforce its regulations and reverse this trend. Given the liberal model's assumption about the state's responsibility to secure the safety of its citizens, the case of airline security prior to 9/11 represents a deviation from the liberal model. This failure arose, in part, from a fragmented security power structure, in which various feudal actors pursued contradictory and competing interests. The feudal model can explain these circumstances better than the liberal one can.

Bouncers, Bodyguards, Bounty Hunters, and Other Free Agents of Private Coercion

Private coercion is controlled by a number of other groups and agents, whose functions do not fit the conventional job characteristics of the "security guard." For example, the lords of the nighttime economy rely heavily on bouncers and other guards to patrol and limit access to their facilities. Bouncers are omnipresent in bars, clubs, and restaurants in big cities. Working in a "largely unregulated zone of venture capitalism," they regularly use physical coercion and violence, unfettered by public oversight, to deal with problematic customers and subjugate the alcohol- and drug-fueled nighttime economy (Hobbs et al. 2003, 28; Lister et al. 2000; Lister et al. 2001; DeMichele and Tewksbury 2004; Monaghan 2002).

Club owners and their bouncers may establish social order where it is lacking, but they serve this function in the name of private, not public, aims. The same was true in the Middle Ages. When the great landlords of ninth-century France used their knights to establish security in the provinces, they did not act in the public interest, but according to a specific set of private objectives.

Bail bondsmen and bounty hunters represent another, often neglected agent of private coercion. Bond enforcement companies play an important role in the American criminal justice system. For a substantial nonrefundable fee, they post bail for criminal defendants who are presumed innocent but cannot afford to make bail. The bond company has complete discretion over who receives assistance, which can be seen as a sort of privatization of imprisonment. Furthermore, if a client does not appear in court, the bondsman or bounty hunter has extensive power to search for and apprehend the defendant. They may "break into homes of defendants without a warrant, temporarily imprison them and move them across state lines without entering into the extradition process" (Liptak 2008).

Unlike the public police, bounty hunters do not require a special form of training or accreditation, and the ambiguity of their work allows them to ignore some federal and state laws that protect the rights of citizens. The feudal label may be especially apt given the fact that posting bail for others in exchange for money is treated as a crime in most Western countries (Liptak 2008).

In response to the increasing problem of identity theft, a number of private firms provide services that help prevent people's identities from being stolen and provide assistance to victims. A related industry, devoted to protecting online information for individuals, corporations, and governments, has also grown substantially in the last decades. Internet security firms not only work in the area of loss prevention, but also play active roles in investigating digital thefts and other cyber crimes and provide high-technology litigation support.

Specialized corporate security agencies perform numerous tasks involving financial and accounting irregularities, forensic computer data discovery, counterfeiting and product reputation protection, employee integrity, workplace stability, executive protection, event security, supply-chain monitoring, eco-terrorism, competitive intelligence gathering, and corporate espionage (Winkler

1997). Corporate spying is an activity that clearly defies free market principles and cannot be explained by the liberal capitalist model of society (Penenberg and Barry 2000a). According to recent reports, it is also widespread: "Almost every Fortune 500 company these days has a 'competitive intelligence' (or C.I.) unit or farms out its spy activities. Coca-Cola, 3M, Dow Chemical, General Electric, and Intel all maintain a staff dedicated to uncovering what business rivals are up to. Motorola hired away a star from the Central Intelligence Agency to create its corporate intelligence division. Ernst & Young, the accounting firm, boasts a 25-member competitive intelligence arm" (Penenberg and Barry 2000b). This form of private coercion urges us, once again, to look beyond the liberal model and adopt the feudal model as a supplementary analytical tool.

Gated Communities

One of the most apparent analogues to medieval society is the contemporary gated enclave or community. Residential areas where public access is restricted are common in most major metropolitan areas. In 2001, the American Housing Survey, conducted by the U.S. Census Bureau, added new questions that identified whether or not a dwelling was "secured with walls or fences." According to the survey, roughly 7 percent of occupied housing units were located in gated communities in 2001. The percentage did not change much in the 2003 and 2005 waves of the survey (U.S. Census Bureau 2008).

The purposes or motives behind the gating phenomena are not uniform. As Blakely and Snyder (1997) discussed in *Fortress America*, the first major study on the subject, these communities can be divided into three types: lifestyle communities, prestige communities, and security zones. Although we should not assume that the three categories are mutually exclusive, the third type is closest to the medieval context and the feudal model's emphasis on private coercion. Not unlike the desperate search for protection in the Middle Ages, entire communities have increasingly enclosed themselves within gates or walls since the early 1980s. Blakely and Snyder described a new security mind-set among many Americans, which has been shaped by growing fears of crime and disorder: "Many feel vulnerable, unsure of their place and the stability of their neighborhoods in the face of rapid change. This is reflected in an increasing fear of crime that is unrelated to actual crime trends or locations, and in the growing number of methods used to control the physical environment for physical and economic security. The phenomenon of walled cities and gated communities is a dramatic manifestation of a new fortress mentality growing in America" (Blackely and Snyder 1997, 1–2).

In some cases, entire residential areas hire security contractors to augment the protection of the public police. For instance, the eighty-block Georgetown community in Washington, D.C., which encompasses roughly six thousand residences, is patrolled by several private guards in cars and on foot. The community group that represents the area and coordinates the added protection openly suggests that public policing efforts are inadequate. Facing what they perceived as "serious and wide-spread community concerns about public safety," their solution, like that of medieval cities, was to take responsibility for their own security.[2]

In urban areas, commercial interests use gates and other infrastructural barriers to ensure security and impede "undesirable" people. As reported in a *New York Times* article about the homeless population in Los Angeles, "Skid Row's street people have been watching their territory shrink for years, as downtown developers open the long-neglected area to gentrification" (Moore 2007). Just as medieval lords erected castles along busy trade routes, the lords of LA's bookstores, DVD shops, financial buildings, cafes, bars, and restaurants build fences and other architectural structures to bolster their "miniature monarchies," and to push and keep out the city's homeless population.

This bifurcation of space, which intentionally separates the upper class from the underclass, exists in subtler forms, and in a variety of social and geographical contexts, from private shopping centers, amusement parks, and college campuses to massive residential estates and high-density apartment and condominium buildings (Shearing and Stenning 1983; Reiner 1992).

This growing level of fortification and increased security has not spread to all areas of the urban and suburban landscape. It would be a mistake to overextend the medieval metaphor and suggest that America has become a land of walled cities, castles, barricades, and defensive infrastructural outcroppings. At the same time, the public's fear of crime and disorder is real, and the proliferation of gated communities comes with real consequences in terms of public access to streets, parks, playgrounds, rivers, lakes, and oceans. At least two aspects of the gated communities—the privatization of the security function in society and the impact of fortification on public access—are contradictory to the liberal model and can be better understood with the feudal model (Shlapentokh with Woods 2007).

2. See the Public Safety Program of the Association of Georgetown at http://www.cagtown.org.

Private Prisons

Another important element of private coercion can be seen in the relatively new trend of privatizing prison systems. While the characteristics of punishment vary dramatically between the medieval and modern contexts, the private control of facilities of incarceration can be found in both periods (Geltner 2006). In contemporary America, the private-detention business expanded in the 1980s as privatization in general became a popular remedy to "inefficient government." In the next decades, given a number of high-profile examples of mismanagement, corruption, abuse, and other failures—including riots and escapes from private prisons—the industry received mixed reviews from policy makers, the public, and the press (Talbot 2008; Butterfield 2004). In a handful of cases, public outrage against the privatization of prisons resulted in mass protests at major American universities (Ellin 2001). In spite of some setbacks, however, the privatization of prisons represents a growing trend in the United States at the start of the twenty-first century.

In theoretical terms, private prisons stray from the liberal model in a number of respects. While public and private prisons may perform similar functions, the underlying motives that shape daily operations differ between the two. Like any other industry, private prisons are driven by profit margins, as opposed to the public will, which is the benchmark of the liberal model. Profit, in turn, depends on the number of inmates. Given the fact that "most private prisons operate on a per diem rate for each bed filled, there is a financial incentive not only to detain more inmates but also to detain them for a longer period of time" (Cheung 2004, 4). As suggested by Nathan, the editor of *Prison Privatisation Report International*, it's "Capitalism 101. You've got to expand your markets—you've got to fill your beds" (Rose 2007).

The political push for increased reliance on private prisons has been driven to a great extent by the Corrections Corporation of America (CCA), the first private company to receive a contract to take over a state prison (in Hamilton, Tennessee, 1984). According to the company itself, "CCA houses approximately 75,000 offenders and detainees in more than 60 facilities, 44 of which are company-owned, with a total bed capacity of more than 80,000."[3] As suggested in a report by the National Institute on Money in State Politics, CCA is also one of the industry's biggest corporate contributors to political campaigns (Bender 2000). During the 1998 election cycle, CCA and other private-prison companies

3. See http://www.correctionscorp.com/about/.

made 1,187 contributions to 636 candidates, totaling more than $862,822. This sum exceeds the contributions of other major groups, such as the National Rifle Association, and does not include the far greater amount of funding used to pay for the services of lobbying firms and other associations (Bender 2000).

At the start of the twenty-first century, campaign financing from private firms was on the rise, along with a general expansion of for-profit prisons (Bender 2000). Moreover, after 9/11, the Bush administration bolstered its efforts to curb illegal immigration, which led to a substantial increase in the number of immigrants in private detention facilities. In 2006, the two biggest prison operators, CCA and Geo Group, housed no fewer than 20 percent of the immigrants being detained (Kolodner 2006).

This kind of influence, as some observers suggest, may explain why the former general consul at CCA, Gustavus Adolphus Puryear, was nominated by the Bush administration in June 2007 to be a federal trial court judge for the Middle District of Tennessee. Given the lack of Puryear's experience in a courtroom, the nomination generated sharp criticism from the media and from politicians, including members of the Senate Judiciary Committee. Senators Arlen Specter and Dianne Feinstein both noted the nominee's "conspicuous lack of trial experience" (Mencimer 2008). Puryear had litigated only two cases and had served as lead counsel on only one of them. These "job experiences" occurred more than a decade prior to being nominated as a federal trial court judge.

Another feudal aspect of private prisons involves the limits on public oversight associated with a firm's access to private resources. The maintenance and development of state prisons and local jails ultimately rely on public funding, which requires voter approval for its disbursement. Private prison companies, in contrast, can use their own funds to build new facilities, speculating on the increased demand for prison space in the future. Meanwhile, as suggested by Cheung (2004, 5), "taxpayers are denied the opportunity to approve or disapprove the building of new facilities while remaining liable for the expenses incurred by the government through their contract with private prison companies."

Disagreements have also arisen as to whether private prisons are exempt from open records laws. In 2008, CCA attempted to withhold information regarding legal settlements, judgments, and complaints against the company. Alex Friedman, an associate editor of the monthly magazine *Prison Legal News*, sued CCA for its refusal to present the documents in accordance with Tennessee's open records laws. Friedman's attorney said that he took the case pro bono because he believed that CCA was intentionally trying to hide damaging information about the company (Associated Press, 2008). Friedman won his case, though attorneys for the company vowed to appeal the ruling.

In summary, the ongoing privatization of prisons encourages a number of feudal tendencies, including public-private collusions, the purchase of political influence, the use of personal relations, limits on public oversight, the direct impact of big money on election campaigns, and the increased control of violence and coercion in private hands.

Debt Collectors

While the systematic collection of debt by private firms is not feudal by definition, collection efforts that utilize coercion, manipulation, threats, and other unscrupulous practices do fit this category. According to reports by the Federal Trade Commission, which regulates the debt-collection industry, complaints about such feudal activities have been on the rise since the 1990s. The agency reported that it received 66,627 consumer complaints against third-party debt collectors in 2005, and 69,204 complaints in 2006, which is nearly six times the number reported in 1999 (Federal Trade Commission 2007). No other industry in the country generated as many complaints. As Chan Sewell (2006) suggested, "the agencies often buy the debt from more established companies for pennies on the dollar and seek to collect even if the debt has been paid or was never valid to begin with. Sometimes, consumers pay up simply because they are worn down by threats from the companies and fear damage to their credit rating."

A new market has grown up around the prospect of collecting extremely old debts. According to industry researchers, debt buyers bought up roughly $110 billion of such debt in 2006, whereas only ten years ago this type of debt was almost never purchased (Weston 2006). Given the inadequacies of record keeping and the incentive to collect on debts even when they are not owed, the new interest in old debts will likely result in more cases of feudal-style harassment and coercion.

According to the Federal Trade Commission, the number one consumer complaint against the industry is that "a collector is attempting to collect either a debt the consumer does not owe at all or a debt larger than what the consumer actually owes" (Federal Trade Commission 2007). Other complaints include repeated calls and continuous harassment, threats of dire consequences if the debt is not paid, and calls to the consumer's place of employment. These problems are not expected to diminish in the future. Given the country's economic troubles and the accumulation of debt in the late 2000s, the collection industry—which relies heavily on private coercion—is likely to grow (Gross 2005).

Another possible boon for collectors may come with the renewed intent of governments to privatize the gathering of state and federal taxes. As Krugman (2007) suggested, "tax farming—giving individuals the right to collect taxes, in return for a share of the take—went out with the French Revolution; now the tax farmers are back." In 2006, as part of a plan by the Bush administration, the IRS turned over information on 12,500 taxpayers to three collection agencies, though people who owed larger debts would continue to be pursued by government officers (Johnston 2006). The measure was part of the administration's broader plan to privatize tax collection.

Conclusion

The size of the private security industry has increased significantly in the last several decades. The lion's share of spending on crime prevention is now being funneled into the private sector. While previous research has stressed the industry's substantial growth trajectory, there has been less emphasis placed on the scope, diversity, and nature of these services. Private coercion plays a role in almost all areas of society and the economy, from education, entertainment, and urban development to globalization and international conflicts. Moving beyond the typical duties of security guards, private individuals, groups, and corporations provide a range of services, from spying on corporate competitors to chasing bail jumpers across the country. These services not only protect people, but also aid in the expansion of wealth and power.

The essence of private coercion conflicts with the state's monopoly on the exercise of legitimate violence, which is, according to Weber and many contemporary scholars, one of the defining characteristics of the modern state. Conventional models of liberal capitalism, though important to any analysis of American society, cannot fully explain the nature of security in the United States. We suggest that the feudal model makes an important contribution to our understanding of the character and consequences of private coercion. Comparisons with the medieval context are especially apt when considering cases in which the private use of force increases the wealth of a few major actors in society, while diminishing the rights of citizens, or the central authority's ability to protect them.

The need for security and the privatized patterns of social interaction that result can be found, to varying degrees, in many social contexts and historical periods. Private coercion has played a socially significantly role in medieval Europe, contemporary America, and many other societies across time and space. Private coercion should be seen as a "sociological universal"—one that shapes and is shaped by both the individual need for safety and the socially constructed motivation for increased economic security. The feudal model is a useful analytical tool for assessing the nature and consequences of private coercion. The model offers an alternative set of ideas about private security services, and could generate new and useful questions on this fundamental aspect of society.

6

Personal Relations in American Politics and Business: A Feudal Phenomenon

One of the most obvious elements of feudalism in contemporary society is the role of personal relations in politics, the economy, and other spheres of social life. There are two types of personal relations. One type is based on the interaction between independent actors who attempt to achieve their goals through mutual cooperation. The other type is based on the clientele principle, or suzerain-vassal relations, which suppose a hierarchy in the relations between people. The second type serves as the main subject of this chapter (Godbout 2000).

A feudal form of personal relations is seen when people use their scarce resources to acquire other benefits, advantages, or "rent," exceeding the level expected by the authoritarian or liberal models. The major social actors who benefit from feudal relations include rich people and corporations, government officials, and individuals who control networks of influential people.

Personal relations play a key role in the process of choosing people for important positions in society, particularly leadership posts in corporate management, politics, and culture. The use of personal relations in the selection of cadres influences the efficiency of major social institutions, as well as the levels of political, economic, and social stability. While in most cases personal preferences and nepotism clearly have a negative effect on the efficiency of social institutions, they also, at times, solidify the social and political order.

In general, there are three ways of selecting cadres and controlling their performance. First, the democratic principle of selection and supervision is based on the merits and competence of workers and on rational decision making, as described by Weber (1978) and Parsons (1951). It supposes that the electorate selects the best-qualified candidates, and that elected bodies supervise the quality of nonelected officials, while market competition ensures that the best managers are positioned in the economic sphere. The intrusion of personal relations into the decision-making process in politics is considered, in democratic societies, as a form of deviance (often illegal) that challenges the fundamentals of society.

The principles of an authoritarian society suppose that only those who are loyal to the leader and the dominant political or religious ideology can be appointed to important positions within the government and party apparatus. While the leadership in such societies is interested in recruiting the most highly qualified individuals to manage the economy and work in the areas of science, technology, education, and the military, loyalty to the top leadership and official ideology, as opposed to one's friends, family members, and immediate supervisors, is a prerequisite for placement. Authoritarian systems attempt to dissuade bureaucrats from selecting people who are loyal to them personally, rather than to the supreme leader or central authority. Given its intolerance for any form of divided loyalty, the system regards nepotism and the formation of clans based on clientele or family ties as crimes, and harshly punishes such disobedience. The hierarchical principles of the authoritarian model held up quite well in the Soviet Union, particularly in Stalin's time.[1]

Unlike the authoritarian model, the feudal model supposes that organizations rely on personal loyalty rather than loyalty to institutions, ideas, or the supreme leader. In an ideal feudal society, a higher lord's emotional and intellectual trust in his or her subordinates would transcend institutional guarantees against treason and serve as the basis for selecting cadres. The decision to install relatives in high government positions and the formation of family clans—a widespread practice in medieval society—were also dictated by the desire for loyal partners and subordinates. While competence was not ignored in the medieval selection process, it was considered less important than the cadre's loyalty to the immediate superior.

1. The evolution in the selection of cadres in the USSR had a tremendous impact on life in Soviet society. In the first period of Soviet history, in the aftermath of the revolution (1920s), the selection of cadres was based on devotion to the cause of the revolution; the apparatchiks thought of themselves as shareholders in a common business. During the next period, with the installation of Stalin's cruel totalitarianism, selection depended on their loyalty to the leader and whether they looked like "soldiers of the party." After Stalin's death and during the softening of the regime, the selection of cadres became influenced by personal loyalty to the individual party bosses, which lowered the quality of the cadres and their performance and opened the way for corruption. The rise in the education level of cadres somewhat countervailed the negative effect of the "personalization" of the cadres policy (see Shlapentokh 1988).

Personal relations of the feudal type have the potential to damage the internal functioning of both public and private organizations. In this chapter, we focus on three types of such relations: the abuse of power inside organizations, the selection of cadres in business and politics based on personal relations (the clientele phenomenon), and the role of family clans and the "American nobility." We will also consider how some actors have attempted to challenge these feudal elements.

Personal Relations in Social Science

Twentieth-century political science and sociology tended to underestimate the role of personal relations in the political and economic establishments and in the formation of key social developments.[2] Those who have broached this topic have generally treated the impact of personal relations as "natural" or implicit, and therefore undeserving of special attention in the study of macro social issues. It is almost impossible to find a discussion of this crucial social phenomenon in texts on sociology and political science. While personal relations have received attention from sociologists and political scientists who examine society at the micro level, most of these studies ignore the distribution of power among the participants of human relations, though feminist studies stand as a notable exception to the rule.

The Disregard of Power in Personal Relations

The egalitarian vision of human relations dominated intellectual movements in sociology and social psychology in the postwar years. Moreno's sociometry (1956), which became popular in the social sciences in the 1950s, assumed social and political equality among participants in various contexts, such as offices or schools. As seen in the works of Blumer and Goffman, symbolic interactionism, which became influential in the 1960s, was another egalitarian perspective on human relations. Interactionists studied the behavior of supposedly equal, independent individuals in small groups, and showed little interest in the impact of these interactions on political or social conflicts (Blumer 1969; Goffman 1959). Later developments in social science only strengthened the

2. Among the social sciences, only anthropology, with its focus on nonmodern societies, was an exception. See the most recent anthropological publications on kinship in Carsten (2004), Holy (1996), and Parkin (1997).

"egalitarian" perception of human relations. Game theory, along with rational choice theory, added to the emphasis placed on equality between the partners in social interactions; the "prisoner's dilemma," popular in social science in the 1960s through the 1980s, also assumed that participants had equal access to information within the context of games.

To their credit, theories of social capital and networks, which rose to prominence in the 1970s and 1980s, drew more attention to personal relations. However, most researchers took the egalitarian approach and assumed the autonomy and independence of individuals, as if none of the participants had an advantage in terms of power (political, economic, or ideological) (Granovetter 1973). The literature on social capital and networks almost completely ignores the unequal distribution of power between actors, dealing with such issues as school boards, scouting, amateur sports leagues, fraternal organizations, and Internet networks (Fine 2001). Putnam (2001), a noted expert on social capital and the author of *Bowling Alone,* talked about networks of people with equal status. Coleman (1990) and Fukuyama (2000) also based their views of social capital and networks on the assumption of equality between participants.

These scholars seemed to overlook an important distinction between types of personal relations. It is one thing to have acquaintances of the same social status, but quite another to receive favors—legal or illegal—from friends or relatives who hold higher positions in government, business, education, or other institutions. People living in both the Middle Ages and modern times have used their family ties and social connections to find protectors, whether among landlords, royal bureaucrats, and the clergy or among CEOs, government bureaucrats, and trade union leaders.

The Nonegalitarian Approach to Personal Relations

Only a few authors who have discussed theories of human relations in the United States have taken the "nonegalitarian" approach and focused on the role of power. Even some of these authors, however, did not pay enough attention to the benefits received by those who hold the power (Eisenstadt and Ronigher 1984, 22, 33; Erber and Gilmour 1994, 5, 6, 68). Prominent authors such as Harold Kelley have talked only about the dominance-submission dimension of human relations in terms of individual differences, which seems to assume that some people choose the position of dominance, while others choose submission. This perspective also seems to reject the idea that the power differential is determined mostly by external factors, such as the social position of the participants before they enter into the interaction (Kelley 1982).

The nonegalitarian approach has been more popular among those who studied the interaction between superiors and subordinates in factories, offices, and hospitals (Brown 1986; Vidal 2007; Coombs 2004). However, they focused mostly on relations that are essentially regulated by the formal rules of the organization. Only in rare cases do they discuss relations based on the abuse of power by superiors for their personal benefit, a phenomenon we treat as feudal. As a matter of fact, as mentioned, only the feminist literature has paid a great deal of attention to the role of power in family relations (Cancian 1985; Therborn 2004; Umberson et al. 1998).

The disregard of personal relations in politics and other spheres of public life may be explained in part by the general belief among many scholars that rationalism is predominant in modern society; merit, not personal loyalty or family ties, determines where people are positioned in government, business, and cultural institutions. Weber, for instance, believed that political and economic relations in liberal society were based on formal rules, and that the personal factor did not play a significant role. Ferdinand Toennies (1887), who followed Weber's vision of modernization, saw *Gemeinschaft*—a concept involving communities with strong face-to-face relations—as a radically different type of organization than *Gesellschaft,* a modern society based strictly on formal principles. Parsons (1951) was also a champion of rationality and universalism. He was confident that, with modernization, people's social status would be less and less determined by inherited or acquired power ("the ascription"), and more by "achievement" or individual merit. For both giants of sociology, lord-vassal relations and the personal bonds of loyalty belonged to the remote past (Beck, Giddens, and Lash 1994).

Kinship as a Factor in Politics

Given their disregard of power in personal relations, social scientists tend to underestimate the contemporary importance of kinship, which was also a key social issue in the Middle Ages (Buss and Kenrik 1989; Kenrik, Ackerman, and Ledlow 2006). Some authors also tend to water down the concept, declaring that any tightly knit group of people, whether a motorcycle club or a drug cartel, is a form of kinship (Hebert 1993). Since 1964, after Hamilton initiated studies on kinship in everyday life, a few scholars began to pay more attention to this issue (Hamilton 1962). The interest increased after Dawkins's (1976) work in the 1970s on the subject of helping behavior (or altruism) and people's willingness to help those who will carry on their genes. Almost all publications on kinship in American society concentrate on relations at the micro level (Szinovácz 1998). In a nearly one-thousand-page edited volume, *Families in the U.S.: Kinship and Domestic Politics,* (Hansen and Garey 1998), none of the sixty-two chapters was devoted to kinship in American politics. The well-founded empirical studies on kinship that exist have not inspired widespread interest in the subject, particularly as it relates to the creation and maintenance of political power.

The Marxist and Feudal Approaches to the Role of Personal Relations in Politics

Similar to Weber and Parsons, orthodox Marxists and leftists (even if for other reasons) also tend to ignore the role of personal relations in politics and business. Their focus on class as the key factor in human relations led to a deemphasis of personal loyalties between individuals of different classes. Some argued that class was the single determinant of people's positions in liberal society. However, the vision of society based on the feudal model, and particularly societies with weak states—as in the cases of Russia and other post-Soviet countries—allows us to see another type of division based on clans, "teams," and "cliques," which unite people who are loyal to the same leader. The members of clans support each other, not because of their common social status or origin, as Marxists like to stress (even if these factors are indeed quite important), but because they share the same fate and will prosper or perish together—the sort of behavior and mentality seen in movies and television shows such as *The Godfather* and *The Sopranos.* Societies are divided into more than rich and poor, educated and noneducated, residents of metropolitan areas and small cities, people living in the east and west, citizens and illegal immigrants; they are also divided into different clans and groups that rely on different "roofs" or "protection rackets" and have different patrons (Shlapentokh with Woods 2007).

Ideal Societies for the Study of Personal Relations: Medieval Western Europe

The importance of personal relations in politics, kinship in particular, reached its peak in the Middle Ages. As Habermas (Habermas, Lennox, and Lennox

1974, 13) suggested, the private sphere was superior to the public one in the time of classic feudalism; the "public sphere was directly linked to the concrete existence of a ruler." As discussed in a reference book on medieval studies, "position, power, and place within society were based not on individual freedoms and impersonal relationships, but instead upon very personal relationships of reciprocal behavior, entered into contractually and described with kinship terminology" (Hekala 1996). In the political realm, personal loyalty and kinship were a person's most important qualities (Fortes 1969). Position and power were based on the "hierarchical principle" and rooted in the social organization of those barbaric societies that replaced the Roman Empire. While Roman law during the golden era of the empire strictly separated public and private domains, barbaric societies did not acknowledge this distinction; the leader of the tribe and those warriors who were personally loyal to him carried out the functions of the state (Shlapentokh with Woods 2007).

Personal relations have served as the basis of organization in politically fragmented societies where the central administration was unable to maintain order and security was provided by a number of powerful social actors (Bloch 1964). In medieval society, almost everyone had his own personal patron, from nobles and merchants to artisans and peasants. Patronage was often hereditary, and children expected to enjoy the same advantages as their parents from being under the protection of the lord. Of course, the character of personal patronage varied depending on the social status of the boss and the client. A vassal who controlled land and one who was landless could not claim the same respect. The same was true about the vassal of a king compared to the vassal of an "ordinary" landlord. While a noble could require decent treatment by his lord, a peasant or a serf was at the total mercy of his "protector."

This feudal ideology was a two-edged sword. It demanded obedience to the boss, but also imposed certain obligations on the lord to care for his vassals (Cantor 1994). Vinogradoff identified ceremonial bonds between the lord and tenant as an important aspect of life in the Middle Ages. "The tenant had to appear in person before the lord, surrounded by his court, kneel before him, put his folded hands into the hand of the lord and promise him loyalty. This act of homage corresponded with the 'investiture' by the lord, who delivered to his vassal a flag, a staff, a charter, or some other symbol of the property ownership" (Vinogradoff 1924; Shlapentokh with Woods 2007, 58).

Loyalty is a leading issue in Shakespeare's plays, such as *King Lear,* in which Cordelia epitomizes loyalty to her father, as well as *Macbeth* and *Much Ado About Nothing.* Loyalty is also praised in almost all of the plays by the authors of classicism, Racine and Corneille first among them, but mocked by the authors of the new, bourgeois era, such as Molière and Beaumarchais. Values such as loyalty and trust, along with boss-client relations, were transferred to the subsequent eras, and became, with differing degrees of intensity, part of cultural life in many contemporary societies, primarily in Europe and Japan.[3]

Kinship in the Middle Ages

Kinship, a special type of personal relation, was very important in the Middle Ages. "People talked not about coworkers, but about kinsmen; not about peers, but about brothers; not about associations, but about fraternities" (Heers and Herbert 1977). The importance of having children, particularly sons, was connected to the basis of the political order. People were interested, if for different reasons, in having big families. The peasants' main motivation was the need for labor; more family members in the nobility meant greater political power and an increase in the size of one's network, which was based on marriages and other network relations (Cantor 1994).

Sabean and his coauthors describe Germany as a particularly good illustration of the political role of kinship. In the thirteenth century, each political unit in Germany was considered a territory to be divided according to the number of sons. This practice permitted the youngest son to marry well and multiplied the number of territories that were ruled by the same dynasties, which was also a guarantee against the extinction of the family. Some territories were ruled by agnates, such as sons-in-law, and not by the male heir (Sabean, Teuscher, and Mathieu 2007).

Feudal Relations and Contemporary Society: The Office

Let us now move to an analysis of feudal-type personal relations in contemporary American society. By referring to "elements of feudal relations" inside organizations, public and private, we mean relations in which a superior is able to use his or her power to extricate illegal favors from subordinates.

3. Feudal values, such as honor, are difficult to explain to the average citizen of a totalitarian society because the total subordination of people to their superiors has made it practically impossible to observe these values. Among more than one hundred participants in the plot to kill Hitler—all German aristocrats—none reported to the Gestapo about the conspiracy (see Gisevius, Dulles, and Hoffmann 1998). In the Soviet Union, even after Stalin's death, where feudal traditions had completely vanished, such a large conspiracy was practically impossible.

Sexual Harassment

The sexual exploitation of subordinates is one area of comparison with feudal relations. Count Almaviva, in Beaumarchais' play *Figaro's Wedding,* does not seem anachronistic to contemporary observers. In the play, the count tried to use the feudal right of the lord to "the first night" with Suzanne, the fiancée of his servant Figaro. The pursuit of sexual favors by bosses is a common phenomenon in American society (Conte 2000). Sexual harassment is found in a variety of contexts—government, business, the military, law enforcement, medicine, academia, and others. Multiple surveys suggest that almost 50 percent of women experience sexual harassment in one form or another sometime in their working lives (Petrocelli and Repa 1998; Paludi and Paludi 2003). The figures are higher in the military, where two-thirds of women have reported being harassed. Sexual harassment occurs at a greater rate in industries traditionally dominated by men (military, mining, law enforcement). Targets of sexual harassment tend to be young (under thirty-five), single, and supervised by a member of the opposite sex. A consistent finding is that only a fraction of employees take formal actions against their harassers (Paludi and Paludi 2003).

Personal Favors

The abuse of power by managers is a lingering societal problem in the United States, especially in the context of corporations. Asking employees to perform personal favors or services (such as running errands) is a widespread form of such abuse. Secretaries (or administrative assistants) are highly susceptible to this type of power abuse because of the arbitrariness entrenched in the professional and personal relations between secretaries and bosses. The higher the position of the boss in the organization, the greater the possibility that subordinates will be asked to perform personal services (Kanter 1993).

In social studies on secretarial work in organizations, performing personal favors for the boss is classified as peripheral labor. Studies show that this type of labor is widespread and suggest that it stems from the status differential between secretaries and bosses. Peripheral labor usually involves physical tasks associated with traditional gender expectations. Peripheral labor is not recognized by the organization and is subject to personal negotiations between the boss and secretary (Wichroski 1994).

Given the difficult economic situation in the United States in the late 2000s, and the pressing problem of job security, it is increasingly important that the issue of power abuse by managers be analyzed. A survey conducted by Randstad USA suggested that many employees may be more willing to go the extra mile to keep their jobs, even if they may need to cross the line between professional, work-related activities and personal ones. Fifteen percent of respondents reported that they were willing to socialize with their boss outside the office, and 11 percent were willing to perform personal favors, such as running errands (Business Wire 2008).

Even though there is not enough academic research on the topic, many books have taken on the topic of power relations at work as practical guides to the inner workings of corporations and other bureaucratic organizations. They teach women and men strategies for how to build ethical relationships in the workplace and how not to comply with the inappropriate demands of managers or coworkers (DeMars 1998; Mandel 2006; Kosmoski and Pollack 2005).

Feudal Relations in American Politics: Clientele and Nepotism

Feudal behavior in politics is widespread in the United States, even if some authors are inclined to either ignore it or to describe American society as a triumph of meritocracy (McNamee and Miller 2004; Mlodinow 2008). There are two types of this behavior: when power is used to create a network of loyal people, a "clientele," and when the network of loyalists is based on kinship or nepotism. In many countries, such as Mexico (Bailey and Godson 2000), post-Soviet Russia (Shlapentokh with Woods 2007), and Italy (Ginsborg 2003; Stille 2003), clientele relations and nepotism play a more important role than in the United States.

The Case of Clientele

The most striking case of feudal behavior in American politics is the selection of cadres by American presidents. In fact, presidents have quite often ignored merit as the main criterion for selecting people for their administrations. This happens mostly because they need to reward their donors with positions in government. President Johnson was notable in this respect. As Mackenzie (1981, 32) suggested, "few Presidents have come to office with a wider range of friends and contacts upon whom to draw in making appointments than Lyndon Johnson." In the first years, Johnson paid a great deal of attention to ideological loyalty, but focused later on personal loyalty. For him it was particularly important that appointees were personally loyal to him, not Robert Kennedy. Merit and professionalism played a lesser role. Johnson's major political appointments were selected in return for political favors, and positions often went to his old senatorial friends or campaign contributors (Schott and Hamilton 1983). Nixon also made several cabinet selections from among his good, personal friends (John Mitchell, Robert H. Finch, and William P. Rogers) (Mackenzie 1981, 41).

President Carter was less engaged in the search for personal loyalty. Nevertheless, among his friends in business who received high positions in his administration were Griffin Bell (attorney general), Bert Lance (Office of Management and Budget), and Jay Solomon (General Services Administration). As had many presidents before him, Carter brought in several people who had participated in his election campaign, including Hamilton Jordan (longstanding manager of his campaign) and Thomas Lance (director of the Office of Budget Management), who had been Carter's head of public transportation in Georgia. During Carter's years, several ambassadorial appointments also went to old friends from Georgia with no experience in foreign affairs (Adams and Kavanagh-Baran 1979, 182). President George W. Bush (along with his father) not only favored his own family, but also encouraged nepotism at all levels of the hierarchy. As described by Bellow, as soon as Bush appeared in the White House he encouraged favoritism in his administration. "Michael Powell, the son of Secretary of State Colin Powell, became chairman of the Federal Communications Commission" (Bellow 2003a). It was no less remarkable that "Elaine Chao, the wife of Senator Mitch McConnell, became Secretary of Labor. Chao's chief labor attorney, Eugene Scalia, is the son of Supreme Court Justice Antonin Scalia" (Bellow 2003a). At the same time, Justice William Rehnquist's daughter received a position in Health and Human Services. The relatives of Vice President Cheney also prospered: "Elizabeth Cheney, his daughter, became a deputy assistant secretary of state, and her husband became chief counsel for the Office of Management and Budget" (Bellow 2003a). Bush appointed then twenty-eight-year-old Strom Thurmond Jr., son of Senator Thurmond, U.S. attorney for South Carolina.

> Helen Thomas, the former UPI Washington correspondent, declared in a column that the Bush administration had become "a family affair, reeking of nepotism." (Nepotism is often said to reek, as though it were a pile of dirty laundry.) "You'd think an administration headed by the son of a former president might be a teensy bit leery of appearing to foster a culture of nepotism," Andrew Sullivan wrote in *The New Republic.*

> Sullivan produced a long list of people who had gotten jobs in Washington through such connections, and concluded, "All this nepotism is a worrisome sign that America's political class is becoming increasingly insular." (Bellow 2003a)

The classic example in the creation of clientele in contemporary America is, of course, Chicago. At the end of the nineteenth century, the Democratic Party created a political machine that dominated the city for decades.

As previously noted, clientele is usually based on the loyalty principle and does not imply that its members are relatives of the boss. However, personal relations based on kinship play a critical role in American politics and business. The creation of clientele who are not relatives of the power holders is only one part of the feudalization of American economic and political life. Nepotism is another, probably more important, part of this process.

Nepotism in Big Business

Small and midsized family businesses play an important role in the U.S. economy. It is almost unavoidable that the founder of a business will often choose to transfer it to his or her heir (Erven 2009). However, the situation is quite different as we move from small to very large businesses (Wagner 2006). Some studies show that the second and, more often, the third generation failed as managers (Chrisman, Chua, and Sharma 2003; Buchholz et al. 1999). It is characteristic that contemporary business recognizes the inefficacy of markets to control the efficacy of managers, by resorting to various consulting and auditing firms for the evaluation of their performance.

Personal relations, in this case kinship based on a family's property, defy market mechanisms. This feudal behavior, with its basis in the monopoly of resources—whether temporary or long term—determines the choices of those who make decisions in corporations, be it a family or a public corporation. According to the logic of the private economy, people have the right to transfer their property to their relatives, whatever their level of competence. However, it is also supposed that a perfect market will correct wrong decisions and will remove, in one way or another, the bad manager who received his or her position based on family ties alone. As numerous data show, though, the market cannot correct bad decisions related to the appointment of relatives in key managerial positions; at best it can only do it with a very big lag time (Bellow 2003b; Conway 2004).

The impact of kinship on the selection of managers is morally condemned in liberal society, even if the business is purely private. All texts suggesting rules for the selection of managers conspicuously ignore kinship as potential grounds for choosing managers (Joint Pension Board 2009). Joseph Schumpeter preached about the innovative character of entrepreneurs and big businesses, and developed the most critical views on the impact of inheritance on economic processes. According to Robert Solow, Schumpeter suggested that there is a mechanism within capitalist society that inevitably causes it to undermine itself. "The children and grandchildren of successful entrepreneurs, precisely the people with the right DNA, are seduced by inherited wealth into intellectual pursuits, the arts, aristocratic habits, perhaps even into left-wing or at least anti-capitalist ideologies. It is not the proletariat that blows up the capitalist edifice, which is in fact good for the proletariat. It is the second generation of successful entrepreneurs that lets the ground floor decay" (Solow 2007; Schumpeter 1954; McCraw 2007).

The Spread of Kinship in Politics

Kinship has almost always played an important role in American politics. At least eight American presidents were relatives: John Quincy Adams, the sixth president, was the son of John Adams, the second president. Benjamin Harrison, the twenty-third president, was the grandson of William Harrison, the ninth president. George W. Bush, the forty-third president, was the son of George H. Bush, the forty-first president. Franklin Roosevelt, the thirty-second president, was the fifth cousin of Theodore Roosevelt, the twenty-sixth president; his spouse, Eleanor, was Theodore Roosevelt's niece.

Many other politicians are involved in kinship relations. Among contemporary examples, we can point to the two Udalls, father and son, U.S. senators. Marc Begich, a senator from Alaska, is the son of a former congressman from the same state (Hulse 2008). Governor Robert Casey helped his son Bob become a senator (Deparle 2006). Senator Chris Dodd could not have made his political career without his father, Senator Thomas Dodd (Bumiller 2007). It is difficult to imagine the election of John McCain as a senator from Arizona without the money of his wife (Dowd 2009). As recognized by Adam Bellow, "all over the country sons and daughters, brothers and sisters, wives and widows of elected officials were strongly in evidence." These include

> Florida's governor, Jeb Bush, re-elected by a healthy margin. In Massachusetts, Mitt Romney, son of the former Michigan governor George Romney, became governor. In New Hampshire, John E. Sununu, son of a former governor and presidential chief of staff, beat the sitting governor, Jeanne Shaheen, for a U.S. Senate seat. In Arkansas, Tim Hutchinson, whose brother Asa was a congressman and is now an undersecretary in the Department of Homeland Security, lost his Senate seat to the state attorney general, Mark Pryor, son of the former Arkansas governor and Senator David Pryor. Lucille Roybal-Allard, who occupies the California congressional seat once held by her father, was also re-elected. And in North Carolina, Elizabeth Dole, the wife of Bob Dole, won a Senate race against Erskine Bowles, a former Clinton chief of staff (and the son of a state politician). Meanwhile, the position of House minority leader was claimed by Representative Nancy Pelosi, the daughter of a five-term Maryland congressman and Baltimore mayor, who had risen swiftly in California politics in part through her skillful use of dynastic connections. Pelosi was opposed by Harold Ford Jr., a young black congressman who had succeeded to his father's seat in Tennessee. (Bellow 2003a, 2003b)

Kinship relations and nepotism that encourage the creation of political clans are more consequential than the casual support of relatives in their job searches. There are a large number of political clans in contemporary America. Family names such as Roosevelt, Rockefeller, Taft, Kennedy, Clinton, Cuomo, Gore, and Paterson remind one of the nobility in France (the Bourbons, Orleans, Anjou, Bourgogne, Artois) or England (the Grosvenors, Cavendishes, and Osborns) (Chaussinand-Nogaret 1985; Sanford and Townsend 1865).

Let us start with the Kennedy family, which has a number of politically active members who closely interact. Some authors, such as Hebert (1993, 19), assert that the existence of the Kennedy's network is beneficial to the country. The functions of the Kennedy clan, however, challenge the essentials of American democracy. Each European aristocratic clan had its recognized founder. The same is true about the Kennedy clan, which was founded by Joseph Kennedy, a leader who "ran the family like a football team" (Klein 2003, 9). The Kennedy clan was like a machine that produced a number of powerful political actors, from presidents and senators to officials of lower status (White 1973).

One recent case that illustrates the role of this clan, and the power of political families in general, involved a much-talked-about senatorial appointment in New York in 2008. With the senate seat up for grabs, Caroline Kennedy emerged as a possible appointee. Before this time, she had mostly been private and had performed minimal public activity (Heymann 2007, 147). Kennedy seemed to want, in the words of an American journalist, "to begin her political career near the top of the ladder" (Nagourney and Confessore 2008). Without a record as a successful politician (she had not held any elected position) and without elaborating her own political program, she insisted, when asked why she wanted to be a senator, "I wouldn't be here if I didn't think I would be the best" (Confessore and Halbfinger 2008). She substantiated her claim to be "the best" based on her "celebrity" and her "political connections."

A host of politicians who were in favor of the Kennedy appointment used her origins as their major argument. The public, for its part, generally accepted her wishes as "normal" and "legitimate." A number of politicians, national and local—among them New York mayor Michael Bloomberg, Senate majority leader Harry Reid, Senator Christopher Dodd, Buffalo Mayor Byron Brown, and several others—supported her candidacy.

In an editorial, the *New York Times* suggested that Kennedy's aristocratic origin was a positive factor. "Ms. Kennedy has much going for her. As a public figure, she carries the glamour and poignancy of her family, the only living child of President John F. Kennedy and Jacqueline Kennedy Onassis. Senator Edward M. Kennedy, an uncle of hers, has reigned for years as the liberal clarion in the Senate. Another uncle, the late Robert Kennedy, was a charismatic senator who represented New York 40 years ago" (*New York Times* 2008b).

Maureen Dowd, a leading columnist at the *New York Times,* was even more enthusiastic. She praised "the magic capital" of Caroline, which will help her "to take care of New York in this time of economic distress" and to direct Congress, which "desperately needs fresh faces and new perspectives, an infusion of class, intelligence, and guts." Maureen Dowd was confident, without putting forth any evidence, that the Senate, which was "shamefully sparse on profiles in courage during Dick Cheney's reign of terror," would be lucky to get her (Dowd 2009).

The fact that Edward M. Kennedy had lobbied Governor David Paterson on Kennedy's behalf did not arouse outrage in society. Another member of the Kennedy clan, Kerry Kennedy, daughter of Senator Robert Kennedy, said (before she promoted the candidacy of her brother Robert Kennedy Jr.), "I think that Teddy and Caroline are so incredibly close, and I can't imagine a better team than the two of them in the Senate from Massachusetts and from New York" (Nagourney and Confessore 2008; Confessore 2008). In the end, Caroline Kennedy, for unclear reasons, withdrew her candidacy. However, this episode in

American political history will remain a typical example of the role of feudal clans in the United States.

The American Nobility

The founding fathers tried to build a new society that would be free from the influence of a noble class. Washington and Lafayette struggled vehemently against rule by a noble class (Lasch 1996, 48). The Constitution mentioned the nobility only in a negative sense, banning the endowment of the title of nobility to anyone. *The Federalist* brims with contempt for the "spirit of clanship" and for "barons and nobles." Yet the founders were not idealists or romantics. Alexander Hamilton had no illusions about human nature when he wrote in *The Federalist* that the "supposition of universal venality in human nature is little less an error in political reasoning, than the supposition of universal rectitude." He knew, in particular, how often the merits of people would be ignored in the process of "appointing offices," and how much this process would be influenced by "private and party likings and dislikes, partialities and antipathies, attachments and animosities" (Hamilton, Madison, and Jay 1788).

Despite the attempts of the founding fathers to build a Jeffersonian democracy, a sort of nobility still emerged in the United States. Of course, no one who belonged to this group had a certificate that proved their noble origins. The nobility in the United States comprised families that had ranked among the wealthiest and most politically powerful groups for at least three or four generations.

The old American aristocracy consisted of two types. One was represented by the Brahmins of Boston (this term compares the leading families of Boston with the highest Hindu caste), who had come to America on the *Mayflower*. Another was the rural ruling class of the South, whose wealth was accumulated in the early nineteenth century (Bowers 2004). Over time, the composition of the American aristocracy changed. Families whose positions were based on newly acquired wealth in the twentieth century claimed to be equals of the old aristocracy.[4] The rivalry between families from the East Coast and the newly rich of the West Coast is a well-known phenomenon (Baltzell 1987).

Close to the American aristocracy are "celebrities," even if this title lasts

4. The same process was well known in the Middle Ages, when the old nobility were shoved out by new families, including those who were granted nobility by a king or those who simply bought it (Baltzell 1987; Burt 1970).

only for the life of its holder (Schickel 1985). The main pool of current celebrities is made up of Hollywood entertainers, the owners and journalists of leading media, and some outstanding politicians who are rich with connections in the worlds of politics and business.

Scholars and writers are not a part of the celebrity club. Theories involving the new "brainy" American elite, the dominance of techno-structure, and the holders of "cultural capital" exaggerate the incorporation of intellectuals into the ruling elite. They underestimate the role of political and economic power in the contemporary world, which continues to control society. Those who possess cultural capital have only a limited impact on social and economic processes. The founders of Microsoft and Google became members of the American elite only after they became billionaires, not because of their intellectual accomplishments.[5] Even if the composition of the American nobility changed over the last two centuries, it is still a powerful social actor, strengthening feudal relations in contemporary politics.

Children of Alumni: The Formation of the American Nobility

Despite the push for equal opportunity in the nation's best universities, the offspring of the rich and powerful have a better chance of being accepted by Harvard and Yale than those of the middle or lower classes. As noted in the *Economist,* "the biggest insult to meritocracy, however, is found in the country's top universities. These institutions, which control access to the country's most impressive jobs, consider themselves far above Washington and its grubby spoils system. Yet they continue to operate a system of 'legacy preferences'—affirmative action for the children of alumni" (*Economist* 2004). According to the article, in most Ivy League colleges, children of alumni make up between 10 percent and 15 percent of every freshman class. "Legatees are two to four times more likely to be admitted to the best universities than non-legatees" (*Economist* 2004). Some university administrators try to justify the "legacies" by citing their need for fund-raising from alumni. Others regard the advantages that legatees receive as either very small, or simply the result of self-selection. It is impossible to verify, but according to the 1990 Department of Education report, "the average Harvard legacy student is 'significantly less qualified' than the average non-legacy student in every area except sports" (*Economist*

5. Unlike American nobles, the Soviet ruling elite was proud to communicate with outstanding intellectuals (Shlapentokh 1990).

2004). The case of the University of Illinois is quite illustrative of the role of personal relations in the admission policies of many American colleges. The conspicuous violation of the merit principle in recruiting students had reached such a level that the governor created a special commission to investigate the matter. It established that the chancellor of the main campus, Richard H. Herman, was the "ultimate decision maker" for politically connected and other favored students. The chancellor ultimately resigned (Steinberg 2009).

Mills (1956) and other Marxist critics of American capitalism (Domhoff 1970, 1980), as well as leftist sociologists in France such as Bourdieu and Passeron (1990), wrote about the role of one's origins in the process of promotion and upward mobility in bourgeois society. However, they connected this phenomenon to the class composition of capitalist society. In fact, we are dealing not with a liberal capitalist society, but with feudal relations. The elite class lives in segregated communities—in some cases, gated communities (as discussed in an earlier chapter)—and "send[s] its children to the same exclusive schools, marr[ies] within its own class, and acts in other ways to pass on its accumulated wealth, position, and privileges" (Bellow 2003a).

The Elitist Justification of Family Nepotism

The feudal or elitist ideology asserts that only the rich and noble have the talent and preparation to run society. The ideology praises family dynasties in politics and business, and sees nepotism as a positive development. It supposes that the offspring of successful families are more likely to perform efficiently in any sphere of public life than people from lower classes. The promotion of members of successful families is seen as a service to society. The ideology, which holds contempt for ordinary people and democratic procedures, is deeply hostile toward social equality and indifferent toward social polarization.

Those who defend the special rights of nobles often cite examples of courage and altruism among this class. The U.S.-made movie *Valkyrie* (2008), for instance, glowingly praised the leading participants (there were more than a hundred of them) who plotted against Hitler in 1944. They were all members of the German nobility. None of them betrayed their comrades-in-arms or made reports to the Gestapo, in order to save their own skins. Polish media, even in communist times, praised the leading Polish noble families (Radziwiłł and Potocki) for refusing to collaborate with the Nazis or the Stalinists.

Despite the strong liberal ideology in the United States, with its focus on political and social equality, some American authors have tried to justify nepotism and other elements of the elitist ideology. Bellow (2003b), for example, develops this line of reasoning in his book *In Praise of Nepotism.* Citing many examples of nepotism among the American elite, Bellow rejects the opinion of those who "voiced alarm that we are returning to a society based on hereditary status, complete with a corporate aristocracy and a political House of Lords." He does not see this trend as "an ominous departure from American principles." He claims to not understand the difference between "the professional dynasties" in music, literature, and the circus, as well as other areas of "entertainment, the arts, and sports," and the political and business dynasties. In the first case, the children inherit real talents and their parents serve as models. In the areas of music and literature, they are literally tested each day by the public. Indeed, who will object to the prominence of dozens of second-generation actors, such as Jane and Peter Fonda or Michael Douglas, or to the fame of Martin Amis, the son of Kingsley Amis? The children of politicians and business moguls, on the other hand, inherit political and economic power, so society must acquiesce to them whatever their actual talents may or may not be.

Without analyzing the political and economic consequences of nepotism, Bellow (2003b, 16) justifies it by referring to "the natural impulse to pass something on to their children, just as children wish to accept whatever their parents have to give." The same logic suggests that greed is "a natural instinct," yet society does many things to control it, to keep it from damaging other people and society in general. Bellow insists, following the elitist ideology, that the best families in America advance the best people to engage in politics and run the economy.

The Fight Against Feudal Privileges

Even if some parts of the population accept certain forms of corruption as normal, society has tried to reduce the role of feudal elements. American society has devised various ways of diminishing the impact of feudal style cadre selection, including the influence of the American aristocracy (old and new) on the political establishment, education, and science. In fact, the fight against nepotism began in this country with the abolition of English inheritance practices in the eighteenth century. Thomas Jefferson was a champion of meritocracy and an enemy of feudal practices, such as inheritance rights and the consolidation of family interests.

Nepotism and Government Regulations

The assassination of President James Garfield on July 2, 1881, by Charles Guiteau, a man greatly disgruntled by unsuccessful efforts to obtain a federal post, increased American public support for civil service reform (Sampson 2001). In 1883, the Pendleton Act was the "first attempt to reduce nepotism in the federal government"; two years later this led to the state civil service reform in the states of New York and Massachusetts (Sampson 2001).

A set of laws and regulations (statutes) was developed over the next few decades to "prevent public agencies from favoritism and conflicts of interest in hiring employees and to ensure that hiring is based solely on merit rather than relationship" (Taylor 2006). The New Deal was a prominent milestone in this war. Nepotism statutes date back to 1933 and have been interpreted by a series of attorney general opinions. The statutes prohibit the "appointment" of a relative to any position of "trust or emolument."[6] The civil rights legislation passed in the 1940s through the 1960s, which was intended to uproot the legal barriers to equal opportunity, including anti-nepotism policies, began to be widely adopted by most large-scale public and private institutions (Bellow 2003b).

Today, almost half the states bar legislators from hiring their relatives. In these states, it is unlawful "for a person or any member of any board, bureau, or commission or employee at the head of any department of this state or any political subdivision of this state to appoint to any position of trust or emolument any person related or connected by consanguinity within the fourth degree or by affinity within the second degree" (Section 2-2-302, MCA). It is also unlawful to "enter into any agreement or any promise . . . to appoint [a relative] to any position of trust or emolument" (Section 2-2-303, MCA; Taylor 2006).

In states where nepotism is not directly prohibited by a statute, special conflict-of-interest laws or hiring guidelines for legislators are designed to restrict nepotism. The states also rely on their ethics committees for advice and authority on nepotism cases. Massachusetts and Pennsylvania, for example, do not have laws that prohibit nepotism, but they do have conflict-of-interest laws (National Conference of State Legislatures 2009). Many states differ in the way they regulate the relationships between legislators and their relatives who serve as employees. Arizona, Iowa, and Mississippi prohibit legislators from

6. "Emolument" is defined as "any perquisite, advantage, profit, or gain arising from the possession of office." "Nepotism" is defined by the statute as "the bestowal of political patronage by reason of relationship rather than merit" (Taylor 2006).

hiring a relative of the third degree by blood or marriage; Texas, Missouri, and Montana hold different restrictions for relatives related by blood than those by marriage (National Conference of State Legislatures 2009).

The creation of a federal civil service, which is supposed to be based on merit and efficiency, was an important development in the war against nepotism. Many institutions explicitly forbid people to work under the direct command of their relatives (Sampson 2001). In some cases, job applicants are asked if they have friends in the given unit. Those who wanted to join the Obama administration filled out a questionnaire as part of a painstaking screening process that was aimed at, among other things, identifying friendly relations that could create a conflict of interest.

Inconsistencies in the anti-nepotism rules have created some problems for the states, though. For example, "under Nebraska's current anti-nepotism law, state employees are only barred from hiring or supervising immediate family members or blood relatives if they live under the same roof" (Boyle 2008). The law is obviously weak and invites violations. According to the *Omaha World-Herald,* in June 2007 the auditors revealed that five daughters of five managers had been hired for temporary summer jobs in the Nebraska Department of Labor and received higher wages than other full-time employees (Boyle 2008).

The Fight Against Nepotism in the Private Sphere

Researchers estimate that the number of organizations that enact formal anti-nepotism policies ranges from 10 to 40 percent. Almost 60 percent of organizations have some kind of informal policy (Ford and McLaughlin 1986; Newgren, Kellogg, and Gardner 1988). The anti-nepotism regulations vary from company to company. Many businesses have enacted no-spouse rules for their employees, prohibiting spouses from working together. Many companies prohibit any relatives from working together. While companies are free to enact anti-nepotism regulations, some have been found to be discriminatory, deemed unconstitutional by the courts, and overturned.

The Fight Against Nepotism in Academia

Most universities have a nepotism policy stating that "no employee may participate in decisions which would involve a direct benefit or detriment (appointment, hiring, retention, promotion, salary, leave of absence) to a relative"

(Taylor 2006). However, in reality, many people—especially in academia—work under the supervision of their relatives. Some additional rules have been developed to ensure that the selection and treatment of employees is fair and based solely on merit. For example, when someone applies for a position that is supervised by a relative, a designated authority may be assigned to oversee the fairness of the situation (Taylor 2006).

The most controversial issue is the employment of marriage partners. Many critics of anti-nepotism laws believe that such laws discriminate against qualified applicants on the basis of marital status and that, in most cases, they discriminate against married women. Several organizations, especially universities and colleges, while being bound by the existing nepotism laws, work to make sure they do not deny an applicant the opportunity for a position because he or she is related to another employee. There is a general rule in many universities that a person related to an employee can be hired under a competitive search by an independent hiring committee. Supervision of a relative-employee is another problematic issue. Some believe that supervision of a relative does not violate the nepotism statutes unless the supervising relative has the authority to select, hire, or provide job-related benefits to the relative-employee (Taylor 2006).

Conclusion

Feudal-type personal relations permeate the fabric of society. Contrary to the assumption that the participants of personal relations represent equal partners, there is an unequal distribution of power in many spheres of life, from families to private firms to government offices. The abuse of power by bosses, a common occurrence, is evidence of the feudal character of American society. The reliance on personal relations, nepotism, or loyalty in decision-making processes in business and politics contradicts the principles of political equality and meritocracy. When used as the basis for selecting cadres, these feudal elements hinder the efficiency of the given organization.

The impact of kinship, a special type of personal relations, on American political and economic life deserves special attention. Kinship interferes with the promotion of qualified people to important positions in society. It forms the basis of powerful political clans, which unceremoniously influence the outcome of elections and other democratic processes.

These clans are part of the American nobility, who, not unlike the medieval nobility, play a significant role in political life, challenging democratic and egalitarian principles. American society is well aware of the consequences of feudal personal relations. While some attempts have been made to diminish nepotism and the use of personal relations in the decision-making processes in government and business, this fight has been only moderately successful.

Conclusion

The country's social, political, and economic ills are recurrent and widespread, but they cannot be explained by some fatal flaw in the essence of liberal democracy. As discussed throughout the book, many of these problems are generated by the liberal segment's coexistence with other types of social organization, feudalism in particular. The feudal model attempts to recast a number of "temporary deviations" from the liberal model as stable social patterns.

The model emphasizes certain aspects of corporations, particularly their persistent use of financial resources to acquire additional (often illegal) revenue, which they do not deserve according to the principles of liberal capitalism. Large concentrations of money diminish competition in the economy and politics and foster corruption, both of which have become typical aspects of American life. Large corporations extract monopolistic privileges from the central government in exchange for various resources (rent-seeking activity). Corporations also participate in political processes, elections in particular, and damage the democratic principle of political equality. At the same time, private firms, contrary to the Marxist perspective, do not always behave as a united front in politics. Both collusion and conflicts play important roles in corporate political activities.

The feudal model can also be used to examine social relations inside corporations and other complex organizations. Over the last several decades, as the size and global reach of many corporations increased, the various subunits or divisions within them tended to receive greater authority and independence, while the relative strength of the central authority diminished. Although the current forces of globalization may be intensifying the fragmentation of authority in some organizations, the internal struggle for power is a universal phenomenon that can be found across different organizations and time periods.

The variables shown to be related (directly or indirectly) to such feudal struggles within organizations include decentralization, structural interdependence, uncertainty, informal power, and personal relations. Greater attention to these factors is needed, given the limited nature of this analysis and its weighty implications for modern organizations. The feudal model contributes to the literature on organizations by directing attention to an alternative set of ideas, identifying "sociological universals," and encouraging and directing further inquiry on intraorganizational conflict.

One of the key functions of any society is to provide its members with safety and security. In the United States and other Western countries, increasingly, private firms are performing the task of protecting individuals, groups, and assets. Private security services—another key feudal element in contemporary society—not only secure life and property, but also facilitate the expansion of private wealth and power, while reshaping the relationship between public and private governance. The independent control of violent force also played an important role in the political and economic developments of western Europe in the Middle Ages.

The essence of private security conflicts with the state's monopoly on the exercise of legitimate violence, which is, according to Weber and many contemporary scholars, one of the defining characteristics of the modern state. Conventional models of liberal capitalism, though important to any analysis of American society, cannot fully explain the nature of security in the United States. Comparisons with the medieval context are especially apt when considering cases in which the private use of force increases the wealth of a few major actors in society, while diminishing the rights of citizens, their access to public spaces, and the central authority's ability to protect them. The feudal model provides a unique historical lens through which to reexamine the broad spectrum of activities related to the private sector's use of violence.

The reliance on personal relations in politics and business is another feudal characteristic of the contemporary United States. The abuse of power by bosses who demand various personal favors and privileges from their subordinates stands as crass evidence of the vitality of feudalism in society. The use of power by officials and managers, from presidents and CEOs to heads of local offices, for the sake of promoting and rewarding individuals in exchange for personal loyalty (allegiance to a higher lord, as opposed to kingdom, company, or country) threatens the principles of political equality and meritocracy.

Kinship relations and nepotism influence the selection of people for key positions in society. As the basis of powerful political clans, kinship plays a role in elections and other political processes. Political clans based on kinship exist as a sort of American nobility—similar in many respects to the medieval nobility—which challenges democratic and egalitarian principles. A reliance on the bonds of loyalty, kinship, and personal relations, though functional in many respects, tends to downgrade the efficiency and legitimacy of social institutions.

The central elements of the feudal model (the weakness of the state, feudal conflicts and collusions between and within organizations, personal relations, nepotism, elitism, and private coercion) explain many aspects of both medieval Europe and the contemporary United States that cannot be understood using the liberal or authoritarian models. Most societies reflect all three models, suggesting that a segmented approach to social analysis is needed.

To illustrate the usefulness of this approach, we turn now to one of the most important social events of the twenty-first century thus far: the financial crisis of 2008–9. Consensus among experts about the cause of major historical events, from the fall of Rome to World War I, is rare. The world financial crisis is no exception. At the start of the crisis, most economists and politicians fell into one of two groups—advocates of either the neoclassical (liberal) or Keynesian (or authoritarian) model. The feudal model, however, was absent from mainstream debate over the cause of the crisis. As a result, the political activities of big financial corporations and the personal relations between Wall Street and the government were mostly ignored.

Before the crisis, advocates of the liberal model were confident in their perspective and believed that it provided a sufficient understanding of American society and its economy. For Milton Friedman, given his unbounded belief in the economic efficacy of private initiative, private property and free market regulation were the keys to stable economic performance. The believers in the market's ability to regulate itself were not alarmed by the rapid changes in the financial markets of the 1980s and 1990s, including the emergence of hedge funds, derivatives, structured investment vehicles, and asset-backed securities. Robert Lucas, a Nobel Prize winner and ardent believer in the market's ability to sustain equilibrium, dismissed the Keynesian critique and the demand for active state intervention in economic processes. In an interview in 1999, Lucas said, "I think Keynes's actual influence as a technical economist is pretty close to zero, and it has been close to zero for 50 years" (DeVroey 2004).

There are several other noted proponents of market mechanism. Lawrence

Summers, only a year before he became an articulate supporter of state regulation in the Obama administration, dismissed warnings about the inability of the new financial system to manage risk.[1] Ben Bernanke, the man who succeeded Alan Greenspan as the chair of the Federal Reserve Board, was also a great admirer of the market. In 2006, he said: "The management of market risk and credit risk has become increasingly sophisticated. Banking organizations of all sizes have made substantial strides over the past two decades in their ability to measure and manage risks" (Johnson 2009a). Timothy Geithner, then the head of the New York Federal Reserve and the future treasury secretary, suggested in May 2007 that the national financial institutions were in good health, and praised derivatives as a brilliant innovation that helped the economy (Becker and Morgenson 2009).

The crisis, of course, triggered a counteroffensive against belief in the market's ability to regulate itself. The emerging critics of the liberal model ranged from orthodox Marxists to Keynesians. The crisis suddenly brought forth from oblivion ideas found in Marx's *Capital,* which suggested that the capitalist economy was a dynamic system with tendencies that would destroy the equilibrium of the market and endanger its existence. There was a renewed interest in Marx as an "influential" critic of capitalism among a range of thinkers, such as the Nobel Prize–winning economist Amartya Sen (2009) and Rowan Williams (2008), the archbishop of Canterbury. Some Marxists attacked the neoclassical model using the old dogmas from *Capital,* which suggested that the declining rate of profitability was the major cause of the crisis. Others focused on the Marxist dogma involving the accumulation of capital, which inexorably leads to crisis, and in this case, "the financialization of capital" and the increased market vulnerability that comes with it (McNally 2008).

The most active critics of the liberal model were mainstream economists with Keynesian views. In the years before the crisis, opposition to this model was quite weak and remained outside mainstream economics. One of the most consistent critics was Joseph Stiglitz (2002), who insisted that, given the lack of perfect information among economic actors, state action was needed. Another, earlier critic of the neoclassical model was Robert Solo (1967), who saw the American economy as an interaction between three types of organization—the decentralized market, the centralized (state) economic organization, and the organizational market-negotiated form (corporations). Several other economists critiqued Friedman's neoclassical model, including Robert

1. Regarding the confrontation between Summers and Rajan, see Krugman (2009a).

Reich, Paul Krugman, and Brad DeLong. A few other economists expressed their misgivings about the future of unregulated financial markets (Rajan 2005).

As the crisis unfolded in the United States and elsewhere, the Keynesians went on the offensive, suggesting that the market is doomed without the state taking an active role. Several prominent economists defended the state's role as a regulator. During the crisis, Joseph Stiglitz said that "the Chicago School [Friedman's place of residence] model bears the blame for providing a seemingly intellectual foundation for the idea that markets are self-adjusting and the best role for government is to do nothing" (Lippert 2008). He was joined by others, such as Krugman, Johnson, and Galbraith.

The advocates of the liberal model tried, even during the crisis, to defend the market's effectiveness and reject the Keynesian remedy of massive government spending. They continued to believe in Say's law from the early nineteenth century, which suggested that the interaction between supply and demand guaranteed market equilibrium. They built up two types of defense. One was directly aimed at the supporters of authoritarian models. They blamed the crisis on a federal government that was "too interventionist," diminishing the market's ability to regulate itself.

This argument was leveled by libertarians from the CATO institute, as well as by such economists as Thomas Woods, the author of *Meltdown,* and Luigi Zingales, who criticized the Federal Reserve Board and the federal government's fiscal policy, suggesting that it encouraged the dispersal of subprime mortgages to people who could not afford to buy homes (Woods 2009; Zingales 2009; Hart and Zingales 2008). The belief in market self-regulation was upheld by several dozen economists who signed "Cochrane's petition," which was pushed forward by the prominent economist John Cochrane from the University of Chicago and John Coleman from Duke University in September 2008 (Cochrane 2008).

Both schools seemed to rely on theories of human nature when defending their models. Liberals exonerated the market by suggesting that it was distorted by "greed." Even those who look to "greed" as the cause of the crisis differ from each other, depending on their particular focus. Does greed refer to ordinary people who grabbed cheap credit or CEOs of financial institutions who increased the volume of their risky transactions to gain hefty bonuses, or both? Among those who advanced the "greed" theory with a focus on Wall Street was the former Federal Reserve chairman, Alan Greenspan. "Those of us who have looked to the self-interest of lending institutions to protect shareholders' equity, myself included, are in a state of shocked disbelief." Greenspan added, "I think we can sum up the cause of our current economic crisis in one word—GREED" (Andrews 2008). Luigi Zingales saw the "erratic behavior" of Ben Bernanke, the head of the Federal Reserve Board, as one of the main causes of the crisis. Instead of "greed" or a "lack of confidence," some authors focused on "responsibility," or rather the lack of it (Brooks 2009a).

As the cause of the crisis, Robert Shiller (2008a, 2008b) cited several psychological features, such as the "exuberant irrationality" of "Wall Street tycoons," the excessive trust in "Wall Street titans," and the lack of interest in the ideas of "financial theorists." George Akerlof, a Nobel Prize–winning economist, and Shiller (2009) named eight psychological traits that are accountable for the failure of market regulations. These authors, according to many reviewers of their book, were inspired not only by Keynes's phrase "animal instincts," but also by Keynes's belief in the activist role of the state (Uchitelle 2009).

While the authoritarian and liberal models played central roles in the debates over the economic crisis, the feudal model was largely ignored. The feudal model supposed the crucial role of feudal actors in American society—beginning with corporations. The crisis revealed that a small number of feudal actors had become so big that the fate of the nation depended on their survival. One of the leading arguments from the White House under both Bush and Obama was that it was impossible to allow several American financial institutions to collapse, because they were "too big to fail," a phrase coined during the crisis by Summers and Rubin (Rich 2009). In fact, the heads of large financial corporations, "the princes of the financial world," as Simon Johnson named them, have played a crucial role in American society and its economy since the late nineteenth century (Johnson 2009a). Their role has been the subject of a vehement debate both in this country and around the world. However, in the last two decades some of these corporations, such as Lehman Brothers and AIG, became intertwined with other major institutions to the point that a collapse would deliver a painful, almost lethal blow to the whole economy of the United States and abroad. It was remarkable that, according to national polls, 32 percent of Americans named "corporate America" as the biggest threat to the country, while 55 percent said "big government" (Brooks 2009b). These numbers are good indicators of the relative role of all three models in the public mind.

By the beginning of this century, financial corporations had accumulated tremendous resources, earning 41 percent of total domestic corporate profits (in 1985 it was only 16 percent). In 1982, the average compensation in financial corporations was about the same as in other corporations. By 2007, it was almost two times higher. As Johnson (2009a) said, the political balance of power, as it was shaped before the crisis, gave the financial sector a veto over public policy. CEOs received their bonuses like feudal lords earned their spoils of war. He describes "the blocking power of big banks" (Johnson 2009b). The size of their incomes was not determined by market laws, but by the monopoly of power, given the fact that the boards of directors were submissive and endorsed their bonuses. In 2006, the CEO of Merrill Lynch, O'Neal, received a $14 million bonus; in 2007, his bonus reached $162 million, even though his company was already in decay. In October 2008 (a time when the company was close to bankruptcy), the last Merrill Lynch CEO, John Thain, shamelessly demanded that his board of directors approve a bonus of $30 million and agreed in December, given the media pressure, to take a lower bonus of $10 million. Nell Minow, a prominent journalist, author, and cofounder of research body the Corporate Library, collected a monumental amount of data about the excessive payment of CEOs in corporations, who, without any external supervision and without the consent of stockholders, assigned themselves immense salaries and benefits, like feudal barons in their fiefdoms (Monks and Minow 2008).[2]

Paul Volcker, the former Federal Reserve Board chairman, claimed, "I don't see a relationship between the extremes of income now and the performance of the economy." Volcker insisted that the fabulous revenues of financiers in the early 2000s had nothing to do with their talents or actions (Uchitelle 2007). Volcker was seconded by Nobel Prize–winning economist Paul Krugman, who insisted that "there's no longer any reason to believe that the wizards of Wall Street actually contribute anything positive to society, let alone enough to justify those humongous paychecks." He added that "it's hard to think of any major recent financial innovations that actually aided society," and that "Wall Street is no longer, in any real sense, part of the private sector. It's a ward of the state, every bit as dependent on government aid as recipients of Temporary Assistance for Needy Families, aka 'welfare'" (Krugman 2009b).

It is not surprising that financial corporations became the key players in American politics, given their role as donors in elections and their lobbying efforts over the last decade. The two major culprits in the subprime crisis, Fannie Mae and Freddie Mac, made gigantic contributions to the coffers of both parties. In 2006, Fannie Mae donated $1.3 million, giving 53 percent of this sum to the Republicans, which held the majority in Congress. In 2007, when the majority belonged to the Democrats, 56 percent of Fannie Mae's $1.1 million donations were sent to the Democratic Party. In the same year, Freddie Mac

2. For more about Minow's work, see Owen (2009).

donated $555,700, with 53 percent going to the Democrats. According to the Center for Responsive Politics, fifteen of the twenty-five lawmakers who have received donations from the two companies since the 1990 election are members of the House Financial Services Committee; the Senate Banking, Housing, and Urban Affairs Committee; the Senate Finance Committee; or the Ways and Means Committee. Among those who received money from both companies were Christopher Dodd, John Kerry, Barack Obama, Hilary Clinton, Rahm Emanuel, Jack Reed, Barney Frank, and several other leading Democrats (Mayer 2008).

The financial corporations were able to press the White House and Capitol Hill to create the necessary conditions for achieving huge financial enrichments based on speculative ventures. The companies easily convinced the administration and the legislators that, as Simon Johnson wrote, "the economy was fundamentally sound and that the tremendous growth in complex securities and credit-default swaps was evidence of a healthy economy where risk was distributed safely. The great wealth that the financial sector created and concentrated gave bankers enormous political weight—a weight not seen in the U.S. since the era of J. P. Morgan (the man)" (Johnson 2009a).

The crisis revealed the vital role personal relations play in politics, an essential element of the feudal model. Lawrence Summers, Obama's chief economic adviser and the architect of his economic reforms, was supposed to curb the power of the financial lords. Before his appointment, however, he was closely connected to one of the leading hedge funds, D. E. Shaw. As compensation, he received $5.2 million from this firm in 2008, even though he worked there only one day a week. Citigroup and Goldman Sachs paid him $2.7 million in speaking fees.

Summers served at another hedge fund, Taconic Capital Advisors, from 2004 to 2006, while still president of Harvard (Becker and Morgenson 2009). As was noted in the *New York Times*, "some of his critics worry that such ties raise questions about whether the government's ever-changing effort to bolster the financial industry will benefit Wall Street in general, and hedge funds in particular, at the expense of taxpayers" (Story 2009).

Those institutions were not merely the beneficiaries of taxpayers' bailouts. They had access. Henry Paulson, another former CEO of Goldman Sachs, was George Bush's treasury secretary (Johnson 2009a). No less remarkable are the Wall Street ties of Timothy Geithner, Obama's treasury secretary and the major architect of his financial reforms. As the editors of the *New York Times* wrote, "An examination of Mr. Geithner's five years as president of the New York Fed, an era of unbridled and ultimately disastrous risk-taking by the financial industry, shows that he forged unusually close relationships with executives of Wall Street's giant financial institutions." The newspaper continued, "His actions, as a regulator and later a bailout king, often aligned with the industry's interests and desires, according to interviews with financiers, regulators and analysts and a review of Federal Reserve records" (Becker and Morgenson 2009). The future treasury secretary entertained close, private relations with the senior executives from the major financial corporations, particularly Citigroup, and ignored the fact that the bank was in serious trouble.

Of special importance is the existence of close connections between Wall Street and the New York branches of the Federal Reserve Board. Geithner's predecessors Gerald Corrigan and William Donough found jobs as CEOs in investment banks, while William Dudley, a former CEO of Goldman Sachs, replaced Geithner as the chairman of the New York Federal Reserve. In the opinion of some current and former Federal Reserve Board officials, the New York Federal Reserve is not the eye of the government but an agent of the bankers (Becker and Morgenson 2009). Arthur Levitt Jr., a former chairman of the Securities and Exchange Commission, became an adviser to the Carlyle group after leaving his post at the SEC. He is also known for making Bernie Madoff a member of an SEC committee (Solomon 2009).

The financial companies were also able to recruit participants into their risky and often semilegal activities. These were not only people from the political establishment, but also the cream of the academic world. Medieval barons did the same thing in their day, inviting the best minds in their country to their courts. Nobel Prize winners Myron Scholes and Robert Merton were members of the board of directors of Long-Term Capital Management, a hedge fund that operated in the 1990s. As Johnson wrote, the migration of academics to financial corporations increased their status in society. Numerous editorials in the *Wall Street Journal* and speeches in Congress glorified their activities.

The financial oligarchy of Wall Street was able to create its own ideology, which praised its large institutions and its power, and described it as a precondition for the country's major geopolitical role in the world (Johnson 2009a). Only a few months before the crisis, Sanford Weill, the former head of Citigroup, boasted to journalists about the achievements of financial tycoons. "People can look at the last 25 years and say this is an incredibly unique period of time," Mr. Weill said. "We didn't rely on somebody else to build what we built, and we shouldn't rely on somebody else to provide all the services our society needs" (Uchitelle 2007).

Taken alone, none of the three models—liberal, feudal, or authoritarian—can fully explain the financial crisis; all of them are necessary. To ignore the special role of financial corporations as feudal actors and their relations with the federal government would leave the puzzle of the financial crisis unsolved.

Contemporary American society is in many ways a liberal society, wherein democracy and markets play key roles. At the same time, many of its most important elements do not fit this model. To describe America today using only the language of democracy and free markets would be a disservice to social science and the public. Any honest observer knows that democratic and market principles are often violated. Of course, some people tend to explain these deviations as temporary or accidental circumstances, or as inherent flaws in liberal democracy. We contend that both approaches are problematic. These "deviations" should be seen as persistent feudal and authoritarian elements that coexist in American society and endanger the principles of liberal capitalism.

References

Ackoff, Russell Lincoln, Frederick Edmund Emery, and Brent D. Ruben. 2005. *On purposeful systems: An interdisciplinary analysis of individual and social behavior as a system of purposeful events.* New Brunswick, N.J.: Aldine Transaction.

Adams, Bruce, and Kathryn Kavanagh-Baran. 1979. *Promise and performance: Carter builds a new administration.* Lexington, Mass.: Lexington Books.

Ades, Alberto, and Rafael Di Tella. 1999. Rents, competition, and corruption. *American Economic Review* 89:982–94.

Adler, Patricia A., and Peter Adler. 1988. Intense loyalty in organizations: A case study of college athletics. *Administrative Science Quarterly* 33 (3): 401–17.

Agrawal, R. R. 1990. *The medieval revival and its influence on the romantic movement.* New Delhi: Abhinav.

Akerlof, George A., and Robert J. Shiller. 2009. *Animal spirits: How human psychology drives the economy, and why it matters for global capitalism.* Princeton: Princeton University Press.

Alsayyad, Nezar, and Ananya Roy. 2006. Medieval modernity: On citizenship and urbanism in a global era. *Space and Polity* 10 (1): 1–20.

Ambrosea, Maureen L., Mark A. Seabright, and Marshall Schminke. 2002. Sabotage in the workplace: The role of organizational injustice. *Organizational Behavior and Human Decision Processes* 89 (1): 947–65.

An, Soontae, and Lori Bergen. 2007. Advertiser pressure on daily newspapers: A survey of advertising sales executives. *Journal of Advertising* 36 (2): 111–22.

Analoui, Farhad. 1995. Workplace sabotage: Its styles, motives, and management. *Journal of Management Development* 14 (7): 48–65.

Andersen, Margaret, and Howard F. Taylor. 2002. *Sociology: Understanding of a diverse society.* Belmont, Calif.: Wadsworth.

Anderson, Paul F., and Terry M. Chambers. 1985. A reward/measurement model of organizational buying behavior. *Journal of Marketing* 49:7–23.

Anderson, Perry. 1974a. *Passages from antiquity to feudalism.* London: NLB.

———. 1974b. *Lineages of the absolutist state.* London: NLB.

Andrews, Edmond. 2008. Greenspan concedes error on regulation. *New York Times,* October 23.

Aries, Philippe, and George Dubuis, eds. 1985. *L'histoire de la vie privee.* Paris: Seuil.

Arnold, Thurman Wesley. 1940. *The bottlenecks of business.* New York: Reynal and Hitchcock.

Ashford, Douglas E. 1986. *The emergence of the welfare states.* Oxford: Blackwell.

Associated Press. 2008. Private prison company must produce records. July 29.

Auger, Deborah A. 1999. Privatization, contracting, and the states: Lessons from state government experience. *Public Productivity and Management Review* 22 (4): 435–54.

Avant, Deborah D. 2005. *The market for force: The consequences of privatizing security.* Cambridge: Cambridge University Press.
Babbie, Earl R. 1983. *Sociology: An introduction.* Belmont, Calif.: Wadsworth.
Backman, Clifford R. 2003. *The worlds of medieval Europe.* New York: Oxford University Press.
Bailey, John J., and Roy Godson, eds. 2000. *Organized crime and democratic governability: Mexico and the U.S.-Mexican borderlands.* Pittsburgh: University of Pittsburgh Press.
Bailyn, Bernard. 1967. *The ideological origins of the American revolution.* Cambridge: Harvard University Press.
Baker, Robert Lewis. 1961. *The English customs service, 1307–1343: A study of medieval administration.* Philadelphia: American Philosophical Society.
Baltzell, Edward Digby. 1987. *The protestant establishment: Aristocracy and caste in America.* New Haven: Yale University Press.
Barclay, Donald W. 1991. Interdepartmental conflict in organizational buying: The impact of the organizational context. *Journal of Marketing Research* 28 (2): 145–59.
Barendse, R. J. 2003. The feudal mutation: Military and economic transformations of the ethnosphere in the tenth to thirteenth centuries. *Journal of World History* 14 (4): 503–29.
Bauman, Zygmunt. 2007. *Consuming life.* Cambridge: Polity Press.
Beard, Charles Austin. 1968. *An introduction to the English historians.* New York: B. Franklin.
Beck, Elwood Merideth. 1974. Conflict, change and stability: A reciprocal interaction in schools. *Social Forces* 52 (4): 517–31.
Beck, Ulrich, and Elisabeth Beck-Gernsheim. 1995. *The normal chaos of love.* Trans. Mark Ritter and Jane Wiebel. Cambridge: Polity Press.
Beck, Ulrich, Anthony Giddens, and Scott Lash. 1994. *Reflexive modernization: Politics, tradition, and aesthetics in the modern social order.* Stanford: Stanford University Press.
Becker, Jo, and Gretchen Morgenson. 2009. Geithner, as member and overseer, forged ties to finance club. *New York Times,* April 26.
Behan, Richard W. 2001. *Plundered promise: Capitalism, politics, and the fate of the federal lands.* Washington, D.C.: Island Press.
Bellow, Adam. 2003a. In praise of nepotism. *Atlantic Monthly,* July/August.
———. 2003b. *In praise of nepotism: A natural history.* New York: Doubleday.
Bender, Edwin. 2000. Private prisons, politics, and profits. *National Institute on Money in State Politics.* http://www.followthemoney.org.
Bendix, Reinhard. 1963. Concepts and generalizations in comparative sociological studies. *American Sociological Review* 28 (4): 532–39.
Bennett, Larry. 1997. *Neighborhood politics: Chicago and Sheffield.* New York: Garland.
Benson, J. Kenneth. 1973. The analysis of bureaucratic-professional conflict: Functional versus dialectical approaches. *Sociological Quarterly* 14 (3): 376–94.
Benton, John F. 1962. *Annals of the American Academy of Political and Social Science* 340:144–45.
Berelson, Bernard R., Paul F. Lazarsfeld, and William N. McPhee. 1954. *Voting behavior.* Chicago: University of Chicago Press.
Berg, John C. 1994. *Unequal struggle: Class, gender, race, and power in the U.S. Congress.* Boulder: Westview.

Berle, Adolf Augustus, and Gardiner C. Means. 1968. *The modern corporation and private property.* New York: Harcourt, Brace and World.

Best, Paul J., Kul B. Rai, and David F. Walsh. 1986. *Politics in three worlds: An introduction to political science.* New York: Wiley.

Bishop, Thomas Brad. 1988. The law of shoplifting: A guide for lawyers and merchants. *Cumberland Law Review* 19:43–74.

Bislev, Sven. 2004. Globalization, state transformation, and public security. *International Political Science Review* 25 (3): 281–96.

Blackshaw, Tony. 2005. *Zygmunt Bauman.* London: Routledge.

Blackwater shootings killed 17. 2007. *USA Today,* November 7. http://www.usatoday.com/news/world/iraq/2007–10–07-blackwater-investigation_N.htm.

Blakely, Edward James, and Mary Gail Snyder. 1997. *Fortress America: Gated communities in the United States.* Washington, D.C.: Brookings Institution Press.

Blanchard, Olivier. 2003. *Macroeconomics.* Upper Saddle River, N.J.: Prentice Hall.

Blau, Peter M. 1970. A formal theory of differentiation in organizations. *American Sociological Review* 35:201–8.

———. 1972. Interdependence and hierarchy in organizations. *Social Science Research* 1:1–24.

Bloch, Marc. 1961. *Feudal society: The growth of ties of dependence.* Trans. L. A. Manyon. Chicago: University of Chicago Press.

———. 1964. *Feudal society: The growth of ties of dependence.* Trans. L. A. Manyon. Chicago: University of Chicago Press.

———. 1989. *Feudal society: The growth of ties of dependence.* 2nd ed. Trans. L.'A. Manyon. Chicago: University of Chicago Press.

Blumer, Herbert. 1969. *Symbolic interactionism: Perspective and method.* Englewood Cliffs, N.J.: Prentice-Hall

Bornstein, Morris, ed. 1994. *Comparative economic systems: Models and cases.* Burr Ridge, Ill.: Irwin.

Bourdieu, Pierre. 1984. *Distinction: A social critique of the judgment of taste.* Trans. Richard Nice. Cambridge: Harvard University Press.

Bourdieu, Pierre, and Jean-Claude Passeron. 1990. *Reproduction in education, society, and culture.* Trans. Richard Nice. Newbury Park, Calif.: Sage.

Bowers, Andy. 2004. What's a Boston Brahmin? And has Kerry really earned the name? *Slate,* March 1.

Bowie, Nolan. 2007. Treating money as free speech. *Boston Globe,* July 16.

Bowman, Scott R. 1996. *The modern corporation and American political thought: Law, power, and ideology.* University Park: Pennsylvania State University Press.

Boycko, Maxim, Andrei Shleifer, and Robert W. Vishny. 1996. A theory of privatization. *Economic Journal* 106 (435): 313.

Boyle, Andy. 2008. Lawmakers consider tougher anti-nepotism rules. *Omaha World-Herald,* January 28.

Braithwaite, John. 1985. White collar crime. *Annual Review of Sociology* 11:1–25.

Braudel, Fernand. 1992. *Civilization and capitalism, fifteenth–eighteenth century: The perspective of the world.* Berkeley: University of California Press.

Brehm, John, and Scott Gates. 1999. *Working, shirking, and sabotage: Bureaucratic response to a democratic public.* Ann Arbor: University of Michigan Press.

Brewer, Anthony. 1980. *Marxist theories of imperialism: A critical survey.* Boston: Routledge and Kegan Paul.

Broder, John. 2008. Obama cites attack ads as a failing of the system. *New York Times,* June 21.

Brooks, David. 2009a. Big-spending conservative. *New York Times,* April 20.

———. 2009b. Yanks in crisis. *New York Times,* April 23.

Brown, Elizabeth A. R. 1974. The tyranny of a construct: Feudalism and historians of medieval Europe. *American Historical Review* 79 (4): 1063–88.

Brown, J. A. C. 1986. *The social psychology of industry: Human relations in the factory.* New York: Penguin.

Brubaker, Rogers. 1984. *The limits of rationality: An essay on the social and moral thought of Max Weber.* London: Allen and Unwin.

Buchanan, James, Robert Tollison, and Gordon Tullock, eds.1981. *Toward a theory of the rent seeking society.* College Station: Texas A&M University Press.

Bucher, Rue. 1970. Social process and power in a medical school. In *Power in organizations,* ed. Mayer N. Zald, 3–48. Nashville: Vanderbilt University Press.

Bucher, Rue, and Joan Stelling. 1969. Characteristics of professional organizations. *Journal of Health and Social Behavior* 10:3–15.

Buchholz, Barbara B., Margaret Crane, Ross Crane, and Ross Nager. 1999. *The family business answer book.* Paramus, N.J.: Prentice Hall.

Buckle, Stephen. 1991. *Natural law theory and the theory of property: Grotius to Hume.* Oxford: Clarendon.

Bumiller, Elisabeth. 2007. Dodd's other campaign: Restoring Dad's reputation. *New York Times,* September 24.

Burawoy, Michael. 1979. *Manufacturing consent: Changes in the labor process under monopoly capitalism.* Chicago: University of Chicago Press.

Burns, James MacGregor, Jack W. Peltason, Thomas E. Cronin, and David B. Magleby. 2000. *Government by the people.* 3rd ed. Englewood Cliffs, N.J.: Prentice Hall.

Burris, Val. 1987a. Business support for the new right. *Socialist Review* 91:33–63.

———. 1987b. The political partisanship of American business: A study of corporate political action committees. *American Sociological Review* 6:732–44.

———. 2001. The two faces of capital: Corporations and individual capitalists as political actors. *American Sociological Review* 66 (3): 361–81.

Burris, Val, and James Salt. 1990. The politics of capitalist class segments. *Social Problems* 37:601–19.

Burt, Nathaniel. 1970. *First families: The making of an American aristocracy.* Boston: Little, Brown.

Busch, Lawrence. 2000. *The eclipse of morality: Science, state, and market.* New York: Aldine de Gruyter.

Bushnell, P. Timothy, Vladimir Shlapentokh, Christopher K. Vanderpool, and Jeyaratnam Sundram, eds. 1991. *State organized terror: The case of violent internal repression.* Boulder: Westview.

Business Wire. 2008. Focusing on employees can pay future dividends. http://www.businesswire.com/portal/site/home/permalink/?ndmViewId=news_view&newsId=20081020005014&newsLang=en.

Buss, David, and Douglas Kenrik. 1989. Evolutionary social psychology. In *Handbook of social psychology,* vol. 2, ed. Daniel T. Gilbert, Susan T. Fiske, and Gardner Lindzey. Oxford: Oxford University Press.

Butler, Arthur G., Jr. 1973. Project management: A study in organizational conflict. *Academy of Management Journal* 16 (1): 84–101.

Butterfield, Fox. 2004. Justice dept. report shows trouble in private U.S. jails preceded job fixing Iraq's. *New York Times,* June 6.

Cain, Bruce E., John Ferejohn, and Fiorina Morris. 1987. *The personal vote: Constituency service and electoral independence.* Cambridge: Harvard University Press.

Cain, Peter J., and Mark Harrison, eds. 2001. *Imperialism: Critical concepts in historical studies.* New York: Routledge.

Cancian, Francesca. 1985. Gender politics: Love and power in the private and public spheres. In *Gender and the life course,* ed. Alice Rossi. New York: Aldine Transaction.

Cantor, Joseph E. 2006. Campaign financing. *Congressional Research Service.* http://usinfo.state.gov/infousa/government/elections/docs/CRS%20Campaign%20Finance%205%5B1%5D.4.06.pdf.

Cantor, Norman. 1993. *Civilization of the Middle Ages: A completely revised and expanded edition of medieval history, the life and death of a civilization.* New York: HarperCollins.

———. 1994. *The civilization of the Middle Ages. Revised and expanded ed. of Medieval history: The life and death of a civilization.* New York: HarperCollins.

———, ed. 1999. *The encyclopedia of the Middle Ages.* Viking: New York.

Carson, Kevin A. 2006. Contract feudalism: A critique of employer power over employees. London: Libertarian Alliance.

Carsten, Janet. 2004. *After kinship.* Cambridge: Cambridge University Press.

Cascardi, Anthony J. 1992. *The subject of modernity.* Cambridge: Cambridge University Press.

Case, Karl E., and Ray C. Fair. 1996. *Principles of microeconomics.* 4th ed. Upper Saddle River, N.J.: Prentice Hall.

———. 2002. *Principles of macroeconomics.* 6th ed. Upper Saddle River, N.J.: Prentice Hall.

Cavanagh, John, and Jerry Mander, eds. 2002. *Alternatives to economic globalization: A better world is possible.* San Francisco: Berrett-Koehler.

Cazel, Fred, ed. 1961. *Feudalism and liberty: Articles and addresses of Sidney Painter.* Baltimore: Johns Hopkins University Press.

Chamberlin, Henry Barrett. 1932. Some observations concerning organized crime. *Journal of Criminal Law and Criminology* 22 (5): 652–70.

Chang, Myong-Hun, and Joseph E. Harrington Jr. 2000. Centralization vs. decentralization in a multi-unit organization: A computational model of a retail chain as a multi-agent adaptive system. *Management Science* 46 (11): 1427–40.

Chappell, Henry W. 1982. Campaign contributions and congressional voting: A simultaneous probit-tobit model. *Review of Economics and Statistics* 64:72–83.

Chaussinand-Nogaret, Guy. 1985. *The French nobility in the eighteenth century: From feudalism to enlightenment.* Trans. William Doyle. Cambridge: Cambridge University Press.

Cheung, Amy. 2004. Prison privatization and the use of incarceration. *The sentencing project.* http://www.sentencingproject.org.

Cheung, Steven N. S. 1987. Economic organization and transaction costs. In *The new Palgrave: A dictionary of economics,* 2:55–58.

Chibnall, Marjorie. 1986. *Anglo-Norman England, 1066–1166.* New York: Basil Blackwell.

Chrisman, James J., Jess H. Chua, and Pramodita Sharma. 2003. Current trends and future directions in family business management studies: Toward a theory of the family firm. Coleman White Paper Series. http://www.usasbe.org/knowledge/whitepapers/chrisman2003.pdf.

Chubais, Anatolii. 2002. Interview with *Moskovskie Novosti,* July 29.

Citizens Association of Georgetown. Public Safety Program. http://www.cagtown.org.

Clark, Ian. 2000. *Governance, the state, regulation, and industrial relations.* London: Routledge.

Clarke, Thomas, and Christos Pitelis, eds. 1993. *The political economy of privatization.* London: Routledge.

Cobban, Alfred. 1999. *The social interpretation of the French revolution.* Cambridge: Cambridge University Press.

Cochrane, John H. 2008. Mortgage Protest Letter. http://faculty.chicagobooth.edu/john.cochrane/research/Papers/mortgage_protest.htm.

Cohen, Adam, and Elizabeth Taylor. 2000. *American pharaoh: Mayor Richard J. Daley: His battle for Chicago and the nation.* Boston: Little, Brown.

Colander, David C., ed. 1984. *Neoclassical political economy: The analysis of rent-seeking and DUP activities.*Cambridge, Mass.: Ballinger.

Coleman, James S. 1990. *Foundation of Social Theory.* Cambridge: Harvard University Press.

Collins, Randall. 2005. Weber and the sociology of revolution. In *Max Weber's economy and society: A critical companion,* ed. Charles Camic, Philip S. Gorski, and David M. Trubek. Stanford: Stanford University Press.

Colvin, Howard Montagu. 1982. *The history of the king's works.* London: H. M. Stationery Office.

Confessore, Nicholas. 2008. If not one Kennedy, perhaps another, a third Kennedy says. *New York Times,* December 8.

Confessore, Nicholas, and David M. Halbfinger. 2008. As a candidate, Kennedy is forceful but elusive. *New York Times,* December 28.

Conte, Alba. 2000. *Sexual harassment in the workplace: Law and practice.* Gaithersburg, Md.: Panel.

Conway, Brendan. 2004. The new nepotism. *Public Interest* 154 (Winter): 130–35.

Coombs, Maureen A. 2004. *Power and conflict between doctors and nurses: Breaking through the inner circle in clinical care.* London: Routledge.

Cornforth, Maurice, ed. 1978. *Rebels and their causes: Essays in honor of A. L. Morton.* London: Lawrence and Wishart.

Corporate Crime Reporter. 2009. Louisiana most corrupt state in the nation, Mississippi second, Illinois sixth, New Jersey ninth. http://www.commondreams.org/news2007/1008–04.htm.

Corrections Corporation of America. http://www.correctionscorp.com.

Cortés, Fernando, Adam Przeworski, and John Sprague. 1974. *Systems analysis for social scientists.* New York: Wiley.

Corwin, Ronald G. 1970. *Militant professionalism: A study of organizational conflicts in high schools.* New York: Appleton-Century Crofts.

Coser, Lewis A. 1977. *Masters of sociological thought: Ideas in historical and social context.* 2nd ed. New York: Harcourt Brace Jovanovich.

Coulanges, Fustel de. 1923. *Histoire des institutions politique de l'ancienne France.* Paris: Hachette.

Craven, Laura. 2008. Newark ex-mayor Sharpe James is convicted of fraud. http://www.nj.com/news/index.ssf/2008/04/newark_ex_mayor_sharpe_james_convicted.html.

Croly, Herbert. 1909. *The promise of American life.* New York: Macmillan.

Cunningham, William, John Strauchs, and Clifford Van Meter. 1990. *Private security trends, 1970–2000.* The Hallcrest Report II. Boston: Butterworth-Heinemann.

Curtis, Michael, Jean Blondel, and Bernard E. Brown. 1993. *Introduction to comparative government.* 3rd ed. New York: HarperCollins.

Dahl, Robert. 2006. *On political equality.* New Haven: Yale University Press.

Dalton, Melville. 1950a. Conflicts between staff and line managerial officers. *American Sociological Review* 15 (3): 342–51.

———. 1950b. Unofficial union-management relations. *American Sociological Review* 15 (5): 611–19.

———. 1955. Industrial controls and personal relations. *Social Forces* 33 (3): 244–49.

———. 1959. *Men who manage: Fusions of feeling and theory in administration.* New York: Wiley.

Danilov, Viktor. 2000. Rossiiskoie pravitel'stvo w dwazatom weke. In *Kuda idet Rossia: Gosudarstvo, Obshchestvo, Lichnost,* ed. T. I. Zaslavskaia. Moscow: Vysshaia shkola sotsial'nykh i ekonomicheskikh nauk.

Danley, John R. 1994. *The role of the modern corporation in a free society.* Notre Dame: University of Notre Dame Press.

Davey, Monica. 2008. Gov. Rod R. Blagojevich of Illinois. *New York Times,* December 9.

Davis, Melissa G., Richard J. Lundman, and Ramiro Martinez Jr. 1991. Private corporate justice: Store police, shoplifters, and civil recovery. *Social Problems* 38 (3): 395–411.

Davis, Natalie Z. 2000. *The gift in sixteenth-century France.* Oxford: Oxford University Press.

Dawkins, Richard. 1976. *The selfish gene.* Oxford: Oxford University Press.

Deacon, Bob, and Paul Stubbs. 1998. International actors and social policy development in Bosnia-Herzegovina: Globalism and the "new feudalism." *Journal of European Social Policy* 8 (2): 99–115.

Dean, Trevor. 2001. *Crime in medieval Europe, 1200–1550.* New York: Longman.

DeLeon, Peter. 1993. *Thinking about political corruption.* Armonk: M. E. Sharpe.

DeMars, Nan. 1998. *You want me to do what? When, where, and how to draw the line at work.* New York: Simon and Schuster.

DeMichele, Matthew T., and Richard Tewksbury. 2004. Sociological explorations in site-specific social control: The role of the strip club bouncer. *Deviant Behavior* 25:537–58.

Demski, Joel S. 2003. Corporate conflicts of interest. *The Journal of Economic Perspectives* 17 (2): 51–72.

Deparle, Jason. 2006. A high-profile ouster in Pennsylvania. *New York Times,* November 8.

Desveaux, James A., Evert A. Lindquist, and Glen Toner. 1994. Organizing for policy innovation in public bureaucracy: AIDS, energy, and environmental policy in Canada. *Canadian Journal of Political Science* 27 (3): 493–528.

Deutsch, Morton. 1973. *The resolution of conflict: Constructive and destructive processes.* New Haven: Yale University Press.

DeVroey, Michel. 2004. Lucas on involuntary unemployment. *Cambridge Journal of Economics* 28:397–411.

Diamond, Larry. 2002. Thinking about hybrid regimes; categorizing political regimes: New data for old problems. *Journal of Democracy* 13 (2): 21–35.

Diamond, Peter A. 2003. Papers and proceedings of the one hundred fifteenth annual meeting of the American Economic Association, January 3–5, Washington, D.C., 338–42.

Dilger, Robert Jay, Randolph R. Moffett, and Linda Struyk. 1997. Privatization of municipal services in America's largest cities. *Public Administration Review* 57 (1): 21–26.

DiMaggio, Paul J., and Walter W. Powell. 1983. The iron cage revisited: Institutional isomorphism and collective rationality in organizational fields. *American Sociological Review* 48 (2): 147–60.

Dirks, Raymond, and Leonard Gross. 1974. *The great Wall Street scandal.* New York: McGraw-Hill.

Dobb, Maurice Herbert. 1947. *Studies in the development of capitalism.* New York: International Publishers.

Dogan, Mattei, ed. 2003. *Elite configurations at the apex of power.* Boston: Brill.

Domhoff, George William. 1970. *The higher circles: The governing class in America.* New York: Random House.

———, ed. 1980. *Power structure research.* Beverly Hills: Sage.

Domingues, Patricio, Bruno Sousa, and Luis Moura Silva. 2007. Sabotage-tolerance and trust management in desktop grid computing. *Future Generation Computer Systems* 23 (7): 904–13.

Donahue, John D. 1989. *The privatization decision.* New York: Basic Books.

Donovan, John C., Richard E. Morgan, Christian P. Potholm, and Marcia A. Weigle. 1993. *People, power, and politics: An introduction to political science.* 3rd ed. Lanham, Md.: Littlefield Adams.

Douglas, David Charles. 1969. *The Norman achievement, 1050–1100.* London: Eyre and Spottiswoode.

Dowd, Maureen. 2009. Sweet on Caroline. *New York Times,* January 6.

Downey, H. Kirk, and John W. Slocum. 1975. Uncertainty: Measures, research, and sources of variation. *Academy of Management Journal* 18 (3): 562–78.

Drew, Elizabeth. 1983. *Politics and money: The new road to corruption.* New York: Macmillan.

Drew, Katherine Fischer. 2004. *Magna Carta.* Westport, Conn.: Greenwood.

Drucker, Peter F. 1993. *Concept of the corporation.* New Brunswick, N.J.: Transaction.

Drudge, Michael W. 2008. Pork barrel spending emerging as presidential campaign issue: Candidates, critics differ on definition of and remedies for the practice. http://www.america.gov/st/elections08english/2008/August/200808011815041cnirellep0.1261713.html.

Dubin, Robert. 1957. Power and union-management relations. *Administrative Science Quarterly* 2 (1): 60–81.

Dubuis, Pierre. 1995. *Les vifs, les morts et le temps qui court: familles valaisannes 1400–1550.* Lausanne: Section d'histoire, Faculté des lettres, Université de Lausanne.

Duby, Georges. 1977. *The chivalrous society.* Trans. Cynthia Postan. London: Edward Arnold.

———. 1998. *Féodalité.* Paris: Presses Universitaires de France.

Duffy, Eamon. 1997. *Saints and sinners: A history of the popes.* New Haven: Yale University Press.

Dunham, Douglas W. 1986. Inmates' rights and the privatization of prisons. *Columbia Law Review* 86 (7): 1475–504.

Dutton, John M., and Richard E. Walton. 1966. Interdepartmental conflict and cooperation: Two contrasting studies. *Human Organization* 25:207–20.

Duus, Peter. 1993. *Feudalism in Japan.* 3rd ed. New York: McGraw-Hill.

Eagles, Munroe, Larry Johnston, and Christopher Holoman. 2004. *Politics: An introduction to democratic government.* Peterborough, Ont.: Broadview Press.

Economist. 2004. The curse of nepotism. January 8.

Ehrlich, Stanislaw. 1982. *Pluralism on and off course.* Oxford: Pergamon Press.

Eisenstadt, Shmuel Noah, and Luis Roniger. 1984. *Patrons, clients, and friends: Interpersonal relations and the structure of trust in society.* Cambridge: Cambridge University Press.

Eitzen, D. Stanley, and Maxine Baca Zinn. 1993. *In conflict and order: Understanding society.* 6th ed. Boston: Allyn and Bacon.

———. 2004. *Social problems.* Boston: Pearson.

Ekelund, Robert B., Robert F. Hebert, and Robert D. Tollison. 1989. An economic model of the medieval church: Usury as a form of rent seeking. *Journal of Law, Economics, and Organization* 5 (2): 309.

Elias, Norbert. 1982. *Power and civility.* Trans. Edmund Jephcott. New York: Pantheon Books.

———. 1998. *On civilization, power, and knowledge: Selected writings.* Chicago: University of Chicago Press.

Ellickson, Robert C. 1991. *Order without law: How neighbors settle disputes.* Cambridge: Harvard University Press.

Ellin, Abby. 2001. A food fight over private prisons. *New York Times,* April 8.

Epstein, Edwin M. 1969. *The corporation in American politics.* Englewood Cliffs, N.J.: Prentice Hall.

Erber, Ralph, and Robin Gilmour. 1994. *Theoretical frameworks for personal relationships.* Hillsdale, N.J.: Lawrence Erlbaum Associates.

Erickson, Merle, Brian W. Mayhew, and William I. Felix Jr. 2000. Why do audits fail? Evidence from Lincoln savings and loan. *Journal of Accounting Research* 38 (1): 165–94.

Ericson, Richard E. 2000. The post-Soviet Russian economic system: An industrial feudalism? In *Russian crisis and its effects,* ed. Tuomas Komulainen and Iikka Korhonen, 133–66. Helsinki: Kikimora.

Erven, Bernard L. 2009. Management succession issues in family business. http://www.fambiz.com/Orgs/Cornell/articles/real/erven.cfm.

Espeland, Wendy, and Michael Sauder. 2007. Rankings and reactivity: How public measures recreate social worlds. *American Journal of Sociology* 113 (1): 1–40.

Etzioni, Amitai. 1964. *Modern organizations.* Englewood Cliffs, N.J.: Prentice Hall.

———. 1988. *Capital corruption: The new attack on American democracy.* New Brunswick, N.J.: Transaction.

Evans, Peter B., Dietrich Rueschemeyer, and Theda Skocpol, eds. 1985. *Bringing the state back in.* Cambridge: Cambridge University Press.

Evans, Peter B., and John Stephens. 1988. Development and the world economy. In *Handbook of sociology,* ed. Neil Smelser, 739–73. Newbury Park, Calif.: Sage.

Fairbanks, Charles H., Jr. 1999. The feudalization of the state. *Journal of Democracy* 10 (2): 47–53.

———. 2000. The feudal analogy. *Journal of Democracy* 11 (3): 34–36.

Falk, William W., Michael D. Grimes, and George F. Lord III. 1982. Professionalism and conflict in a bureaucratic setting: The case of a teachers' strike. *Social Problems* 29 (5): 551–60.

Farmer, D. J. 2006. Wal-Mart: Neo-feudal (k)night? *Administrative Theory and Praxis* 28:148–61.

Federal Trade Commission. 2007. Federal trade commission annual report. Fair debt collection practices act. http://www.ftc.gov/reports/fdcpa07/P0748032007FDCPAReport.pdf.

Feigenbaum, Harvey, Jeffrey Henig, and Chris Hamnett. 1999. *Shrinking the state: The political underpinning of privatization.* Cambridge: Cambridge University Press.

Ferguson, Niall. 2001. *The cash nexus: Money and power in the modern world, 1700–2000.* New York: Basic Books.

Ferguson, Thomas. 1995. Golden rule: The investment theory of party competition and the logic of money-driven political systems. Chicago: University of Chicago Press.

Fichter, Joseph. 1971. *Sociology.* 2nd ed. Chicago: University of Chicago Press.

Fine, Ben. 2001. *Social capital versus social theory: Political economy and social science at the turn of the millennium.* New York: Routledge.

Fink, Clinton. 1968. Some conceptual difficulties in the theory of social conflict. *Journal of Conflict Resolution* 12:412–60.

Finn, Chester E., Bruno V. Manno, and Gregg Vanourek. 2000. *Charter schools in action: Renewing public education.* Princeton: Princeton University Press.

Fisch, Jill E. 1991. Frankenstein's monster hits the campaign trail: An approach to regulation of corporate political expenditures. *William and Mary Law Review* 32:587–643.

Fischer, Markus. 1992. Feudal Europe, 800–1300: Communal discourse and conflictual practices. *International Organization* 46 (2): 427–66.

Fitzpatrick, Sheila. 1982. *The Russian Revolution.* Oxford: Oxford University Press.

Ford, R., and F. McLaughlin. 1986. Nepotism: Boon or bane. *Personnel Administrator* 31:79–89.

Forst, Brian, and Peter K. Manning. 1999. *The privatization of policing: Two views.* Washington, D.C.: Georgetown University Press.

Fortes, Meyer. 1969. *Kinship and the social order: The legacy of Lewis Henry Morgan.* Chicago: Aldine.

Fowler, Kenneth. 2001. *Medieval mercenaries: The great companies.* Oxford: Blackwell.

Fox, William S., and Michael H. Wince. 1976. Structure and determinants of occupational militancy among public school teachers. *Industrial and Labor Relations Review* 30:47–58.

Frank, Andre Gunder. 1967. *Capitalism and underdevelopment in Latin America: Historical studies of Chile and Brazil.* New York: Monthly Review Press.

Frank, Isnard Wilhelm. 1995. *A concise history of the mediaeval church.* New York: Continuum.

Fraser, Antonia, ed. 2000. *The Middle Ages.* Berkeley: University of California Press.

Freeman, Samuel. 2001. Illiberal libertarians: Why libertarianism is not a liberal view. *Philosophy and Public Affairs* 30 (2): 105–51.

Freidson, Eliot. 1970a. *Profession of medicine: A study of the sociology of applied knowledge.* New York: Dodd, Mead.

———. 1970b. *Professional dominance: The social structure of medical care.* New York: Atherton Press.

Frendreis, John P. and Richard W. Waterman. 1985. PAC contributions and legislative behavior: Senate voting on trucking deregulation. *Social Science Quarterly* 66:401–12.

Fukuyama, Francis. 2000. Social capital. In *Culture Matters,* ed. Lawrence Harrison and Samuel P. Huntington. New York: Basic Books.

Galal, Ahmed, and Mary M. Shirley, eds. 1994. *Does privatization deliver? Highlights from a World Bank conference.* Washington, D.C.: World Bank.

Galambos, Louis. 1988. What have CEOs been doing? *Journal of Economic History* 48 (2): 243–58.

Galambos, Louis, and Joseph Pratt. 1988. *The rise of the corporate commonwealth: U.S. business and public policy in the twentieth century.* New York: Basic Books.

Galbraith, John Kenneth. 1956. *American capitalism: The concept of countervailing power.* Boston: Houghton Mifflin.

Gallup. 2006. Three questions and answers on congressional corruption. http://www.gallup.com/poll/23170/Three-Questions-Answers-Congressional-Corruption.aspx.

Ganshof, François Louis. 1952. *Feudalism.* Trans. Philip Grierson. London: Longmans, Green.

———. 1964. *Feudalism.* Trans. Philip Grierson. New York: Harper and Row.

Garland, David. 1993. *Punishment and modern society: A study in social theory.* Studies in crime and justice. Chicago: University of Chicago Press.

Gauvard, Claude. 1999. Fear of crime in late medieval France. In *Medieval crime and social control,* ed. Barbara A. Hanawalt and David Wallace. Minneapolis: University of Minnesota Press.

Geltner, Guy. 2006. Medieval prisons: Between myth and reality, hell and purgatory. *History Compass* 4 (2): 261–74.

Gerlach, Michael L. 1992. *Alliance capitalism: The social organization of Japanese business.* Berkeley: University of California Press.

Giacalone, Robert A., and Paul Rosenfeld. 1987. Reasons for employee sabotage in the workplace. *Journal of Business and Psychology* 1 (4): 367–78.

Gibbs, Marion. 1953. *Feudal order: A study of the origins and development of English feudal society.* New York: Henry Schuman.

Gibbs, Nancy, Michael Duffy, Karen Tumulty, and Michael Weisskopf. 1997. Legal tender. *Time* 149 (11).

Giddens, Anthony. 1976. *New rules of sociological method: A positive critique of interpretative sociologies.* New York: Basic Books.

———. 1991. *Modernity and self-identity: Self and society in the late modern age.* Stanford: Stanford University Press.

Ginsborg, Paul. 2003. *Italy and its discontents: Family, civil society, state, 1980–2001.* New York: Palgrave Macmillan.

Gisevius, Hans Bernd, Allen W. Dulles, and Peter Hoffmann. 1998. *To the bitter end: An insider's account of the plot to kill Hitler, 1933–1944.* New York: Da Capo Press.

Glaeser, Edward L., and Claudia Goldin, eds. 2006. *Corruption and reform: Lessons from America's economic history.* Chicago: University of Chicago Press.

Gleason, Abbott. 1995. *Totalitarianism: The inner history of the cold war.* New York: Oxford University Press.

Glionna, John M. 2008. A voice for rural women of China. *Los Angeles Times,* January 2.

Goffman, Erving. 1959. *The presentation of self in everyday life.* Garden City, N.Y.: Doubleday.

Godbout, Jacques. 2000. Le don, la dette et l'identité: Homo donator vs. homo aeconomicus. Paris: La Découverte / MAUSS.

Goode, William J. 1972. Presidential address: The place of force in human society. *American Sociological Review* 37:507–19.

Gordley, James. 1991. *The philosophical origins of modern contract doctrine.* Oxford: Oxford University Press.

Gordon, Leonard, and Patricia Harvey. 1978. *Sociology and American social issues.* Dallas: Houghton Mifflin.

Gouldner, Alvin Ward. 1954. *Patterns of industrial bureaucracy.* Glencoe, Ill.: Free Press.

Gradstein, Mark. 1993. Rent seeking and the provision of public goods. *Economic Journal* 103 (420): 1236–43.

Granovetter, Mark S. 1973. The strength of weak ties. *American Journal of Sociology* 78 (6): 1360–80.

Green, Mark. 2004. *Selling out: How big corporate money buys elections, rams through legislation, and betrays our democracy.* New York: HarperCollins.

Green, Roger. 2003. Markets, management, and "reengineering" higher education. *Annals of the American Academy of Political and Social Science* 585:196–210.

Greenberg, Stanley B. 2004. *The two Americas: Our current political deadlock and how to break it.* New York: Thomas Dunne Books.

Grenzke, Janet M. 1988. Comparing contributions to U.S. House members from outside their districts. *Legislative Studies Quarterly* 13:83–103.

Grinberg, Ruslan. 2006. Interview with *Moskovskii Komsomolets,* March 31.

Gross, Daniel. 2005. Repo men: Debt collectors don't send thugs with baseball bats anymore. Now they sic lawyers on you. *Slate,* November 2. http://www.slate.com/id/2129294/.

Grossman, Mark. 2003. *Political corruption in America: An encyclopedia of scandals, power, and greed.* Santa Barbara: ABC-Clio.

Gudkov, Lev. 2000. O negativnoi identfikatsii. *Monitoring of Public Opinion* 5 (49): 35–44.

Guenée, Bernard. 1991. *Between church and state: The lives of four French prelates in the late Middle Ages.* Trans. Arthur Goldhammer. Chicago: University of Chicago Press.

Guriev, Sergei. 2001. Industral'nyi feudalism: nizkaia geograficheskaia mobilnost' trudovykh resursov meshaet perestroike ekonomiki. *Ekspert,* April 9.

Habermas, Jürgen, Sara Lennox, and Frank Lennox. 1974. The public sphere: An encyclopedia article. *New German Critique* 3 (Autumn): 45–48.

Hall, John Whitney. 1962. Feudalism in Japan: A reassessment. *Comparative Studies in History and Society* 5(1):15–51.

Hamilton, Alexander, James Madison, and John Jay. [1787] 1901. *The federalist: A commentary on the constitution of the United States.* Introduction by Edward Gaylord Bourne. New York: M. Walter Dunne.

Hamilton, William Donald. 1964. Genetical evolution of social behavior. *Journal of Theoretical Biology* 7 (1): 1–16.

Hammond, John L., and Barbara Hammond. 1969. *The rise of modern industry.* New York: Harper and Row.

Hampton, Jean. 1986. *Hobbes and the social contract tradition.* New York: Cambridge University Press.

Hanawalt, Barbara A., and David Wallace, eds. 1999. *Medieval crime and social control.* Minneapolis: University of Minnesota Press.

Handel, Michael J., ed. 2003. *The sociology of organizations: Classic, contemporary, and critical readings.* Thousand Oaks, Calif.: Sage.

Handler, Edward, Lawerence Godtfredsen, and John Mulkern. 1980. Diversity and cohesion in corporate political behavior: A microanalysis of the campaign contribution strategies on corporate political action committee. *Proceedings of the Academy of Management,* 361–65.

Hansen, Karen V., and Anita Ilta Garey, eds. 1998. *Families in the U.S.: Kinship and domestic politics.* Philadelphia: Temple University Press.

Harbring, Christine, Bernd Irlenbusch, Matthias Kräkel, and Reinhard Selten. 2007.

Sabotage in corporate contests—an experimental analysis. *International Journal of the Economics of Business* 14 (3): 367–92.

Harding, Richard. 2001. Private prisons. *Crime and Justice* 28:265–346.

Harrington, Michael. 1969. *The other America: Poverty in the United States.* New York: Macmillan.

Harris, Charles Wesley. 1995. *Congress and the governance of the nation's capital: The conflict of federal and local interests.* Washington, D.C.: Georgetown University Press.

Harris, Lloyd C., and Emmanuel Ogbonna. 2006. Service sabotage: A study of antecedents and consequences. *Journal of the Academy of Marketing Science* 34 (4): 543–58.

Hart, Oliver, Andrei Shleifer, and Robert W. Vishny. 1997. The proper scope of government: Theory and an application to prisons. *Quarterly Journal of Economics* 112 (4): 1127–61.

Hart, Oliver, and Luigi Zingales. 2008. Economists have abandoned principle. *Wall Street Journal,* December 3.

Hartz, Louis. 1955. *The liberal tradition in America: An interpretation of American political thought since the revolution.* New York: Harcourt, Brace and World.

Hayek, Friedrich August. 1973. *Law, legislation, and liberty: A new statement of the liberal principles of justice and political economy.* Chicago: University of Chicago Press.

Healy, Paul M., and Krishna G. Palepu. 2003. The fall of Enron. *Journal of Economic Perspectives* 17 (2): 3–26.

Hebert, Ernest. 1993. *The kinship.* Hanover, N.H.: University Press of New England.

Heers, Jacques, and Barry Herbert. 1977. *Family clans in the Middle Ages: A study of political and social structures in urban areas.* Amsterdam: North-Holland.

Heiser, Richard R. 2000. Castles, constables, and politics in late twelfth-century English governance. *Albion: A Quarterly Journal Concerned with British Studies* 32 (1): 19–36.

Hekala, Tamsin. 1996. Who's a relative? Kinship terminology in the Middle Ages. http://www.the-orb.net/essays/text03.html.

Hellriegel, Don, Wendell French, and Richard B. Peterson. 1970. Collective negotiations and teachers: A behavior analysis. *Industrial and Labor Relations Review* 23:380–96.

Henneman, John B. 1971. *Royal taxation in fourteenth century France: The development of war financing, 1322–1356.* Princeton: Princeton University Press.

Herndon, James F. 1982. Access, record, and competition as influences on interest group contributions to congressional campaigns. *Journal of Politics* 44:996–1019.

Heymann, C. David. 2007. *American legacy: The story of John and Caroline Kennedy.* New York: Simon and Schuster.

Hilferding, Rudolf. 1981. *Finance capital: A study of the latest phase of capitalist development.* Ed. T. B. Bottomore. London: Routledge and Kegan Paul.

Hilton, R. H. 1966. *A medieval society: The West Midlands at the end of the thirteenth century.* London: Weidenfeld and Nicolson.

Hobbs, Dick, Philip Hadfield, Stuart Lister, and Simon Winlow. 2003. *Bouncers: Violence and governance in the night-time economy.* Oxford: Oxford University Press.

Hobsbawm, Eric J. 1990. *Echoes of the Marseillaise: Two centuries look back on the French Revolution.* New Brunswick: Rutgers University Press.

Hodge, Graeme A. 2000. *Privatization: An international review of performance.* Boulder: Westview.

Hodson, Randy. 1997. Individual voice on the shop floor: The role of unions. *Social Forces* 75 (4): 1183–212.

Hohenstein, Kurt. 2007. *Coining corruption: The making of the American campaign finance system.* DeKalb: Northern Illinois University Press.

Hollister, Charles Warren. 1960. The significance of scutage rates in eleventh- and twelfth-century England. *English Historical Review* 75 (297): 577–88.

———. 1976. Normandy, France, and the Anglo-Norman regnum. *Speculum* 51 (2): 202–42.

Holsti, Ole R., Terrence P. Hopmann, and John D. Sullivan. 1985. *Unity and disintegration in international alliances: Comparative studies.* New York: Wiley.

Holton, Robert J. 1985. *The transition from feudalism to capitalism.* Basingstoke: Palgrave Macmillan.

Holy, Ladislav. 1996. *Anthropological perspectives on kinship.* Chicago: Pluto Press

Hopkins, Raymond F. 1972. Security authority: The view from the top. *World Politics* 24 (2): 271–92.

Horowitz, Irving, and May Strong. 1971. *Sociological realities: A guide to the study of society.* New York: Harper and Row.

Hough, Jerry F. 1980. *Soviet leadership in transition.* Washington, D.C.: Brookings Institution.

Hoy, Wayne K., and Richard Rees. 1974. Subordinate loyalty to immediate superior: A neglected concept in the study of educational administration. *Sociology of Education* 47 (2): 268–86.

Hulse, Carl. 2008. Famed name is double-edged as two Udalls run. *New York Times,* July 7.

Innes, Matthew. 2000. *State and society in the early Middle Ages: The middle-Rhine valley, 400–1000.* Cambridge: Cambridge University Press.

Jackall, Robert. 1988. *Moral mazes: The world of corporate managers.* New York: Oxford University Press.

Jacob, Philip E., and James V. Toscano, eds. 1964. *The integration of political communities.* Philadelphia: Lippincott.

Jain, Arvind K., ed. 1998. *Economics of corruption.* Dordrecht: Kluwer Academic Publishers.

James, Edward. 1982. *The origins of France: From Clovis to the Capetians, 500–1000.* London: Macmillan.

Janin, Hunt. 2004. *Medieval justice: Cases and laws in France, England, and Germany: 500–1500.* Jefferson, N.C.: McFarland.

Jehn, Karen A. 1997. A qualitative analysis of conflict types and dimensions in organizational groups. *Administrative Science Quarterly* 42 (3): 530–57.

Jessup, Dorothy K. 1978. Teacher unionization: A reassessment of rank and file motivations. *Sociology of Education* 51 (1): 44–45.

Jha, Vishwa Mohan. 2000. A review of *The Feudalism Debate* by Harbans Mukhia. *Social Scientist* 28 (11/12): 70–89.

Johnson, Allan G. 1995. *The Blackwell dictionary of sociology: A user's guide to sociological language.* Malden, Mass.: Blackwell.

Johnson-Cartee, Karen S., and Gary A. Copeland. 1991. *Negative political advertising: Coming of age.* Hillsdale, N.J.: Lawrence Erlbaum Associates.

Johnson, Simon. 2009a. The quiet coup. *Atlantic Monthly,* May.

———. 2009b. In banking, bigger is not better. *New York Times,* October 22.

Johnston, David. 2008. In Blagojevich case, is it a crime, or just talk? *New York Times,* December 15.

Johnston, David Cay. 2006. I.R.S. enlists help in collecting delinquent taxes. *New York Times,* August 20.

Johnston, David, and John M. Broder. 2007. FBI says guards killed 14 Iraqis without cause. *New York Times,* November 14.

Joint Pension Board. 2009. Selecting, reviewing, and replacing investment managers. http://www.uwo.ca/humanresources/docandform/docs/pension/governance/mgrdoc.pdf.

Jomo, Kwame Sundaram. 2003. Rethinking economic discrimination. *American Economic Review* 93 (2): 338–42.

Jones, Brian J., Bernard J. Gallagher, and Joseph A. McFalls. 1995. *Sociology: Micro, macro, and mega structures.* Fort Worth, Tex.: Harcourt College.

Jones, Rhys. 1999. Mann and men in a medieval state: The geographies of power in the Middle Ages. *Transactions of the Institute of British Geographers* 24 (1): 65–78.

Josephson, Matthew. 1962. *The robber barons: The great American capitalists, 1861–1901.* New York: Harcourt, Brace.

Jouvenel, Bertrand de. 1951. *Ethics of redistribution.* Cambridge: Cambridge University Press.

Juravich, Tom. 1985. *Chaos on the shop floor: A worker's view of quality, productivity, and management.* Philadelphia: Temple University Press.

Kahn, Paul W. 2005. *Putting liberalism in its place.* Princeton: Princeton University Press.

Kahn, Robert L. 1964. *Organizational stress: Studies in role conflict and ambiguity.* New York: Wiley.

Kale, Prashant, Jeffrey H. Dyer, and Harbir Singh. 2002. Alliance capability, stock market response, and long-term alliance success: The role of the alliance function. *Strategic Management Journal* 23 (8): 747–67.

Kanter, Rosabeth Moss. 1993. *Men and women of the corporation.* New York: Basic Books.

Karstedt, Susanne. 2000. Knights of crime: The success of "premodern" structures in the illegal economy. In *Social dynamics of crime and control: New theories for a world in transition,* ed. Susanne Karstedt and Kai-D Bussmann, 53–68. Oxford: Hart.

———. 2003. Legacies of a culture of inequality: The Janus face of crime in post-communist countries. *Crime, Law, and Social Change* 40 (2/3): 295–320.

Kau, James B., and Rubin, Paul H. 1982. *Congressmen, constituents, and contributors.* Boston: Martinus Nijhoff.

Kawata, Junichi, ed. 2006. *Comparing political corruption and clientelism.* Burlington, Vt.: Ashgate.

Kaye, Harvey J. 1984. *The British Marxist historians: An introductory analysis.* Cambridge: Polity Press.

Keim, Gerald D., and Carl P. Zeithaml. 1986. Corporate political strategy and legislative decision making: A review and contingency approach. *Academy of Management Review* 11 (4): 828–43.

Kelley, Harold H. 1979. *Personal relationships: Their structures and processes.* Hillsdale, N.J.: Lawrence Erlbaum Associates.

Kelly, Christine A. 2001. *Tangled up in red, white, and blue: New social movements in America.* Lanham, Md.: Rowman and Littlefield.

Kenrik, Douglas, Josh Ackerman, and Suzan Ledlow. 2006. Evolutionary social psychology: Adaptive predispositions and human culture. In *Handbook of social psychology,* ed. John Delamater. New York: Springer.

Kerfoot, Karlene M. 2007. Leadership, civility, and the "no jerks" rule. *Nursing Economics* 25 (4): 223–26.

Khanna, Tarun, Ranjay Gulati, and Nitin Nohria. 1994. Alliances as learning races. *Academy of Management Proceedings:* 42–46.

Khanna, Vikramaditya S. 2003. *Corporate crime legislation: A political economy analysis.* Michigan Law and Economics Research Paper No. 03–012 and Boston University School of Law Working Paper No. 03–04, September.

Killing, Peter J. 1983. *Strategies for joint venture success.* New York: Praeger.

Kirkpatrick, David D. 2007. Use of bundlers raises new risks for campaigns. *New York Times,* August 31.

Kirst, Michael W. 1970. *The politics of education at the local, state, and federal levels.* Berkeley: McCutchan.

Kiser, Edgar, and Joshua Kane. 2001. Revolution and state structure: The bureaucratization of tax administration in early modern England and France. *American Journal of Sociology* 107 (1): 183–223.

Kleck, Gary. 1988. Crime control through the private use of armed force. *Social Problems* 35 (1): 1–21.

Klein, Edward. 2003. *The Kennedy curse: Why tragedy has haunted America's first family for 150 Years.* New York: St. Martin's Press.

Kogut, Bruce. 1988. Joint ventures: Theoretical and empirical perspectives. *Strategic Management Journal* 9 (4): 319–32.

———. 1989. The stability of joint ventures: Reciprocity and competitive rivalry. *Journal of Industrial Economics* 38 (2): 183–98.

Kolb, Deborah M., and Linda L. Putnam. 1992. The multiple faces of conflict in organizations. *Journal of Organizational Behavior* 13 (3): 311–24.

Kolodner, Meredith. 2006. Immigration enforcement benefits prison firms. *New York Times,* July 19.

Konchalovskii, Andrei. 2006. Koruptsia? Kak eto po russki. *Argumenty Nedeli,* November 23. http://www.konchalovsky.ru.

Kosmoski, Georgia J., and Dennis R. Pollack. 2005. *Managing difficult, frustrating, and hostile conversations: Strategies for savvy administrators.* Thousand Oaks, Calif.: Corwin Press.

Kreps, Gary A., ed. 1989. *Social structure and disaster.* Newark: University of Delaware Press.

Krueger, Anne O. 1974. The political economy of the rent-seeking society. *American Economic Review* 64 (3): 291–303.

Krugman, Paul. 2007. Hired gun fetish. *New York Times,* September 28.

———. 2009a. Making banking boring. *New York Times,* April 9.

———. 2009b. Money for nothing. *New York Times,* April 26.

Kulish, Nicholas, and Thom Shanker. 2008. NATO's leader says the alliance remains unified on troops for Afghan mission. *New York Times,* February 10.

Kunda, Gideon. 1992. *Engineering culture: Control and commitment in a high-tech corporation.* Philadelphia: Temple University Press.

Kuper, Leo, and Michael G. Smith, eds. 1969. *Pluralism in Africa.* Berkeley: University of California Press.

Laclau, Ernesto. 1971. Feudalism and capitalism in Latin America. *New Left Review* 67:19–38.

Laffey, Mark. 2004. The red herring of economism: A reply to Marieke de Goede. *Review of International Studies* 30 (3): 459–68.

Lakoff, George, and Mark Johnson. 1980. *Metaphors we live by.* Chicago: University of Chicago Press.

Lambsdorff, Johann Graf. 2007. *The institutional economics of corruption and reform: Theory, evidence, and policy.* Cambridge: Cambridge University Press.

Landsberger, Henry A. 1961. The horizontal dimension in bureaucracy. *Administrative Science Quarterly* 6 (3): 299–332.

Lange, Mark, and Ellen Rose. 2007. For fairer campaigns: Full, public funding. *Christian Science Monitor,* October 29.

Larson, Magali S. 1977. *The rise of professionalism: A sociological analysis.* Berkeley: University of California Press.

Lasch, Christopher. 1996. *The revolt of the elites: And the betrayal of democracy.* New York: W. W. Norton.

Latynina, Yulia. 2000. Access Code. On *Moscow Echo Radio,* May 19.

———. 2001. Zakhvat: Segodniashnii peredelk sobstvennoti kak ekonomika voiny. *Novaia Gazeta,* March 26 and 28.

———. 2002. Feodalnye woiny oligarkhov. *Komsomol'skaia Pravda,* December 10.

———. 2005. Okhota na iziubra. Moscow: Eksmo.

Lee, Guy Carleton. 1900. *Source-book of English history.* New York: Henry Holt.

Lee-Chai, Annette Y., and John A. Bargh, eds. 2001. *The use and abuse of power: Multiple perspectives on the causes of corruption.* Philadelphia: Psychology Press.

Lefebvre, Georges. 2005. *The coming of the French Revolution.* Trans. R. R. Palmer. Princeton: Princeton University Press.

Le Goff, Jacques. 1988. *Medieval civilization, 400–1500.* Trans. Julia Barrow. New York: Blackwell.

Levitsky, Steven, and Lucan A. Way. 2002. Elections without democracy: The rise of competitive authoritarianism. *Journal of Democracy* 13 (2): 51–65.

Lewicki, Roy J., Stephen E. Weiss, and David Lewin. 1992. Models of conflict, negotiation, and third party intervention: A review and synthesis. *Journal of Organizational Behavior* 13 (3): 209–52.

Lewin, Moshe. 1988. *The Gorbachev phenomenon: A historical interpretation.* Berkeley: University of California Press.

Lieven, Anatol. 1998. *Chechnya: Tombstone of Russian power.* New Haven: Yale University Press.

Light, Donald, and Suzanne Infeld Keller. 1982. *Sociology.* New York: Knopf.

Lindahl, Martin L., and William A. Carter. 1959. *Corporate concentration and public policy.* Englewood Cliffs, N.J.: Prentice-Hall.

Lindblom, Charles E. 1988. *Democracy and market system.* Oslo: Norwegian University Press.

Linowes, David F. 1988. *Privatization: Toward more effective government: Report of the President's Commission on Privatization.* Chicago: University of Illinois Press.

Lippert, John. 2008. Friedman would be roiled as Chicago disciples rue repudiation. Bloomberg.com, December 23. http://www.bloomberg.com/apps/news?pid=20601109&sid=a3GVhIHGyWRM&refer=home.

Liptak, Adam. 2008. Illegal globally, bail for profit remains in U.S. *New York Times,* January 29.

Lister, Stuart, Philip Hadfield, Dick Hobbs, and Simon Winlow. 2001. Accounting for bouncers: Occupational licensing as a mechanism for regulation. *Criminology and Criminal Justice* 1 (4): 363–84.

Lister, Stuart, Dick Hobbs, Steve Hall, and Simon Winlow. 2000. Violence in the night-time economy; bouncers: The reporting, recording, and prosecution of assaults. *Policing and Society* 10 (4): 383–402.

Loader, Ian, and Neil Walker. 2007. *Civilizing security.* Cambridge: Cambridge University Press.

Luhmann, Niklas. 1995. *Social systems.* Trans. John Bednarz Jr. and Dirk Baecker. Stanford: Stanford University Press.

Luke, Timothy W. 1989. *Screens of power: Ideology, domination, and resistance in informational society.* Urbana: University of Illinois Press.

Luo, Michael. 2008a. Ready to attack Obama, if some money arrives. *New York Times,* June 21.

———. 2008b. Study: Many Obama small donors really weren't. *New York Times,* November 24.

Maasen, Sabine, and Peter Weingart. 2000. *Metaphors and the dynamics of knowledge.* New York: Routledge.

Mackenzie, G. Calvin. 1981. *The politics of presidential appointments.* New York: Free Press.

Mackrell, John Q. C. 1973. *The attack on "feudalism" in eighteenth-century France.* London: Routledge and Kegan Paul.

Malbin, Michael J. 1979. Campaign financing and the "special interests." *Public Interest* 56 (Summer): 21–42.

Mandel, Debra. 2006. *Your boss is not your mother: Eight steps to eliminating office drama and creating positive relationships at work.* Chicago: Agate.

Mankiw, N. Gregory, and Robert B. Harris. 1998. *Principles of microeconomics.* 1st ed. New York: Dryden.

———. 2001. *Principles of macroeconomics.* 2nd ed. New York: Harcourt College.

———. 2007. *Principles of macroeconomics.* 4th ed. Mason, Ohio: Thomson South-Western.

Manning, Peter K. 2008. *The technology of policing: Crime mapping, information technology, and the rationality of crime control.* New York: New York University Press.

Markoff, John. 1996. *The abolition of feudalism: Peasants, lords, and legislators in the French Revolution.* University Park: Pennsylvania State University Press.

Martin, John Levi. 2005. The objective and subjective rationalization of war. *Theory and Society* 34 (3): 229–75.

Marx, Karl. 1906. *Capital: A critique of political economy.* New York: Modern Library.

Marx, Karl, and Friedrich Engels. 1908. *Manifesto of the Communist Party.* Chicago: Charles H. Kerr.

Matei, Sorin. 2004. The emergent Romanian post-communist ethos: From nationalism to privatism. *Problems of Post-Communism* 51 (2): 40–47.

Matthews, Owen, and Anna Nemsova. 2006. The new feudalism: Forget corruption in Putin's Russia, the nexus of payoffs and patronage is almost medieval, touching every aspect of life. *Newsweek International,* October 23.

Mayer, Lindsay Renick. 2008. Fannie Mae and Freddie Mac invest in democrats. OpenSecrets.org. July 16. http://www.opensecrets.org/news/2008/07/top-senate-recipients-of-fanni.html.

Mayhew, Leon. 1984. In defense of modernity: Talcott Parsons and the utilitarian tradition. *American Journal of Sociology* 89 (6): 1273–305.

McChesney, Fred S. 1997. *Money for nothing: Politicians, rent extraction, and political extortion.* Cambridge: Harvard University Press.

McConnell, Campbell R., and Stanley L. Brue. 2006. *Macroeconomics: Principles, Problems, and Policies.* New York: McGraw-Hill/Irwin.

McCraw, Thomas K. 2007. *Prophet of Innovation: Joseph Schumpeter and creative destruction.* Cambridge: Harvard University Press.

McGrath, Phyllis S. 1979. *Redefining corporate-federal relations.* New York: Conference Board.

McGuire, Jean B. 1984. Strategies of school district conflict. *Sociology of Education* 57 (1): 31–42.

McIntire, Mike, and Jeff Zeleny. 2008.Obama's effort on ethics bill had role in governor's fall. *New York Times,* December 9.

McNally, David. 1993. *Against the market: Political economy, market socialism, and the Marxist critique.* London: Verso.

———. 2008. From financial crisis to world slump: Accumulation, financialization, and the global slowdown. http://marxandthefinancialcrisisof2008.blogspot.com.

McNamee, Stephen J., and Robert K. Miller Jr. 2004. *The meritocracy myth.* Lanham, Md.: Rowman and Littlefield.

McPherson, R. Bruce. 1988. Superintendents and the problem of delegation. *Peabody Journal of Education* 65 (4): 113–30.

Meier, Artur. 1990. Abschied von der sozialistischen staendegesellschaft. *Politik und Zeitgeschichte* 16 (17): 3–14.

Mencimer, Stephanie. 2008. Meet Bush's prison nominee. *MotherJones,* February 20.

Metzger, Gillian E. 2003. Privatization as delegation. *Columbia Law Review* 103 (6): 1367–502.

Michels, Robert. 1915. *Political parties: A sociological study of the oligarchical tendencies of modern democracy.* New York: Hearst's International Library.

Middleton, Kent, and Bill Chamberlin. 1988. *The law of public communication.* White Plains, N.Y.: Longman.

Migdal, Joel S. 1988. *Strong societies and weak states: State-society relations and state capabilities in the third world.* Princeton: Princeton University Press.

Miller, George A., and Oleg I. Gubin. 2000. The structure of Russian organizations. *Sociological Inquiry* 70 (1): 74–87.

Miller, T. Christian. 2005. Private security guards in Iraq operate with little supervision. *Los Angeles Times,* December 4.

Mills, C. Wright. 1956. *The power elite.* New York: Oxford University Press.

Mills, Kenneth, William B. Taylor, and Sandra Lauderdale Graham, eds. 2002. *Colonial Latin America: A documentary history.* Wilmington, Del.: S. R. Books.

Mintzberg, Henry. 1979. *The structuring of organizations: A synthesis of the research.* Englewood Cliffs, N.J.: Prentice Hall.

Mitchell, William C., and Michael C. Munger. 1991. Economic models of interest groups: An introductory survey. *American Journal of Political Science* 35 (2): 512–46.

Mizruchi, Mark S. 1996. What do interlocks do? An analysis, critique, and assessment of research on interlocking directorates. *Annual Review of Sociology* 22:271–98.

———. 2004. Berle and Means revisited: The governance and power of large U.S. corporations. *Theory and Society* 33 (5): 579–617.

Mizruchi, Mark S., and Thomas Koenig. 1986. Economic sources of corporate political consensus: An examination of interindustry relations. *American Sociological Review* 51 (3): 482–91.

———. 1988. Economic concentration and corporate political behavior: A cross-industry comparison. *Social Science Research* 17 (4): 287–305.

Mlodinow, Leonard. 2008. The meritocracy paradox. Forbes.com. April 10 http://www.forbes.com/2008/04/10/performance-pay-meritocracy-oped-utopia08-cx_lm_0410mlodinow.html.

Moe, Ronald C. 1987. Exploring the limits of privatization. *Public Administration Review* 47 (6): 453–60.

Monaghan, Lee. 2002. Regulating "unruly" bodies: Work tasks, conflict and violence in Britain's nighttime economy. *British Journal of Sociology* 53 (3): 403–29.

Monks, Robert A. G., and Nell Minow. 2008. *Corporate governance.* Chichester: John Wiley and Sons.

Monson, Robert J., and Mark W. Cannon. 1965. *The makers of public policy: American power groups and their ideologies.* New York: McGraw-Hill.

Moore, Barrington, Jr. 1966. *Social origins of dictatorship and democracy: Lord and peasant in the making of the modern world.* Boston: Beacon Press.

Moore, Solomon. 2007. Some respite, if little cheer, for skid row homeless. *New York Times,* October 31.

Moreno, Jacob Levy. 1956. *Sociometry and the science of man.* New York: Beacon House.

Morgan, Gareth. 1981. The schismatic metaphor and its implications for organizational analysis. *Organization Studies* 2 (1): 23–44.

Morton, Adam David. 2005. The age of absolutism: Capitalism, the modern states-system and international relations. *Review of International Studies* 31 (3): 495–517.

Moss, Michael, and Leslie Eaton. 2001. A nation challenged: Aviation security; security firms ever mindful to cut costs. *New York Times,* November 15.

Mueller, Dennis C. 1990. The economics of special privilege and rent seeking. *The Economic Journal.* 100 (402): 976–8. Oxford: Blackwell.

———. 2003. *Public choice III.* Cambridge: Cambridge University Press.

Mukhia, Harbans, ed. 2000. *The feudalism debate.* New Delhi: Manohar.

Mulkern, John R., Eric Handler, and Lawrence Godtfredsen. 1981. Corporate PACs as fundraisers. *California Management Review* 23 (3): 49–55.

Murphy, Cullen. 2003. Feudal gestures: Why the Middle Ages are something we can still look forward to. *Atlantic Monthly* 292 (3): 135–37.

Murphy, Kevin R. 1993. *Honesty in the workplace.* Pacific Grove, Calif.: Brooks/Cole.

Murray, V. V., and Allan F. Corenblum. 1966. Loyalty to immediate superior at alternate hierarchical levels in a bureaucracy. *American Journal of Sociology* 72 (1): 77–85.

Nagourney, Adam, and Nicholas Confessore. 2008. As privacy ends for Kennedy, a rough path awaits. *New York Times,* December 16.

Nathan, James A. 1981. The new feudalism. *Foreign Policy* 42 (Spring): 156–66.

National Conference of State Legislatures. 2009. Ethics: Nepotism restrictions for state legislators. NCSL.ORG. http://www.ncsl.org/programs/ethics/e_nepotism.htm.

Neillands, Robin. 2001. *The hundred years war.* London: Routledge.

Newgren, Kenneth E., Calvin E. Kellogg, and William Gardner. 1988. Corporate responses to dual-career couples: A decade of transformation. *Akron Business and Economic Review* 19 (2): 85–96.

New York Times editorial. 2008a. Blackwater's impunity. May 16.

New York Times editorial. 2008b. Another Kennedy for New York? December 16.

New York Times blog. 2009. http://freakonomics.blogs.nytimes.com, comment posted December 7.

Niskanen Jr., William. 1971. *Bureaucracy and representative government.* Chicago: Aldine.

Nörr, Knut Wolfgang. 2000. Harry N. Scheiber: The state and freedom of contract. *American Journal of Comparative Law* 48 (3): 535–41.

Orekhovskii, Petr. 2005. Chem samoupravliat' budem. *Izvestiia,* September 6.

Ortenberg, Veronica. 2006. *In search of the Holy Grail: The quest for the Middle Ages.* New York: Hambledon Continuum.

Osman, Abdulahi A. and Issaka K. Souaré, eds. 2007. *Somalia at the crossroads: Challenges and perspectives in reconstituting a failed state.* London: Adonis and Abbey.

Outhwaite, William. 1994. Public sphere. In *The Blackwell dictionary of twentieth- century social thought,* ed. William Outhwaite and Tom Bottomore, 531. Malden, Mass.: Blackwell.

Owen, David. 2009. The pay problem. *New Yorker,* October 12.

Painter, Sidney. 1961. Feudalism and western civilization. In *Feudalism and liberty: Articles and addresses of Sidney Painter,* ed. Fred A. Cazel Jr. Baltimore: Johns Hopkins Press.

Paludi, Michele, and Carmen A. Paludi Jr. 2003. *Academic and workplace sexual harassment: A handbook of cultural, social science, management, and legal perspectives.* Westport, Conn.: Praeger.

Parfomak, Paul W. 2004. *Guarding America: Security guards and U.S. critical infrastructure protection.* Washington, D.C.: Congressional Research Service.

Park, Seung Ho, and Michael V. Russo. 1996. When competition eclipses cooperation: An event history analysis of joint venture failure. *Management Science* 42 (6): 875–90.

Park, Seung Ho, and Gerardo R. Ungson. 2001. Interfirm rivalry and managerial complexity: A conceptual framework of alliance failure. *Organization Science* 12 (1): 37–53.

Parker, David, and David S. Saal. 2003. *International handbook on privatization.* Cheltenham, U.K.: Edward Elgar.

Parker, Glenn R. 1996. *Congress and the rent-seeking society.* Ann Arbor: University of Michigan Press.

Parker, Suzy. 2006. Our view on government corruption: Scandal? What scandal? Congress ducks ethics reform. http://blogs.usatoday.com/oped/2006/09/our_view_on_gov.html.

Parkin, Robert. 1997. *Kinship: An introduction to basic concepts.* Oxford: Blackwell.

Parsons, Talcott. 1951. *The social system.* Glencoe, Ill.: Free Press.

———. 1952. *The social system.* London: Tavistock.

———. 1967. *Sociological theory and modern society.* New York: Free Press.

———. 1971. *The system of modern societies.* Englewood Cliffs, N.J.: Prentice Hall.

Pastor, James F. 2003. *The privatization of police in America: An analysis and case study.* Jefferson, N.C.: McFarland.

Penenberg, Adam L., and Marc Barry. 2000a. *Spooked: Espionage in corporate America.* Cambridge, Mass.: Perseus.

———. 2000b. Corporate spies; the pizza plot. *New York Times,* December 3.

Percy, Sarah V. 2007. *Mercenaries: The history of a norm in international relations.* Oxford: Oxford University Press.

Pérez-Peña, Richard. 2008. Editor fires parting shot at his chain. *New York Times,* January 22.

Perrett, Geoffrey. 1982. *America in the twenties: A history.* New York: Simon and Schuster.

Petrocelli, William, and Barbara Kate Repa. 1998. *Sexual harassment on the job: What it is and how to stop it.* Berkeley: Nolo Press.

Pfeffer, Jeffrey, and Gerald R. Salancik. 1978. *The external control of organizations: A resource dependence perspective.* New York: Harper and Row.

Phillips, Kevin P. 2003. *Wealth and democracy: A political history of the American rich.* New York: Random House.

Pindyck, Robert, and Daniel Rubinfeld. 1998. *Microeconomics.* Upper Saddle River, N.J.: Prentice Hall.

Pipes, Richard. 1999. *Property and freedom.* New York: Alfred A. Knopf.

Pirenne, Henri. 1937. *Economic and social history of medieval Europe.* New York: Harcourt, Brace.

Polanyi, Karl. 1944. *The great transformation: The political and economic origins of our time.* New York: Rinehart.

Pollert, Anna. 1981. *Girls, wives, factory lives.* London: Macmillan.

Pollock, Frederick, and Frederic W. Maitland. 1968. *The history of English law before the time of Edward I.* 2nd ed. London: Cambridge University Press.

Polsby, Nelson. 1963. *Community power and political theory.* New Haven: Yale University Press.

Pondy, Louis R. 1967. Organizational conflict: Concepts and models. *Administrative Science Quarterly* 12 (2): 296–320.

Postan, Michael. 1944. The rise of a money economy. *Economic History Review* 14 (2): 123–34.

Poulantzas, Nicos Ar. 2000. *State, power, socialism.* New York: Verso.

Prest, Wilfrid. 1991. Judicial corruption in early modern England. *Past and Present* 133 (November): 67–95.

Provine, Doris Marie, and Carroll Seron. 1991. Privatization of judicial services. *Journal of Public Administration Research and Theory* 1 (3): 319–36.

Public Citizen. 2007. Gift rules for congress. *Cleanupwashington.org* http://www.cleanupwashington.org/lobbying/page.cfm?pageid=43.

Putnam, Robert. 2000. *Bowling alone: The collapse and revival of American community.* New York: Simon and Schuster.

Rabkin, Jeremy. 1999. A liberal country, after all. *Public Interest* 134 (Winter): 68–81.

Rajan, Raghuram G. 2005. Has financial development made the world riskier? NBER Working Paper No. W11728. November. http://www.nber.org/papers/w11728.

Reich, Robert. 2007. *Super capitalism: The transformation of business, democracy, and everyday life.* New York: Knopf.

Reiner, Robert. 1992. Policing a postmodern society. *Modern Law Review* 55 (6): 761–81.

Reinstein, Alan, Stephen R. Moehrle, and Jennifer Reynolds-Moehrle. 2006. Crime and punishment in the marketplace: Accountants and business executives repeating history. *Managerial Auditing Journal* 21 (4): 420–35.

Reynolds, Susan. 1994. *Fiefs and vassals: The medieval evidence reinterpreted.* Oxford: Oxford University Press.

Rich, Frank. 2009. Awake and sing! *New York Times,* April 11.

Richardson, Henry Gerald, and George Osborne Sayles. 1963. The governance of mediaeval England from the conquest to magna carta. Edinburgh: University Press.

Ringen, Stein. 2006. Going soft. *Times Literary Supplement,* November 3.

Risen, James. 2008. Iraq contractor in shooting case makes comeback. *New York Times,* May 10.

Robin, Corey. 2004. *Fear: The history of a political idea.* New York: Oxford University Press.

Rodee, Carlton Clymer. 1983. *Introduction to political science.* New York: McGraw-Hill.

Romano, Ruggiero, and Stanley J. Stein. 1984. American feudalism. *Hispanic American Historical Review* 64 (1): 121–34.

Rose, David. Locking in the best price: Private jails. 2007. *Economist,* January 27.

Rose, Nikolas S. 1999. *Powers of freedom: Reframing political thought.* Cambridge: Cambridge University Press.

Rosenau, Pauline Marie. 1992. *Post-modernism and the social sciences: Insights, inroads, and intrusions.* Princeton: Princeton University Press.

Rosenwine, Barbara. 2005. *A short history of the Middle Ages.* Orchard Park, N.Y.: Broadview.

Rotberg, Robert I., ed. 2003. *When states fail: Causes and consequences.* Princeton: Princeton University Press.

Rousseau, Jean-Jacques. [1762] 2006. *The social contract.* Trans. Maurice Cranston. New York: Penguin Books.

Rubin, Miri. 1987. *Charity and community in medieval Cambridge.* Cambridge: Cambridge University Press.

Rutz, Henry J., and Benjamin S. Orlove, eds. 1989. *The social economy of consumption.* New York: University Press of America.

Ryan, Kathleen, and Daniel Oestreich. 1998. *Driving fears out of the workplace: Creating the high-trust, high performance organization.* 2nd ed. San Francisco: Jossey-Bass.

Sabato, Larry. 1984. *PAC Power: Inside the world of political action committees.* New York: Norton.

Sabean, David Warren, Simon Teuscher, and Jon Mathieu, eds. 2007. *Kinship in Europe: Approaches to long-term developments (1300–1900).* New York: Berghahn Books.

Sachs, Jeffrey. 2003. *Macroeconomics in the global economy.* Boulder: Westview.

———. 2008. *Common wealth: Economics for a crowded planet.* New York: Penguin.

Sales, Arnaud. 1991. The private, the public, and civil society: Social realms and power structure. *International Political Science Review* 12 (4) 295–312.

Sampson, Ginger. 2001. To hire (or not to hire) a relative. *National Conference of State Legislatures,* December 2001.

Sanford, John Langton, and Meredith White Townsend. 1865. *The great governing families of England.* London: William Blackwood and Sons.

Sauder, Michael, and Wendy Espeland. 2009. The discipline of rankings: Tight coupling and organizational change. *American Sociological Review* 74 (1): 63–82.

Sauter, Mark, and James Jay Carafano. 2005. *Homeland security: A complete guide to understanding, preventing, and surviving terrorism.* New York: McGraw-Hill.

Savas, Emmanuel S. 1990. A taxonomy of privatization strategies. *Policy Studies Journal* 18:343–65.

Scahill, Jeremy. 2007. *Blackwater: The rise of the world's most powerful mercenary army.* New York: Nation Books.

Scheiber, Harry N., ed. 1998. *The state and freedom of contract.* Stanford: Stanford University Press.

Schickel, Richard. 1985. *Intimate strangers: The culture of celebrity.* New York: Doubleday.

Schlesinger, Arthur M., Jr. 1999. *The cycles of American history.* New York: Houghton Mifflin.

Schmitt, Eric, and Thom Shanker. 2004. Big pay luring military's elite to private jobs. *New York Times,* March 30.

Schott, Richard L., and Dagmar S. Hamilton. 1983. *People, positions, and power: The political appointments of Lyndon Johnson.* Chicago: University of Chicago Press.

Schumpeter, Joseph Alois. 1954. *Capitalism, socialism, and democracy.* London: Allen and Unwin.

Seelye, Katharine Q. 2006. The newspaper publisher who said no to more cuts. *New York Times,* September 28.

Seidenstat, Paul. 2004. Terrorism, airport security, and the private sector. *Review of Policy Research* 21 (3): 275–91.

Sen, Amartya. 2009. Capitalism beyond the crisis. *New York Review of Books,* March 26.

Sennett, Richard. 1992. *The fall of public man: An introduction to their relationships.* New York: Knopf.

Sewell, Chan. 2006. An outcry rises as debt collectors play rough. *New York Times,* July 5.

Shearing, Clifford. 2004. Thoughts on sovereignty. *Policing and Society* 14 (1): 5–12.

Shearing, Clifford, and Philip C. Stenning. 1981. Modern private security: Its growth and implications. *Crime and Justice* 3:193–245.

———. 1983. Private security: Implications for social control. *Social Problems* 30 (5): 493–506.

Sheth, Jagdish N. 1973. A model of industrial buyer behavior. *Journal of Marketing* 37 (4): 50–56.

Shiller, Robert. 2008a. Everybody calm down. A government hand in the economy is as old as the republic. *Washington Post,* September 28.

———. 2008b. *Subprime solution: How today's global financial crisis happened and what to do about it.* Princeton: Princeton University Press.

Shklar, Judith. 1998. *Political thought and political thinkers.* Chicago: University of Chicago Press.

Shlapentokh, Vladimir. 1988. *Soviet ideologies in the period of Glasnost: Responses to Brezhnev's stagnation.* New York: Praeger.

———. 1990. *Soviet intellectuals and political power: The post-Stalin era.* New York: I. B. Tauris.

———. 1996a. Early feudalism: The best parallel for contemporary Russia. *Europe-Asia Studies* 48 (3): 393–411.

———. 1996b. Russia: Privatization and illegalization of social and political life. *Washington Quarterly* 19 (1): 65–85.

———. 1997a. "Normal" Russia. *Current History* 212 (606): 331–36.

———. 1997b. The four faces of mother Russia. *Transition* 4 (5): 60–61.

———. 1998. Four Russias. *Tocqueville Review* 19 (1): 9–34.

———. 2003. Hobbes and Locke at odds in Putin's Russia. *Europa-Asia* 7:981–1007.

———. 2004. Wealth versus political power: The Russian case. *Communist and Post-Communist Studies* 37 (2): 135–60.

———. 2006. *Fear in contemporary society: Its negative and positive effects.* New York: Palgrave Macmillan.

Shlapentokh, Vladimir, Roman Levita, and Mikhail Loiberg. 1997. *From submission to rebellion: The provinces versus the center in Russia.* Boulder: Westview.

Shlapentokh, Vladimir, Eric Shiraev, and Eero Carroll. 2008. *The Soviet Union: Internal and external perspectives on Soviet society.* New York: Palgrave Macmillan.

Shlapentokh, Vladimir, with Joshua Woods. 2007. *Contemporary Russia as a feudal society: A new perspective on the post-Soviet era.* New York: Palgrave Macmillan.

Simmel, Georg. 1968. *The conflict in modern culture, and other essays.* New York: Teachers College Press.

———. 1978. *The philosophy of money.* Boston: Routledge and Kegan Paul.

Simon, David R. 2008. *Tony Soprano's America: The Criminal Side of the American Dream.* New York: Basic Books.

Simon, David R., and D. Stanley Eitzen. 1986. *Elite deviance.* Boston: Allyn and Bacon.

Simon, Herbert A. 1979. Rational decision making in business organizations. *American Economic Review* 69 (4): 493–513.

Simpson, A. W. B. 1998. Land ownership and economic freedom. In Scheiber 1998, 13–43.

Sims, Ronald R., and Johannes Brinkmann. 2003. Enron ethics (or: culture matters more than codes). *Journal of Business Ethics* 45:243–56.

Singer, Peter Warren. 2002. Corporate warriors: The rise of the privatized military industry and its ramifications for international security. *International Security* 26 (3): 186–220.

———. 2003. *Corporate warriors: The rise of the privatized military industry.* Ithaca: Cornell University Press.

Sitkoff, Robert H. 2003–4. Politics and the business corporation. *Regulation* 26:30–36.

Smelser, Neil J. 1994. *Sociology.* Cambridge: Blackwell.

Smith, Clagett G. 1966. A comparative analysis of some conditions and consequences of intra-organizational conflict. *Administrative Science Quarterly* 10 (4): 504–29.

Solo, Robert. 1967. *Economic organizations and social system.* Ann Arbor: University of Michigan Press.

Solomon, Deborah. 2009. Questions for Arthur Levitt. *New York Times,* January 22.

Solow, Robert M. 2007. Heavy thinker. *New Republic Online,* July 12. http://www.powells.com/review/2007_07_12.

Spitzer, Steven, and Andrew T. Scull. 1977. Privatization and capitalist development: The case of the private police. *Social Problems* 25 (1): 18–29.

Sprouse, Martin, ed.1992. *Sabotage in the American workplace: Anecdotes of dissatisfaction, mischief, and revenge.* San Francisco: Pressure Drop Press.

Spufford, Peter. 1988. *Money and its use in medieval Europe.* New York: Cambridge University Press.

Stark, Rodney. 2001. *Sociology.* Belmont, Calif.: Wadsworth.

Stavrakis, Peter J. 1997. *Shadow politics: The Russian state in the twenty-first century.* Harrisburg, Pa.: Strategic Studies Institute, U.S. Army War College.

Steffens, Lincoln. 1931. *The autobiography of Lincoln Steffens.* New York: Harcourt.

Steinberg, Jacques. 2009. University of Illinois chancellor quits over admissions scandal. *New York Times,* October 22.

Stern, Steve J. 1988. Feudalism, capitalism, and the world-system in the perspective of Latin America and the Caribbean. *American Historical Review* 93 (4): 829–72.

Stiglitz, Joseph E. 2002. *Globalization and its discontents.* New York: W. W. Norton.

———. 2003. *The roaring nineties: A new history of the world's most prosperous decade.* New York: W. W. Norton.

Stiglitz, Joseph E., and Carl E. Walsh. 2006. *Principles of microeconomics.* New York: W. W. Norton.

Stille, Alexander. 2003. Italy: The family business. *New York Review of Books,* October 9.

Stokstad, Marilyn. 2005. *Medieval castles.* Westport, Conn.: Greenwood.

Story, Louise. 2009. A rich education for Summers (after Harvard). *New York Times,* April 5.

Strauss, George. 1962. Tactics of lateral relationship: The purchasing agent. *Administrative Science Quarterly* 7 (2): 161–86.

Sugimoto, Yoshio. 2003. *An introduction to Japanese society.* New York: Cambridge University Press.

Sullivan, Harold J. 1987. Privatization of public services: A growing threat to constitutional rights. *Public Administration Review* 47:461–67.

Sutherland, Edwin. 1949. *White collar crime.* New York: Dryden.
Swanson, C. L. 1981. Corporate political participation: From Tillman to the eighties. In *Research in corporate social performance and policy,* ed. L. Preston, 229–48. Greenwich, U.K.: JAI Press.
Sweezy, Paul Marlor. 1978. *The transition from feudalism to capitalism.* London: Verso.
Szinovácz, Maximiliane, ed. 1998. *Handbook on grandparenthood.* Westport, Conn.: Greenwood.
Talbot, Margaret. 2008. The lost children: What do tougher detention policies mean for illegal immigrant families? *New Yorker,* March 3.
Taylor, Leslie C. 2006. What is nepotism? Office of Legal Council, Montana State University. http://www.montana.edu/legalcounsel/nepotism.htm.
Teschke, Benno. 1998. Geopolitical relations in the European Middle Ages: History and theory. *International Organization* 52 (2): 325–58.
Théis, Laurent. 1992. *Histoire du moyen âge français: Chronologie commentée de Clovis à Louis XI, 486–1483.* Paris: Perrin.
Therborn, Göran. 2004. Between sex and power: Family in the world, 1900–2000. London: Routledge.
Thompson, Lyke, and Richard C. Elling. 2000. Mapping patterns of support for privatization in the mass public: The case of Michigan. *Public Administration Review* 60 (4): 338–48.
Tilly, Charles. 1992. *Coercion, capital, and European states, AD 990–1992.* Oxford: Blackwell.
Tocqueville, Alexis de. 1904. *Democracy in America.* Trans. Henry Reeve. New York: D. Appleton.
Toennies, Ferdinand. [1887] 1963. *Community and society (Gemeinschaft und Gesellschaft).* New York: Harper and Row.
Tonsor, Stephen J. 1979. Feudalism, revolution and neo-feudalism: A review article. *Comparative Studies in Society and History* 21 (1): 131–38.
Transparency International. 2007. Corruptions perception index 2007. http://www.transparency.org/policy_research/surveys_indices/cpi/2007.
Treisman, Daniel. 2000. The causes of corruption: A cross-national study. *Journal of Public Economics* 76 (3): 399–457.
———. 2002. Russia renewed? *Foreign Affairs* 81 (6): 58–72.
Trevino, Javier, ed. 2001. *Talcott Parsons today: His theory and legacy in contemporary sociology.* Lanham, Md.: Rowman and Littlefield.
Tullock, Gordon. 1967. The welfare costs of tariffs, monopolies, and theft. *Western Economic Journal* (now *Economic Inquiry*) 5:224–32.
———. 1989. *The economics of special privilege and rent seeking.* Boston: Kluwer Academic.
Turner, Charles. 1992. *Modernity and politics in the work of Max Weber.* New York: Routledge.
Turner, Jonathan. 1985. *Sociology: The science of human organization.* Chicago: Nelson-Hall.
Turow, Scott. 2008. State of shame. *New York Times,* December 10.
Tyson, Ann Scott. 2005. Private security workers living on edge in Iraq. *Washington Post,* April 23.
Uchitelle, Louis. 2007. The richest of the rich: Proud of a new gilded age. *New York Times,* July 15.
———. 2009. Irrational exuberance. *New York Times Book Review,* April 19.
Ullmann, Walter. 1961. *Principles of government and politics in the Middle Ages.* New York: Barnes and Noble.

———. 1988. *Law and jurisdiction in the Middle Ages.* Ed. George Garnett. London: Variorum Reprints.

Ullmann-Margalit, Edna. 1977. *The emergence of norms.* Oxford: Clarendon.

Umberson, Debra, Kristin Anderson, Jennifer Glick, and Adam Shapiro. 1998. Domestic violence, personal control, and gender. *Journal of Marriage and the Family* 60 (2): 442–52.

U.S. Census Bureau. Census, American Housing Survey for the United States. 2008. http://www.census.gov/hhes/www/housing/ahs/ahs.html.

USA Patriot Act. 2001. Uniting and strengthening America by providing appropriate tools required to intercept and obstruct terrorism (USA Patriot Act), Public Law 107–56. http://frwebgate.access.gpo.gov/cgi-bin/getdoc.cgi?dbname=107_cong_public_laws&docid=f:pub1056.107.pdf.

Verdery, Katherine. 1996. *What was socialism, and what comes next?* Princeton: Princeton University Press.

Vidal, Matt. 2007. *Lean enough: Factory relations of production under neoliberal globalization.* Madison: University of Wisconsin Press.

Vinogradoff, Paul. 1908. *English society in the eleventh century: Essays in English mediaeval history.* Oxford: Clarendon.

———. 1924. Feudalism. In *Cambridge medieval history.* Vol. 3, planned by J. B. Bury, ed. Henry Melvill Gwatkin et al., 458–84. Cambridge: Cambridge University Press.

Vogel, David. 1981. The new social regulation in historical and comparative perspectives. In *Regulation in perspective,* ed. Thomas N. McCraw. Cambridge: Harvard University Press.

———. 1983. The power of business in America: A re-appraisal. *British Journal of Political Science* 13 (1):19–43.

Volckart, Oliver. 2002. *Wettbewerb und Wettbewerbsbeschränkung in vormodernen Deutschland, 1000–1800.* Tübingen: Mohr Siebeck.

Wagner, Wolf. 2006. Performance evaluation and financial market runs. http://www.wiwi.uni-konstanz.de/fb/admin/paper/wagner.pdf.

Wallace-Hadrill, Andrew, ed. 1989. *Patronage in ancient society.* New York: Routledge.

Wallander, Celeste A. 2000. Institutional assets and adaptability: NATO after the cold war. *International Organization* 54:705–35.

Wallerstein, Immanuel. 1974. *The modern world-system.* Vol. 1, *Capitalist agriculture and the origins of the European world-economy in the sixteenth century.* New York: Academic Press.

Walton, Richard E., and John Dutton. 1969. The management of interdepartmental conflict: A model and review. *Administrative Science Quarterly* 14 (1): 73–84.

Walton, Richard E., John M. Dutton, and Thomas P. Cafferty. 1969. Organizational context and interdepartmental conflict. *Administrative Science Quarterly* 14 (4): 522–42.

Waquet, Jean-Claude. 1991. *Corruption: Ethics and power in Florence, 1600–1770.* Cambridge: Polity.

Wayne, Leslie. 2008. Candidates forgo soft money, but conventions rake it in. *New York Times,* June 7.

Webb, Diana. 2007. *Privacy and solitude in the Middle Ages.* London: Hambledon Continuum.

Webber, Carolyn, and Aaron Wyldavsky. 1994. Feudalism nothing. In *The Blackwell dictionary of twentieth-century social thought,* ed. William Outhwait and Tom Bottomore. Oxford: Blackwell.

Weber, Max. 1949. *The methodology and the social sciences.* Trans. and ed. Edward A. Shils and Henry A. Finch. Glencoe, Ill.: Free Press.

———. 1965. *Politics as a vocation.* Minneapolis: Fortress Press.

———. 1978. *Economy and society: An outline of interpretive sociology.* Berkeley: University of California Press.

Weick, Karl E. 1976. Educational organizations as loosely coupled systems. *Administrative Science Quarterly* 21 (1): 1–19.

Weidenbaum, M. L. 1986. *Business, government, and the public.* Englewood Cliffs, N.J.: Prentice Hall.

Weigand, Robert E. 1968. Why studying the purchasing agent is not enough. *Journal of Marketing* 32 (1): 41–45.

Weinberg, Meyer, and Oscar E. Shabat. 1965. *Society and man.* Englewood Cliffs, N.J.: Prentice Hall.

Weisman, Jonathan. 2006. Corruption scandals cast shadow on GOP leadership race. *Washington Post,* January 30.

Weizsäcker, Ernst Ulrich von, Oran R. Young, and Matthias Finger. 2005. *Limits to privatization: How to avoid too much of a good thing.* Sterling, Va.: Earthscan.

Wells, Joseph T. 1993. Accountancy and white-collar crime. *Annals of the American Academy of Political and Social Science* 525 (1): 83–94.

Weston, Liz Pulliam. 2006. "Zombie" debt is hard to kill. *MSN Money,* July 24.

Weyl, Walter. 1912. *The new democracy.* New York: Macmillan.

White, Theodore Harold. 1973. *The making of the president, 1972.* New York: Atheneum.

Wiarda, Howard J. 1992. *Politics and social change in Latin America: The distinct tradition.* Boulder: Westview.

Wiarda, Howard J., and Harvey F. Kline, eds. 1979. *Latin American politics and development.* Boston: Houghton Mifflin.

Wichroski, Mary Anne. 1994. The secretary: Invisible labor in the workworld of women. *Human Organization* 53 (1) 33–41.

Wickham, Chris. 2005. *Framing the early Middle Ages: Europe and the Mediterranean 400–800.* Oxford: Oxford University Press.

Williams, Rowan. 2008. Face it: Marx was partly right about capitalism. *Spectator,* September 24.

Williamson, Oliver E. 1975. *Markets and hierarchies, analysis and antitrust implications: A study in the economics of internal organization.* New York: Free Press.

———. 1981. The modern corporation: Origins, evolution, and attributes. *Journal of Economic Literature* 19 (4): 1537–68.

———. 1985. *The economic institutions of capitalism: Firms, markets, relational contracting.* New York: Free Press.

———. 1996. *The mechanism of governance.* New York: Oxford University Press.

Wilson, Ronald C. 1989. *Ancient republicanism: Its struggle for liberty against corruption.* New York: Peter Lang.

Winkler, Ira. 1997. *Corporate espionage: What it is, why it is happening in your company, what you must do about it.* Rocklin, Calif.: Prima Lifestyles.

Wirt, Frederick, and Michael Kirst. 1972. *The political web of American schools.* Boston: Little-Brown.

Wolfe, Martin. 1966. French views on wealth and taxes from the Middle Ages to the old regime. *Journal of Economic History* 26 (4): 466–83.

Wood, Jennifer, and Clifford Shearing. 2007. *Imagining security.* Portland, Ore.: Willan.

Woods, Joshua, and Vladimir Shlapentokh. 2009. The feudal model and the study of modern organizations. *International Journal of Organization Theory and Behavior* 12 (4): 521–37.

Woods, Thomas E. 2009. *Meltdown: A free-market look at why the stock market collapsed, the economy tanked, and government bailouts will make things worse.* Washington, D.C.: Regnery Press.

Wright, Erik Olin. 1998. *The debate on classes.* New York: Verso.

Zald, Mayer Nathan. 1962. Power balance and staff conflict in correctional institutions. *Administrative Science Quarterly* 7 (1): 22–49.

Zeigler, L. Harmon, M. Kent Jennings, and G. Wayne Peak. 1974. *Governing American schools: Political interaction in local school districts.* North Scituate, Mass.: Duxbury Press.

Zernike, Kate. 2008. In Illinois, a virtual expectation of corruption. *New York Times,* December 13.

Zingales, Luigi. 2009. *Economist* debates: Keynesian principles. *Economist,* April 30.

Zinn, Howard. 2003. *A people's history of the United States: 1492–present.* New ed. New York: HarperCollins.

Index

Abramoff, Jack, 36, 47
Adams, Henry, 36
Adams, John, 111
Adams, John Quincy, 111
Adler, Patricia A., 75
Adler, Peter, 75
Akerlof, George, 127
alumni, 115, 127
America, American. *See also* United States
  exceptionalism, 2, 4
  heritage of feudalism, 2, 24, 40
Amis, Kingsley, 117
Amis, Martin, 117
Anderson, Paul F., 66
Anderson, Perry, 6, 12
Anderson, Tom, 37
aristocracy, 11, 20, 114, 117. *See also* nobility
  feudal aristocracy, 14–15
  landed aristocracy, 16, 55
Ashford, Douglas E., 54
attitudes of the public, vii, 30–31, 33, 39, 60, 85, 87, 89, 91, 113, 127. *See also* public choice theory
  toward corruption, 33, 36–37, 94
  toward crime, 14, 93
  toward privatization of prisons, 94–95
authoritarianism or authoritarian model, vii–viii, xi, 3, 5–7, 18–19, 21, 25–26, 28, 31–32, 34–35, 55, 63, 82, 99, 100, 124, 126–27, 131. *See also* regimes
  oligarchic form of, 51

Barclay, Donald W., 70
Bargh, John A., 35
Bauman, Zygmunt, 10
Beaumarchais, Pierre-Augustin, 106–7
Begich, Marc, 111
Bell, Griffin, 109
Bellow, Adam, 109, 111, 117
Bendix, Reinhard, 57
Benson, Kenneth J., 67
Berle, Adolf Augustus, 47, 51
Bernanke, Ben, 125, 127
big money, 33–55
  in political decisions, 34, 37, 44–45, 47, 48–54
Bislev, Sven, 83
Blagojevich, Rod, 37, 43–44
Blakely, Edward James, 92
Bloch, Marc, 12, 14, 24, 63, 74, 80–81
Bloomberg, Michael, 113
Blumer, Herbert, 101
Bourdieu, Pierre, 6, 116
Bowman, Scott R., 41, 50–51
Braithwaite, John, 35
Brown, Byron, 113
Burawoy, Michael, 73
bureaucracy, bureaucrats, viii, 7, 16, 25, 28, 30, 31, 46–47, 56–59, 62, 66–69, 100
bureaucratic model, 25, 57–59, 66–67, 69, 72, 74, 76
Burns, James MacGregor, 48, 54
Bush, George H. W., 45, 47, 111
Bush, George W., 45, 53–54, 95, 97, 109, 111, 127, 129

Cafferty, Thomas P., 70
Cantor, Norman, 22, 24
capitalism, 9, 26, 68, 91, 94, 125
  corporate form of, 79
  liberal form of, vii–viii, x, 5, 7, 97, 122–23, 131
  in the West, 2
Carolingian, 20, 25, 63
Carroll, Eero, 71
Carter, Jimmy, 109
Casey, Bob, 111
Casey, Robert, 111
Cavanagh, John, 50
Chamberlin, Henry, 35
Chao, Elaine, 109
Charlemagne, 13, 20, 25, 36, 61, 63
Charles the Simple, 69
Cheney, Dick, 45, 109, 113
Cheney, Elizabeth, 109

Cheung, Amy, 95
Cheung, Steven N. S., 46
China, vii, 4, 10
church, monasteries, and clergy, 7, 14, 20, 26, 33, 35, 38
  as a social organization, 18
  Catholic, 26, 31, 42
  development of democracy, 20
  influence of, 39–40, 42
clans, clique, 9, 100, 104
  family, 100–101
  Kennedy, the, 112–13
  political, vii, 104, 112–13, 120–21, 124
  spirit of clanship, 114
  warrior, 13
clientele, 38–39, 108, 110
Clinton, Bill, 29, 51, 53, 112
Clinton, Hilary, 129
Coase, Ronald, 33, 48
Cochrane, John, 126
coercion, 8, 12, 96
  by the church, 33
  by debt collectors, 96–97
  physical, 33, 82, 87, 91
  political, 8
  private prisons, in, 94–96
  private, 78–98, 124
Cold War, ix
Coleman, James S., 102
Coleman, John, 126
Collins, Randall, 10
commendation, 80
Communism, Communist, 2–3. *See also* regimes
  feudalism, and, 2–4, 7
  former Communist regimes, 2–3
  post-Communist, 2–3, 8
complex organizations, 5, 11, 58, 63
  conflict inside, 67
  feudalization of, 122
contractors, 31
  military, 84–85
  private, 78, 82, 86–87
  security, 89, 93
contracts
  feudal times, in, 16, 20, 22, 69
  medieval, 23–25, 32
  military based, 15
  political 29, 42–43
  prison, 94–95
  social, 83. See also *The Social Contract*
  union, 71
consumption, 23, 38
Corenblum, Allan F., 75
Corneille, Pierre, 106
corporations, 31, 32, 88, 122, 125
  abuse of power, 107–8
  and big money, 33–55, 127–28, 130–31
  and prisons, 94
  election donations, 51
  feudal relations, 38–39, 56, 99, 127
  high-tech, 75
  influence in politics, vii–viii, 8, 27, 32, 39–40, 43, 46–55, 122, 124, 129
  modern, 74
  multinational, 86
  nepotism, 110
  rent-seeking, 41–43, 46–47
  Russia, in, 3
Corrigan, Gerald, 130
corruption
  feudal elements of, 7, 33–38, 117
  in corporations, viii, 3, 29, 49
  in government, 8, 35–36, 43, 65, 122
  in history, 35
  in modern society, 14, 34, 35, 55
  in politics, 3
  in prisons, 94
  in privatization, 30–31
  in rent-seeking activities, 41, 43–44, 46
Corwin, Ronald G., 66–67
Corzine, Jon, 50
Coulanges, Fustel de, 12
court, 14, 73, 91, 119, 130
  and coercion, 95
  Iraqi, 84
  supreme court, 52
  system, 25
crime
  and prisons, 91
  crime prevention, 87
  digital and cyber, 91
  increasing fear of, 92
  in authoritarian systems, 100
  in medieval times, 14, 80, 82
  in politics, 43
  organized, 5, 35
  public fear of, 95
  prevention, 97
  in the state, 8, 86
  white-collar, 35, 41, 50
Croly, Herbert, 49
Cronin, Thomas E., 48, 54
culture
  and models of society, 57
  in business, 68, 75, 109

medieval, 17, 76
subculture, 75
Cunningham, Randy ("Duke"), 37

Dahl, Robert, 34, 50
Daley, Richard, 37, 44
Daley, Richard, Jr., 44
Dalton, Melville, 61, 64–66, 71–72
Dawkins, Richard, 103
Dean, Trevor, 35
debt collectors, 96
DeLay, Tom, 45
DeLeon, Peter, 50–51
DeLong, Brad, 126
democracy, vii, 3, 46, 50
American representative democracy, 27
and authoritarianism, 3, 6
and business, 54, 68
Athenian, 20, 27
development of, 20
in England, 19
in France, vii
in Iran, vii
Jeffersonian, 27, 34, 51, 114
Kennedy family, 112
liberal, viii, 19, 121, 131
"shareholder democracy," 28
The Social Contract (Rousseau), 25
Western, 2
Dobb, Maurice Herbert, 12
Dodd, Christopher, 111, 113
Dodd, Thomas, 111
Donough, William, 130
Douglas, David Charles, 24
Douglas, Michael, 117
Dowd, Maureen, 113
Drucker, Peter, 51
Duby, Georges, 21
Dudley, William, 130
Dutton, John M., 70

Edward I, 21–22
Edwards, Edwin, 37
egalitarianism, egalitarian approach, vii, 101–2, 121, 124
non-egalitarian approach, 102–3
Elias, Norbert, 61
elitism, 124
and nepotism, 116–17
elitist ideology, 7, 15, 117
Emanuel, Rahm, 129
empire
feudal, 3, 13
Roman, 3, 13, 22, 61, 81, 105
Engels, Friedrich, 11
England, 12, 17, 19, 25, 35, 40, 69, 81, 112
Ericson, Richard E., 3
Enron, 36, 45, 69
estate, 15, 26, 38, 64, 76, 81, 93. *See also* land property
Etzioni, Amitai, 75
extortion, 15, 23, 81

failing states, 5
Farber, Steve, 53
Farmer, D. J., 2
fear
and authoritarianism, 32
and church, 33
and politics, 44
of crime, 80, 82, 92–93
of supervisors, 32
federal
elections, 54
election campaign act, 53
government, 30–31, 36, 118–19, 126, 131
regulations, 46, 89, 91
Federal Reserve Board, 125–28, 130
Federal Trade Commission, 96
Feigenbaum, Harvey, 29–30
Feingold, Russell, 50, 52
Feinstein, Dianne, 95
feudalism, feudal
and law, 5, 13, 15–16, 21–22
and the market, 23, 28–29, 32–33, 35, 55, 61, 67, 81, 92, 110, 128, 131
as a model of society, 1, 3–5, 7, 9–10, 12–14, 16–19, 34–35, 44, 46, 54, 56–61, 67–68, 74–79, 82–84, 88, 90, 92–93, 97–98, 100, 104, 122–24, 127, 129
as ideal type, 1, 4, 8, 10, 17, 19, 57, 79
classic period, 11, 13–14, 105
conflicts, 7, 11, 14, 19, 20, 57, 59, 60–68, 70–74, 76–77, 80, 122, 124
definitions of, 1–5, 8–9, 11–12, 16–17, 24, 58–59
heritage of, 2, 24, 40
in Europe, 3, 106
in Japan, 5, 10, 62, 75, 106
in medieval Europe, ix, 1, 3–5, 7, 9, 13–14, 17, 22, 59, 61, 78, 80, 82–84, 89, 98, 104, 123–24
in the Middle Ages, 13, 15, 20–24, 35, 38, 41, 55, 59, 69, 76, 80–81, 85–86, 91–92, 104–6
legal aspects of, 14–15, 21, 23–24, 42, 45, 60, 100, 102, 122

feudalism (*continued*)
lords, 3, 5, 8, 11, 13–15, 19–26, 35–36, 38–42, 59, 61, 63–64, 66–67, 69, 71–74, 76, 80–82, 88–89, 93, 100, 103, 105, 107, 114, 116–17, 123, 128, 130
military aspects of, 9, 14–16, 24, 39, 41, 59, 63, 73, 76, 80–82
political school of, 9, 12–13
privileges, 23, 55, 117
in Russia, 19–20, 22, 25; contemporary Russia, vii, 2–3, 5, 8, 104, 108
socioeconomic school of, 9, 11–13, 16
universalism and, 16
fiefs, 16, 39
financial crisis of 2008–9, ix–x, 124–31
Fonda, Jane, 117
Fonda, Peter, 117
France, French
medieval, 1, 17, 21, 25, 40
Revolution, 12, 97
Frank, Barney, 129
Fraser, Antonia, 22
Friedman, Alex, 95–96
Friedman, Milton, 124–26
Frist, Bill, 37
Fukuyama, Francis, 102

Galambos, Louis, 46
Galbraith, John Kenneth, 51, 126
Gallagher, Bernard J., 48
Ganshof, François Louis, 12, 21, 24
Garfield, James, 118
Garland, David, 32
Geithner, Timothy, 125, 129–30
Giddens, Anthony, 10, 16
Glaeser, Edward, 35
globalization, 76, 86, 97, 122
graded approach, 6. *See also* hybrid approach
Goffman, Erving, 72, 101
Goldin, Claudia, 35
Gramm, Phil, 45
Grant, Ulysses S., 36
Greece, 4
Greenspan, Alan, x, 125–26
Gregory VII (pope), 20
Guiteau, Charles, 118

Habermas, Jürgen, 16, 104
Hamilton, Alexander, 114
Hamilton, William Donald, 103
Harrison, Benjamin, 111
Harrison, William, 111
Hartz, Louis, 2
Hayek, Friedrich August, 25
Hebert, Ernest, 112
Henry IV, 20
Herman, Richard H., 116
hierarchy, hierarchical principle, 13, 15, 18, 26, 31–33, 38, 56, 59, 62, 64, 69, 73, 75, 99, 100, 105, 109
Hilferding, Rudolf, 41
historical analysis, 9, 11
Hobbes, Thomas, 24–25, 83
holistic approach or vision of the world, 5, 6
Hollister, Charles Warren, 69
Holton, Robert J., 12
humanistic, 57
Hundred Years' War, 23
hybrid approach, 6. *See also* graded approach

ideal types, ix, 1, 4–5, 10, 17, 19, 57, 79, 82, 84
ideology
authoritarian, 100
elitist, 7, 15, 116–17
liberal, 116
oligarchic (or feudal), 51, 105, 116, 130
India, Indian, 4
inequality, 11–12, 34
Iraq war, 84–85
Italy, vii, 44, 108

Jackall, Robert, 74–75
Jagiello, Wladyslaw, 20
Jain, Arvind K., 41
James, Sharpe, 37
Janin, Hunt, 35
Japan, 5, 9–10, 62, 75, 106
Jefferson, William, 37
John (king), 19, 82
Johnson, Allan, 71
Johnson, Lyndon B., 108–9
Johnson, Simon, 126–27, 129–30
Jomo, Kwame Sundaram, 46
Jones, Brian J., 48
Jordan, Hamilton, 109
judicial system, 7–9, 13, 18–19, 29, 35, 42, 53–54, 68, 82–83, 91, 118–19, 120. *See also* law

Karstedt, Susanne, 5
Kelley, Harold, 102
Kennedy, Caroline, 112
Kennedy, Edward M., 113
Kennedy, John F., 112, 113
Kennedy, Joseph, 112
Kennedy, Kerry, 113
Kennedy, Patrick, 85

Kennedy, Robert, 109, 113
Kennedy, Robert, Jr., 113
Kerner, Otto, 44
Kerry, John, 54, 129
Keynes, John Maynard, 124, 127
Keynesian model, 124–26
kings, kingdom, 13–14, 18–23, 25–26, 35–36, 38, 40, 58–59, 61, 63–64, 67, 69, 71, 75, 80–82, 89, 105, 123, 130. *See also individual names of kings*
kinship, 8, 15, 38, 105, 120, 124
  in business, 110–11
  in politics, 103–4, 108, 110–12
  in the Middle Ages, 106
Kolb, Deborah M., 60–61
Krueger, Anne, 41
Krugman, Paul, 97, 126, 128
Kunda, Gideon, 75

Laclau, Ernesto, 6
Lafayette, Gilbert du Motier, 114
Lambsdorff, Johann, 35
Lance, Bert, 109
Lance, Thomas, 109
land property, 26, 38, 64, 76, 81, 93. *See also* estate
Latynina, Yulia, 3
law, 7–9, 13, 18–19, 29, 35, 42, 53–54, 68, 82–83, 91, 118–20. *See also* judicial system
  disrespect for, 21, 52
  in the Middle Ages, 5, 13, 15–16, 21–22
  Roman, 22, 24, 105
Lay, Kenneth, 45
Lee-Chai, Annette Y., 35
Lenin, Vladimir, 41
Levitt, Arthur, Jr., 130
liberal, liberalism, viii, 19–20, 22–25, 49, 103–4, 111, 122
liberal capitalism, vii–viii, x, 5, 7, 97, 116, 122–23, 131
liberal model, viii–ix, 18–19, 21, 27–28, 30, 32, 34–35, 55, 79, 82–85, 88–90, 92–94, 99, 124–27, 131
libertarian, libertarianism, 24, 126
Lindblom, Charles, 50
Lindsey, Lawrence, 45
Locke, John, 24–26, 83
London, 19
Lorenzo, Frank, 47
Louis the Pius, 20
Louis IX, 25
Louis XI, 25
loyalty, 15, 44, 74–76, 100, 103, 105–6, 108–10, 120–24
  culture of, 75–76
Lucas, Robert, 124

MacKenzie, Calvin G., 108
Madoff, Bernie, 130
mafia, vii
Magna Carta, 19, 21, 82
Magyars, 13
managerialism, 51
Mankiw, Gregory, 48
Manning, Peter K., xi, 72, 75
market, ix, 6–7, 10, 12, 18, 23, 27–29, 32–33, 39, 42, 48–49, 55, 61–62, 67, 92, 96, 100, 110, 124–28, 131
  economy, 3, 16, 26
  relations, 30, 35
Martel, Charles, 76
Marx, Karl, ix, 11, 125
Marxists, and Marxism, 6, 11–12, 23, 41–42, 55, 60, 104, 116, 122
McCain, John, 52, 54, 111
McConnell, Mitch, 109
McFalls, Joseph A., 48
McPherson, Bruce R., 75
Means, Gardiner C., 47, 51
media, viii, 39–40, 53, 85–86, 95, 115–16, 128
medieval, 1, 3–5, 8–9, 11–26, 32, 35, 38–41, 55, 58, 61–64, 67, 69, 71, 73–74, 76, 78–82, 86, 89, 92–94, 97–98, 100, 104–5, 121, 123–24, 130
  France, 1, 17, 21, 25, 40
mercenaries, 15, 81–82, 85
Merton, Robert, 130
Michels, Robert, 27, 28
military, 14–16, 24, 39, 41, 59, 64, 73, 76, 80–82, 100, 107
  privatization of, 78–79, 84–86
Mills, C. Wright, 40, 116
Minow, Nell, 128
Mizruchi, Mark S., 41, 47
modernity, modernization, 16–17, 103
Moe, Ronald, 31
Moliere, Jean-Baptiste, 106
monarchism, 19, 25
  absolute monarchy, 11, 13, 15, 32, 61
money, 15, 23, 26, 34, 40–42, 91, 122
  social role of, 23, 39, 41
  in Western society, 14, 28, 34, 37–38, 43, 45, 49, 51–56
monopoly, monopolistic, 8, 14, 27, 33–34, 42, 55, 83–84, 86, 97, 122–23
  of resources, 16, 29, 33, 42, 45, 110
Moreno, Jacob Levy, 101
Mueller, Dennis, 48
multiculuralism, 23
Murray, V. V., 75

Nathan, James, 86, 94
neoclassical economic model or economists, 41, 124–25
nepotism, 8, 15, 34, 74–75, 99, 100, 108–10, 112, 116–21, 124
  in academia, 119–20
networks, 13, 15, 38–40, 47, 49, 64, 90, 99, 102, 106, 108, 112
Nixon, Richard, 109
nobility, 11, 14–16, 20, 21, 55, 106, 112, 116. *See also* aristocracy
  in the United States, 114–15, 117, 121, 124
Nuñez, Fabian, 37

Obama, Barack, viii, 37, 43–44, 52, 54, 119, 125, 127, 129
Occam, William, ix
Occam's razor, ix
Oestreich, Daniel, 32
oligarchs, oligarchy, vii, 18, 27–28, 49, 130
  autonomy of, 8
  conflicts between, 72
  ideology of, 51, 130
  iron law of, 27
O'Neal, Stanley, 128
one-system approach, 5, 18
Otto I, 76

Parsons, Talcott, 5–6, 16, 25, 99, 103–4
Passeron, Jean-Claude, 116
Pastor, James F., 87
Paterson, David, 113
Paulson, Henry, 129
peasants, 11–12, 14, 23, 26, 39, 80, 105–6
Peltason, Jack W., 48, 54
Pepin the Short, 20
Perot, Ross, 50
personal loyalty, 74, 100, 103, 105, 108–9
personal relations, vii, 15, 66, 71–72, 74, 96, 99–107, 110, 116, 120–21, 123–24, 129
Philip I, 69
Pipes, Richard, 22
Plantagenet, Henry, 76
pluralism, 17–21
Poland, 2, 23, 44
  election of the king, 20
  Polish, 20, 116
police and law enforcement, 18, 25–26, 44, 72, 75, 86–87, 89, 91, 93, 107
political financing. *See* big money
political freedom, 19
Polsby, Nelson, 50
Postan, Michael, 23, 41
post-Communist, 2–3
Poulantzas, Nicos Ar., 42
Powell, Colin, 109
Powell, Michael, 109
Powell, Paul, 44
property, 13–14, 22, 26, 34, 38–39, 55, 65, 78–81, 105, 110, 123
  private, 22–33, 47, 124
privatization, 28–30, 32, 86, 94
  capitalist aspects of, 28
  feudal aspects of, 29, 96
  of the military, 78–79, 84–86
  political aspects of, 28–30
  in Russia, 29
  of security, prisons, 8, 91, 93–94, 96
  in United States, viii, 29–31, 94
privilege, privileged, 10, 23, 33–34, 40, 42–43, 55, 64, 116–17, 122–23
public attitudes. *See* attitudes of the public
public choice theory, 30
public life, 22, 116
Puryear, Gustavus Adolphus, 95
Putnam, Linda L., 60–61
Putnam, Robert, 102

Racicot, Marc, 45
Racine, Jean, 106
Reed, Jack, 129
regime, 22, 33, 79
  authoritarian, vii, 3, 5–6, 21, 26, 32, 63, 99, 127, 131. *See also* authoritarianism
  Communist, 2, 116
  post-Communist, vii, 2–3, 6–8
  totalitarian, vii, 22, 35
Rehnquist, Justice William, 109
Reich, Robert, 41, 50, 126
Reid, Harry, 113
religion, church, 7, 13–14, 16, 18–20, 25–26, 33, 38–40, 42, 64
  Catholic church, 20, 26, 31–33, 42
  Christian, Christianity, 40
  Protestant church, 20
rent-seeking activity, 41–48, 50, 122
  consequences of, 45
  cost and efficiency, 44–45
  in the Middle Ages, 41
  legal and illegal, 42
  privileges from, 42
  rent givers, 43
  state regulation, 46
  technology of, 46
Rezko, Antoin, 37
Robin, Corey, 32

Rodee, Carlton Clymer, 48
Roman Empire, 3, 13, 22, 61, 80, 105
Roosevelt, Eleanor, 111
Roosevelt, Franklin, 111
Roosevelt, Theodore, 111
Rose, Nikolas S., 78
Rostenkowski, Dan, 37
Rotberg, Robert I., 8
Rousseau, Jean-Jacques, 25
Rove, Karl, 45
Rowland, John, 37
royal power, 20–22, 25
Ryan, George, 37
Ryan, Kathleen, 32

Sabean, David Warren, 106
Sachs, Jeffery, 29
safety and security, 7–8, 14, 17, 78, 82–84, 89, 90, 93, 98, 105, 123
  companies, 78–79, 85, 87–89, 91
  gated communities (enclaves), 79, 88, 92–93, 116
  industry of, 78–79, 86–88, 97
  in the Middle Ages, 64, 73, 80, 82, 91
  private security, viii, 8, 78–79, 82, 85–90, 93, 97–98, 123
Scalia, Antonin, 109
Scalia, Eugene, 109
Schlesinger, Arthur M., Jr., 2
Scholes, Myron, 130
Schumpeter, Joseph Alois, 51, 111
segmented approach, x, 5–7, 17–19, 21, 26, 32, 124
Sen, Amartya, 125
Sewell, Chan, 96
sexual harassment, 107
Shakespeare, William, 105
Shearing, Clifford, 87
Shiller, Robert, 127
Shklar, Judith, 32
Shleifer, Andrei, 29
Simmel, Georg, 4, 17
Simon, Herbert, 71
Simpson, A. W. B, 5, 24
Singer, Peter Warren, 86
Sitkoff, Robert, 50
Smelser, Neil J., 5, 47
Snyder, Mary Gail, 92
social capital, 102
The Social Contract (Rousseau), 25
social institutions, 6, 99, 124
social organizations, ix, 5, 17–18, 24, 32, 40, 122
sociology, formal, 4
sociology, social psychology, and social sciences, in general, ix, 10, 17, 35, 47, 58, 101–3
Solo, Robert, 6, 49, 125
Solomon, Jay, 109
Solow, Robert, 111
Sorich, Robert, 37
Soviet Union, USSR, vii, 2, 21, 29, 70, 100
Specter, Arlen, 95
Stalin, Josef, 100
state, the, 1, 3, 8, 12–15, 18, 20, 25, 27–28, 33, 42, 48, 55, 82–84, 86, 89, 97, 118, 123, 125–27
  autonomy of, viii
  strengths of, 8, 63, 76, 122
  weaknesses of, 3, 7, 9, 18, 33, 35, 85, 89–90, 104, 124
Stavrakis, Peter J., 3
Steffens, Lincoln, 36, 49
Stenning, Philip C., 87
Stevens, Ted, 37
Stiglitz, Joseph, 29, 49, 125–26
Summers, Lawrence, 29, 125, 127, 129
Sutherland, Edwin, 49
Sweezy, Paul Marlor, 12

taxes, 22–23, 25, 36, 42, 48, 81, 97
terrorism, 37, 84–86, 89, 91
Teschke, Benno, 76
Thain, John, 128
Thurmond, Strom, 109
Thurmond, Strom, Jr., 109
totalitarianism, 10
  totalitarian, vii, 22, 24, 35
trade unions, 31, 49, 51, 102
Traficant, Jim, 37
transition societies, 2
Transparency International, 35–36
Treisman, Daniel, 3, 34
Tocqueville, Alexis de, 14–15
Toennies, Ferdinand, 103
Tollison, Robert D., 42
Torricelli, Robert, 37
Turow, Scott, 54

United States, vii–x, 4–10, 17, 34, 36, 42, 46–48, 52, 78–79, 84–86, 88–89, 94, 102, 107–8, 114, 116, 123–24, 126, 129
  textbooks in, 17, 46–48, 86
universalism in social science, 4–5, 16, 57, 66

vassal relations, 5, 13–14, 24, 61, 73–74, 99, 103, 105
Vinogradoff, Paul, 12, 40, 80, 105

violence, 8, 14, 18, 79–84, 86, 91, 96–97, 123
in the Middle Ages, 21, 76
Vogel, David, 46
Volcker, Paul, 128

Walton, Sam, 2, 70
war, 14, 83, 89. *See also individual wars*
during the Middle Ages, 22–23, 39, 70, 76, 81
Washington, George, 114
Waxman, Henry, x
Weber, Max, 1, 4, 10, 16–17, 56–57, 74–76, 83–84, 97, 99, 103–4, 123
Weick, Karl E., 63
Weill, Sanford, 130
Weyl, Walter, 49
Wickham, Chris, 38–39
William the Bastard, 69
William the Conqueror, 25–26, 81
Williams, Rowan, 125
Williamson, Oliver, 25, 33, 48–49
Woods, Thomas, 126
World War I, 124
Wright, Eric Olin, 6
Wyldavsky, Aaron, 5

Zingales, Luigi, 126–27

